THE AGE OF FENTANYL

Brodie Ramin, M.D.

THE AGE OF FENTANYL

Ending the Opioid Epidemic

DUNDURN
TORONTO

Publisher: Scott Fraser | Acquiring editor: Kathryn Lane | Editor: Dominic Farrell
Cover designer: Sophie Paas-Lang
Cover image: unsplash.com/James Wheeler
Printer: Marquis Book Printing Inc.

Library and Archives Canada Cataloguing in Publication

Title: The age of fentanyl : ending the opioid epidemic / Brodie Ramin, M.D.
Names: Ramin, Brodie, 1982- author.
Description: Includes bibliographical references and index.
Identifiers: Canadiana (print) 20190231890 | Canadiana (ebook) 20190231904 | ISBN 9781459746701 (softcover) | ISBN 9781459746718 (PDF) | ISBN 9781459746725 (EPUB)
Subjects: LCSH: Opioid abuse. | LCSH: Fentanyl. | LCSH: Opioids—Overdose. | LCSH: Fentanyl—Overdose.
Classification: LCC RC568.O45 R36 2020 | DDC 362.29/3—dc23

Canada Council for the Arts Conseil des arts du Canada

We acknowledge the support of the Canada Council for the Arts and the Ontario Arts Council for our publishing program. We also acknowledge the financial support of the Government of Ontario, through the Ontario Book Publishing Tax Credit and Ontario Creates, and the Government of Canada.

Printed and bound in Canada.

VISIT US AT

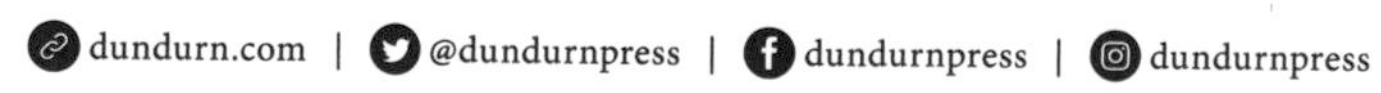

Dundurn
3 Church Street, Suite 500
Toronto, Ontario, Canada
M5E 1M2

To those we have lost, those still fighting, and everyone working to end this epidemic.

Contents

Introduction

The nurse on the phone told me Amber had been eating breakfast an hour earlier, she had seemed well, but now she was hardly breathing. She wouldn't wake up. When I entered the room, she was unconscious. She looked so peaceful, her long black hair spread across the pillow. I placed an oxygen meter on her right index finger and saw the blue sapphire glow under her nails, the sign of hypoxia I had seen in my textbooks. The oximeter beeped into life and confirmed what we could see with our own eyes: Amber was dying.

The most accurate sign of an opioid overdose is a person taking fewer than twelve breaths a minute. Try breathing only once every five seconds. If you wait too long, your brain stem takes over and forces you to breathe. Amber was breathing once every ten seconds.

She had been admitted two days earlier to the third floor of the Toronto hospital where I was a fourth-year medical student on the internal medicine ward. Amber had come to the emergency room with a fever on Sunday night. Every part of her body hurt, and her chest felt heavy; she thought she had the flu. Her doctor knew she was using needles.

It was 2009, and more men and women like Amber were walking into emergency rooms across North America with track marks, abscesses, and infections deep in their bodies. More were coming in by ambulance after overdosing, as well.

Amber was anxious, especially when she was told she had a murmur in her heart. She said no one had told her that before. Not that she'd been to the doctor in a while. Her mother drank and her father was long gone. Her teachers cared about her, but she had left school and home at sixteen.

The first time Amber snorted heroin, she forgot, for a while, about her mother, her absent father, the men who had hurt her, and the small room where she lived with her latest boyfriend. The heroin travelled to the opioid receptors in her central and peripheral nervous system. The opioid flooded her brain with the pleasure molecule dopamine. She felt no pain. It was like floating in a pool of warm salt water.

She had been injecting for only a month when her fevers started. The heart murmur and the red sores on her arms, quickly identified as track marks by her doctor, led to the diagnosis of endocarditis, an infection in her heart, which took her some time to understand. A mass of bacteria was coalescing on her heart's tricuspid valve, sending waves of bacteria and debris ricocheting through her body with every heartbeat. We could see the mass, called a vegetation, using an echocardiogram, an ultrasound of the heart. We gave her penicillin and treated her fever.

When she overdosed in her hospital bed, we administered the antidote: naloxone. The naloxone entered her IV, pulsed into her vein, and then filtered through to all the opioid receptors in her body. The tiny molecules displaced any opioids in her system and blocked the opioid receptors. In a few seconds, she sat up with a start, eyes wide, her black hair whipping around.

"Shit!" she exclaimed.

She looked around in anger.

"What did you do to me?"

The naloxone had put her into immediate opioid withdrawal, but after a few minutes she calmed down. We explained to her that she had stopped breathing. We had needed to give her oxygen — to put a mask on her and squeeze air into her lungs with a bag valve mask — to help her breathe. She had overdosed. She had been using heroin in her room again. Her boyfriend had smuggled it in; they couldn't stop using. As we reminded her, she nodded. Yes, it was true, that was what had happened. She had never been given naloxone before, so she had never been so rudely awakened from a drug-induced slumber. It would still be a few years before naloxone would be found in every paramedic's bag and every pharmacy, before it would be pressed into the hands of people who use drugs across the continent.

Amber was the first patient I had ever treated for an opioid overdose. She was the first patient with whom I discussed getting addiction treatment and trying methadone — something she was seriously considering, especially now that she had this *thing* growing in her heart.

I had no special interest in addiction medicine at that time. I had done my master's thesis on tobacco control and I was interested in infectious diseases like HIV and hepatitis. If someone had told me I would end up as an addiction doctor, working on the front lines of the opioid epidemic — first the OxyContin wave, then heroin, then fentanyl — I would not have believed it.

But the epidemic called my name.

Opioids, like fire, like floods, like disease, have been killing for millennia. There have been waves of deaths caused by drugs in the past, and there have been moral panics about them. What is different this time is the durability of the epidemic. If we trace it back to the early 1990s, we see that it has been with us for a quarter century, first hiding, lurking below public awareness, and now frightfully obvious. The other thing that is different this time is the scale of the epidemic. Opioid overdoses have become the number-one cause of accidental death in North America, reaching into every level of society and pushing down life expectancy. The final thing that is different is fentanyl.

We have been hit by three waves, so far, of the North American opioid epidemic. In the 1990s, as more doctors prescribed more opioids to ease pain, patients began to die from those medications. That was the first wave. The second wave began in 2010, as heroin became increasingly competitive with prescription opioids in terms of cost and purity, and new heroin distribution networks spread across the continent. The third wave began only a few years later, in 2013. We are being hit by the third wave now, and it's much worse than the wave of the 1990s, worse than what occurred in 2010. The third wave is being driven by fentanyl.[1]

On February 13, 2017, Ottawa Public Health and the Ottawa Police Service released an alert titled "Potential Risk of Overdose from Counterfeit Prescription Pills." The notice warned that "illicit fentanyl has been detected in counterfeit pills manufactured to resemble prescription pills like Percocet. The presence of illicit fentanyl significantly increases the risk of overdose; it is fatal in very small amounts."[2] I began to hear about the fake Percocet tablets from patients around the same time. The full force of the third wave was about to crash down on the continent.

The next day, February 14, 2017, Chloe Kotval died of an overdose. She was fourteen years old; in a photo, her shoulder-length brown hair frames her brown eyes; a subtle smile brightens her oval face. Two weeks later, the Ottawa police confirmed that pills found near her body had tested positive for fentanyl. More teens died in the same neighbourhood, and parent groups demanded action; some parents got a naloxone kit and had an agonizing discussion with their children about opioid use.

Sam Quinones wrote of the epidemic in his powerful book *Dreamland: The True Tale of America's Opiate Epidemic*:

> This epidemic involved more users and far more death than the crack plague of the 1990s, or the heroin plague in the 1970s; but it was happening quietly.... Via pills, heroin had entered the mainstream. The new addicts were football players and cheerleaders; football was almost a gateway to opioid addiction. Wounded soldiers returned from Afghanistan hooked on pain pills and died in America. Kids got hooked in college and died there.... They were the daughters of preachers, the sons of cops and doctors, the children of contractors and teachers and business owners and bankers.[3]

When first setting out to write *Dreamland*, Quinones was sitting in a tavern in Covington, Kentucky, when he fell into conversation with an elderly woman. He told her he was just beginning a book about the epidemic. She invited him to sit down and introduced herself as Carol Wagner: "Carol went on to tell me of her handsome, college-educated son, Chad, who was prescribed OxyContin for his carpal tunnel syndrome, grew addicted, and never got unstuck after that. He lost home and family and five years later lay dead of a heroin overdose in a Cincinnati halfway house." Quinones was "stunned that so random an encounter in America's heartland could yield such personal connections to heroin."[4]

The opioid epidemic has spread across North America like spilled ink across the page.

In 2018 Evan Wood, a pioneer in addiction and harm-reduction research in Canada, observed, "Every indication is that North America's opioid-overdose crisis is not abating, and experts have recently estimated that overdoses could kill more than half a million Americans over the next decade."[5] In 2017 and again in 2018, almost fifty thousand Americans and more than four thousand Canadians died from opioids. Nearly every year has seen big increases in the number of people killed by opioids; in recent years, these increases have been driven by fentanyl.

In October 2018, all twenty-one samples of drugs tested at my clinic in Ottawa, which were sold on the street as heroin, contained fentanyl; zero samples contained heroin. Of the fifteen samples thought to be speed or crystal meth, five contained fentanyl. In that unusually warm fall of 2018, without any prompting from me, patients were talking about the power of this synthetic opioid.

"The down has got a real hold on me now. I didn't even like down before, but the purple stuff, I think it's the fentanyl, I can't stop. Whenever I see someone doing it or someone offers it to me, I have to use," Clara told me one afternoon. "It's so easy to get, it's cheap, only twenty bucks for half a point."

She looked away for a moment, then continued, "I can't expect anyone to help me. I'm not helping myself. I've been so fucked up since I started on fentanyl. Yes, I was using before, but now all I can think about is getting my next point of fentanyl. The first thing I have to do is stop using."

Even people who weren't using fentanyl were affected, as my next patient told me: "I missed my appointment yesterday because I went to a wake. My friend overdosed on one of those new kinds of fentanyl, the kind you can't come back from."

The idea that there was a kind of fentanyl you could not come back from had entered the minds of people who used drugs in towns and cities across the continent. The world was changing.

But there was also good news that day.

"Doc, I haven't used in a month," Joel told me.

I was surprised. Joel had been my patient for three years and I'd never seen him go more than three days without smoking, injecting, swallowing, or snorting an opioid.

"That's amazing. How did you do it?"

"I was tired of fucking up. I just woke up the other day and I didn't feel like using." He grinned.

I looked at his matted blond hair and his pale cheeks, marked with a few days of stubble, and then back at his smile. It was different. That smile had been driven away by terrible withdrawal symptoms, sleepless nights smoking crack and injecting heroin, the police pounding on his door, and jail time. The smile I saw that day wasn't rueful, ironic, or self-deprecating. It wasn't the smile I had seen a few months earlier when he told me, "I've gotten very good at crime. I'm not proud of it."

This new smile changed his face.

Almost every day, amid the daily assault of dark news and pessimism about the epidemic, I see the light of such small successes. In the safety of my office, face to face with a huge photo of a traditional rehab scene — a tranquil mountain lake just as the sun is about to set — a patient will unwrap layers of shame and trauma and share their fragile victories.

I have seen how exquisitely delicate these periods of recovery can be, so I treat them with great care. We talk about how to nurture their success, how to incubate this new-found freedom from opioids.

But each time I see some light, I am reminded that the tragedies have not stopped. At meetings of physicians, this reminder comes as a simple line on a graph labelled "Overdose Deaths." For too many years the line pointed up, indicating that the number of deaths from opioids continued to climb. Overdoses are dragging down life expectancy for entire swathes of the population and destroying families and communities in the process. Life expectancy in the United States declined for two years in a row because of the rising death toll. One morning, I opened a journal to see a simple statistic: 115 lives are ended by opioid overdoses every day in the United States.

The news is filled with overdoses, but death is only the final frame for those whose lives have been marred by lost careers, ruined relationships, sickness, jail time, and secret misery.

"I haven't told my dad that I relapsed. I was doing so good. He keeps asking why I'm losing so much weight — I think he knows," Carl told me recently as sweat poured down his angular face and he looked at me through swollen pupils.

We talked about increasing his dose of buprenorphine, and we booked a follow-up visit in a week to reassess his use. I looked at his urine drug screen, which was positive for heroin, fentanyl, and cocaine, and thought about our visits two years earlier, when Carl had celebrated a whole year without drug use.

"Why do you want to stop using this time?" I asked.

"I'm getting tired of watching all my friends die. I look around to all the people I got into this mess with and they're all gone. Why should I wait to quit when I'm fifty, when the damage is already done?"

The next week Carl came back to share his success.

"My cravings are much better now. I started reading this book. It's the first time I've read a novel."

Carl told me he went three days without injecting fentanyl. I noticed he wasn't sweating as much as at our last visit and his pupils weren't as big. I increased his dose of buprenorphine again, and we made a plan to meet in another week. Carl was on the first rung of the ladder. We talked about his supports. His girlfriend was still using heroin and cocaine, but she was also trying to quit. His dad supported him, but Carl was keeping the truth from him. He had recently seen a psychiatrist and was on a mood-stabilizing medication. His sleep was getting better as his opioid withdrawal symptoms were treated by his buprenorphine. He hadn't missed an appointment with me for several months. Things were starting to come together for Carl.

The next day, Pamela sat down in front of me with a strained smile, which then transformed into a face of agony. "I need to get out of this city," she said. "I just found out another friend of mine died. We were supposed to meet up yesterday, but she never came. I called her like ten times yesterday, but it went to her voice mail. Then today I heard she was found in the stairwell across the street from my place."

The tears streamed down her face, and I felt her raw emotions wash over me.

In the hallway that leads to the drop-in area of our clinic, there is an overdose memorial wall filled with names and photos. Sometimes people write messages of farewell next to the faces. I knew that Pamela's friend would be one more name on the wall, one more face.

As the death rate climbed, stories like Pamela's became commonplace. She was the last person to talk to the recently deceased; he was texting at the time; they had used the same heroin. Pamela reflected on her own life that day, wondering why she hadn't died, exuding the classic survivor guilt seen in every epidemic or natural disaster. *There but for the grace of God go I.*

"I must have tolerance, I must have, because I've been using the same fentanyl as everyone that died," she told me through her tears.

Overdose deaths ricochet through the community, affecting everyone differently, adding to the burden of fear, guilt, and trauma. They affect people in many ways. Julian was working in a hotel when a teenager overdosed in the lobby. He tried to resuscitate him using a naloxone kit and the rudimentary CPR he had learned in high school.

"We were trying to resuscitate a dead kid. He was like only nineteen. It was fucking terrible," he told me afterward.

Other times, the consequences are more unexpected.

"A guy at the shelter overdosed and set the bed on fire. Now I've got nowhere to sleep," Larry told me when I asked him where he was living. This time there was no death, because the fire alerted the shelter workers, who dragged the young man out of the burning room and were able to administer naloxone before calling both the paramedics and the fire department.

Sometimes weeks will go by without anyone mentioning an overdose. Everyone relaxes a little, maybe gets a little complacent about where they are getting their drugs from or how much they use in one shot, and then there is another death.

How did we get to this point? The ancient Egyptians cultivated poppies and wrote prescriptions for opium on medical papyri. The word *opium* itself comes from the Greek word for poppy juice, *opion*. We have engineered the poppy to make powerful medicines to control pain. Opioids make people feel euphoric, tranquil, free. They calm people living with ceaseless anxiety or sadness. As our bodies become tolerant to opioids we need to use more, and the more we use, the more the opioids quiet our level of consciousness, even our will to breathe.

A friend who took opioids for two days after an injury told me, "I've never felt better in my life; I was so happy and I got so much done." Another doctor told me she wasn't going to stop prescribing opioids: "[They] work; I'm careful with them and they help people." People feel good when they take them, and doctors feel good when they can relieve their patients' suffering.

But opioids give pleasure, and pleasure is a trap.[6] Pamela told me that heroin is like an abusive lover; it gets under your skin and into your mind. Opioids make you feel high and then bring you down. They make you feel calm and safe and then smother you in your sleep. All you can think about is your next point of heroin or your next pill of Percocet, but more than anything, you want to stop using. You want to get away. You fight, but the opioid fights back. It gives you chills and drenching night sweats; it makes you vomit; it makes you want to jump out of your skin; it makes you crazy with revulsion and desire. It is the perfect biological weapon, designed to target the pleasure centres of the brain. People from every walk of life have been swept up in the flood of opioids made available by doctors and dealers, and pilfered from medicine cabinets.

Sandra, a thirty-year-old veteran of the street, looked at me and asked a simple question: "What's going on? Why is this happening?" Like Sandra, I wanted to understand why opioids work so well and kill so easily. I wanted to understand the history that brought us to this point. Finally, I wanted to learn about the weapons we have available to fight against this scourge — treatment, prevention, harm reduction — and make a battle plan, a call to arms, to beat this thing. We are in a race against death. Every day we do not solve the epidemic, more lives are lost.

Opioids are the catalyst of a story that is as complex as the lives they touch. We will travel into darkness with patients like Carl and Pamela, but we will also see their light. We will see that science can be a weapon for good as hope emerges in the form of methadone, buprenorphine, naloxone, and new treatments to come, technologies we cannot even imagine. And we will meet the champions fighting the disease: the nurses, the social workers, the doctors, the people who use drugs, and the visionaries. This is a story of hope.

CHAPTER 1
Knocking at the Door

One week started with frantic knocking on the bathroom door at my clinic. A young woman had gone inside, but something wasn't right; she wasn't answering the persistent banging on the door. As the staff's panic rose, the door was unlocked and the pale, auburn-haired girl slumped forward, a needle at her side. Everyone knew she had overdosed, and they had the antidote naloxone at hand, but they also knew it was too late. She was too cold; fumbling fingers found no pulse. In the eye of the storm, she lay still, receiving ministrations of medication, oxygen, and CPR. She was pushed and implored to return to life, but she had already gone. Opioids had taken her.

Few people grow up wanting to work in addictions. I certainly didn't. My childhood memories of substance use involve snatches of conversations and films. My parents discussing Amsterdam's heroin problem and the use of methadone as a treatment on a trip when I was seven. The unspooling of a man's life owing to alcoholism in a black-and-white film I watched in grade-nine health class. I was sheltered from drugs at school and in my community; they were hidden and suppressed. I went into medicine with plans to become an infectious diseases doctor, treating tuberculosis and HIV in the slums of East Africa. But in downtown Toronto, on medicine and infectious disease wards, in the shelters and outpatient clinics, I came face to face with addiction again and again.

Three men sat at the front of our lecture hall, each looking as unremarkable as the next. "I am an alcoholic," one of them said. Our instructor spoke to us about alcoholism while the men added the details of their lives and experiences to his broad outline of facts and diagnoses. After that day, I was awoken to the presence of addiction all around us. I learned that one in six people has a substance use disorder during their lifetime and that many of them hide it well. The mask slips when their body rebels or they overdose. I saw that hospitals were filled with untended and hidden addictions. This thin man with the long brown beard injects cocaine; that woman is in alcohol withdrawal; this man's heart is infected with bacteria that were forced into his vein through the tip of a syringe.

Working in Toronto's homeless shelters and downtown hospitals, I saw opioid addiction at its most raw: the oozing, swollen abscesses from dirty needles and the fevers arising from bacteria run amok in the blood. The cliché I learned from watching old episodes of *ER* was "treat them and street them." I never heard anyone actually use that term during my training, but we saw the revolving door of care for the tiny percentage of patients, those with the worst addictions, who would return, either in withdrawal or after overdoses, time and again. The acute issues were treated with world-class care and the patients were discharged back to the street or the shelter. Many times we tried to get them into treatment or to a methadone clinic or into housing, and sometimes it worked. I learned of the cruel interplay between opioid addiction, homelessness, disease, and poverty.

While I kept my interest in infectious diseases, I found it was addiction that was infecting and upending the lives of my patients with HIV and hepatitis C. And while so much had changed in the treatment of HIV since the widespread introduction of antiretrovirals in the mid-1990s, very little had changed in the treatment of addictions. HIV was no longer leading to AIDS, but addiction to opioids, alcohol, and tobacco was still taking the lives of my patients. I decided to train more in addiction medicine, and because of the depth of the need, every year I do a little more addiction medicine and a little less of everything else.

* * *

In 2006 I sat with my classmates and with dentistry and pharmacy students to learn about working together to treat pain. It was Pain Week at the University of Toronto. In a huge hall, our teachers spoke in sombre tones about the World Health Organization's (WHO's) pain ladder, the need to work up slowly in response to a patient's suffering, from ibuprofen and acetaminophen to codeine, then up the ladder to morphine, hydromorphone, and fentanyl. They told us to be cautious and diligent, but in the emergency rooms and clinics, we saw our supervisors handing over handwritten prescriptions for hundreds of tablets of Percocet or for fentanyl patches that some patients admitted to misusing.

This situation was replayed in hospitals and clinics across the continent, where the seemingly unstoppable force of addiction repeatedly smashed into the fragile ramparts constructed to maintain prudent opioid prescribing. One common dilemma for physicians was separating addiction from the genuine needs of people suffering with chronic pain. A typical conversation went like this:

"I don't have an addiction. I just have pain."

"I see you have a lot of pain. You had a bad car accident and you've been on opioids for the past ten years."

"That's right, but my doctor wants to cut me off."

"Do the opioids work for you?"

"Yes, but my pain is still really bad."

"So why do you want to stay on the opioids?"

"Because they're the only thing that works."

"But they're not working."

"I don't have enough, so sometimes I need to take extra."

"Where do you get extra from?"

And that was when the whole story would come out: getting a few Percocets from a friend, then finding that chewing or snorting the pills made them work better, then starting to buy stronger opioids on the street. The more conversations like this I've had, the more I've been able to put the whole picture together for myself and for my patients who have resisted believing they have a problem with opioids.

These conversations have become easier in recent years because the culture of prescribing opioids has changed so dramatically. More awareness of the opioid epidemic means patients accept that they can no longer just storm out of your office and find a willing prescriber down the street; they accept that they need to work to find new and safer ways to manage their pain and their addiction.

A big reason these conversations have become easier is the work of Nora Volkow, the great-granddaughter of the Russian revolutionary leader Leon Trotsky. Volkow directs the National Institute on Drug Abuse (NIDA), a massive, multibillion-dollar addiction research and funding body. She has been called a general in the drug war — not the war on drugs, but the fight to combat and treat addiction in the brain and in society. Her life changed in 1981 when, as a newly minted physician, she read an article describing the use of positron emission tomography (PET) scanning to image the brain in real time. "It blew my mind," she said of that eureka moment.[1] Brain imaging became her passion. She looked into brains afflicted by mental illnesses like schizophrenia and explored the effects of cocaine on the ebb and flow of dopamine in the brain.

A competitive swimmer and serious runner, she learned to change her own brain's chemistry through exercise before she, or anyone else, understood the role of dopamine and other neurochemicals in shaping human motivation. Even as she led NIDA, she continued to build on her research into the brain and the science of addiction.

I remember one of my own eureka moments when, as a young addiction doctor, I read her paper on the neurobiology of addiction. I was sitting in a hotel room in Orlando as my children drifted to sleep, and I was transfixed by the awesome clarity and power of her science. So much of what I had been studying and attempting to explain to patients and their families came together.

Understanding that addiction is a chronic brain disease allows us to move past the counterproductive, blame-based explanations for it and the stigmatization of those who suffer from it. As the writer Lorna Crozier put it, "Those who know little about substance abuse see it as something unsavoury and shameful. Why don't the drunks, the junkies, the smokers, the bulimics just smarten up? Pull themselves up by the bootstraps. Get some willpower. Stop."[2]

As I sat in that Orlando hotel room, I read that a "more comprehensive understanding of the brain disease model of addiction may help to moderate some of the moral judgment attached to addictive behaviours and foster more scientific and public health–oriented approaches to prevention and treatment."[3] It can help remove stigma and foster compassion toward people with addictions.

Science can also explain why certain substances are addictive and others are not. Opioids are addictive because they release a cascade of pleasure-inducing molecules in the brain. We have opioid receptors scattered throughout our brain, our nerves, our lungs, and our intestines. When opioids enter the brain, our pain is numbed and we feel euphoric. But the brain is also where our respiration and alertness is controlled, and when opioids lock on to receptors in the brain stem, they reduce the drive to breathe. This manipulation in the centre of our brain is what makes opioids so alluring and so deadly. Someone who takes opioids will appear drunk, nod off, and speak in slurred confusion as the opioids turn down their level of consciousness.

Addiction is about dopamine. Addictive substances push dopamine to high, often massively elevated, levels in the *nucleus accumbens*, the reward centre of the brain. This is the *high* of the street vernacular. You get high, then you come down. You get dope, then you get dope sickness. You use. You need a fix, a drink, a toke. Stimulating the opioid receptors leads to a cascade in the brain that ends with increased dopamine.[4] The writer William S. Burroughs described the experience of using opioids vividly in *Naked Lunch*: "Morphine hits the backs of the legs first, then the back of the neck, a spreading wave of relaxation slackening the muscles away from the bones so that you seem to float without outlines, like lying in warm salt water."

Floating on a cloud is a common description of the first high.

Opioids constrict the pupils. Tiny pinpoint pupils are a sign of an opioid overdose, although other drugs, such as benzodiazepines and antipsychotics, can also constrict the pupils. When opioids hit smooth muscles in the bronchi of the lungs, they block the cough reflex, which is why heroin was originally marketed as a cough medicine and used to treat tuberculosis. When opioids hit the smooth muscles in the intestines, they paralyze the bowel, which leads to constipation, a near universal experience among opioid users.

A long-term effect of opioids is their impact on hormones. Opioids get into the hypothalamus and inhibit the release of two master hormones that control the production of sex hormones, including testosterone. Women will often stop having their periods after prolonged opioid use and men will notice reduced libido and increasing problems with erectile dysfunction.[5]

Many opioids are consumed in one form but are transformed — or *metabolized* — to become something different in the body. These metabolites may or may not be active. An older opioid that was widely misused was Demerol. It was pernicious because of the toxic accumulation of active metabolites, one of which caused seizures. Heroin is metabolized to morphine and to 6-monoacetylmorphine, both of which are active in the brain. Heroin is particularly reinforcing because it can pass quickly through the blood–brain barrier and work at high levels in the brain.[6]

Opioids affect the brain's response to stimuli and impair decision-making. We are all creatures of habit, and addiction is a deeply ingrained habit. Think about an activity or food you love; then think about all the context that makes the experience so great. I love to run. So when I get out my running clothes and put on my running shoes, my brain knows that I'm about to experience the rush of neurochemicals associated with exercise. When you smell your favourite food, you start salivating before a morsel has passed your lips. So it is with drugs. Entering a room where you have used drugs or taking out the equipment to smoke or inject a drug leads your dopamine-producing cells to start firing in anticipation of the rush to come. Repetition turns opioid use into an automatic and compulsive behaviour. These changes in the brain endure; they last years after drug use stops, which is why addiction is a chronic disease.[7]

* * *

A few years ago, I was at a meeting about opioid addiction. To try to get us to understand the effect of the drug, one of the doctors in the room told a story from his youth about hiking through a rural area in Thailand with a companion.

"My friend was really starting to get on my nerves," he said. "We'd been arguing about where we were going to travel next, and we were worried about running out of money. Then one evening, a group of men invited us to sit with them while they smoked opium. We both tried it, and when I inhaled on the pipe, I felt all my worries disappear and I felt so much love for my friend."

For at least the first few dozen times a person uses an opioid, even a small amount, they feel euphoric; they feel no pain; they get sedated. But with extended opioid use — and this is a reason opioids do not actually work very well for chronic pain in the long term — people develop a tolerance. The brain is modified if exposed on a recurrent basis to a drug — any drug — and becomes less sensitive to that drug. The release of dopamine is diminished and so the euphoric effect of opioids is muted with recurrent use. One patient told me that he sometimes felt like every time he used heroin, he was actually chasing his "very first high." The first high is the best, and for someone predisposed to becoming addicted, nothing else in life compares with the calm and warmth they experience the first few times they use a drug.

Ann Marlowe, a Harvard-educated writer, described this experience in her addiction memoir, *How to Stop Time: Heroin from A to Z*: "The nearest I can come to explaining to someone who doesn't take illegal drugs the unrecapturable specialness of your first heroin high is to invoke the deep satisfaction of your first cup of coffee in the morning. Your subsequent coffees may be pleasant enough, but they're all marred by not being the first. And heroin use is one of the indisputable cases where the good old days really were the good old days. The initial highs did feel better than the drug will ever make you feel again."[8]

The tragedy for nearly all people who use drugs is that they never return to that initial state of bliss. With repeated use, smaller and smaller amounts of dopamine are released. People need to increase the quantity and frequency of opioid use. Even worse, they become less sensitive to the stimulation for non-drug-related rewards, and they lose motivation to do quotidian and necessary activities such as show up at work and maintain their relationships. The joys of drug use plateau and then decline, but so do the joys of life. Food doesn't taste as good, careers become a barrier to using drugs, and love feels less like love.

It gets worse. Not only does the brain's reward system flatline, but there is a concurrent rise of the brain's *anti-reward system*, the network of brain pathways involved in stress and negative emotions. Chronic drug use makes the anti-reward system overactive. That is why people who use opioids chronically are more likely to develop depression and to stop caring about every aspect of life other than drugs. People who use opioids are pulled to the rewards of drugs while also being pushed to avoid withdrawal, depression, and pain. Over a short period of time, a person transitions from taking drugs in order to get high to using them to get a brief respite from depression.[9] Rather than using to get the feeling of floating on a cloud, people begin to seek opioids to make the pain stop.

As Kevin put it one morning, as snow fell on the streets outside, "I've been taking everything I can get my hands on to kill the fucking pain." It wasn't pain from an injury or arthritis he was describing; it was the deeper and more pervasive pain of withdrawal and the anti-reward system.

He needed to vent. "The government says don't use drugs because you might overdose, but they don't say your life will also be shit for twenty years."

It doesn't have to be shit, I tried to tell him. He kept refusing to get on to an effective dose of methadone or buprenorphine, always agreeing to take a starting dose for a few days but then missing his appointment and showing up in bad withdrawal a few weeks later. I tried to explain that this pain, this depression, gets better with treatment involving a steady dose of an opioid substitute. But I knew he had to make his own decision about treatment. Although he would show flashes of anger against me, against the government, against the bullshit, he kept coming back, and I felt that was, at the least, a small victory.

One of the reasons that Kevin kept using opioids and coming back for opioid treatment was that he was anxious to prevent withdrawal. Withdrawal from a drug produces the direct opposite of the drug's usual effects. So if drug use makes you feel calm, withdrawal makes you anxious. In withdrawal, freedom from pain becomes a world of pain. Sleepiness becomes insomnia; constipation becomes diarrhea. It is no wonder, then, that people who use opioids are so incredibly motivated to find them at all costs. They don't just want to get high; they desperately want to avoid entering the world of withdrawal. I've heard the state of withdrawal compared with having a plastic bag over your face; you will do anything to get it off, commit any crime.

And you don't have a lot of time. The effects of short-acting opioids such as heroin last for a matter of hours. If more opioids aren't found within twelve hours, a person will sense the early warning signs, perhaps a little sweating or a little nausea, and they will know that withdrawal is to come. If they can't get their hands on an opioid, often because they are broke or in jail, full-scale withdrawal ensues. These acute withdrawal symptoms can last for days but will usually resolve within a week. They are followed by weeks to months of protracted withdrawal symptoms that include fatigue, depression, low appetite, and insomnia.[10]

Early in my training I was taught that full-scale opioid withdrawal is similar to a flu-like illness and that it is not fatal. This was used to justify withholding opioids from patients. But then attitudes became more sympathetic. Another addiction doctor asked me, "Have you ever had the flu? It's like torture. It's inhumane to deny treatment to someone in withdrawal." So now we are more likely to offer opioid substitution when someone is in withdrawal, a treatment that rapidly alleviates withdrawal symptoms, cravings, and the risk of relapse.

Untreated withdrawal causes avoidable suffering. It is also dangerous. The first step in the conventional treatment approach for opioid addiction in North America used to require the patient to go to detox and suffer through withdrawal; for most patients that was where treatment ended. Doctors came to realize that patients who went to detox often went back to their old environments and soon relapsed. These patients were at even greater danger than most people who were actively using drugs; in rehab they had lost their tolerance to opioids, so if they tried using the same doses they had been habituated to in the past, they could very easily overdose. Indeed, this happened many times. Now health care providers avoid relying on the stand-alone detox period. Instead, they either connect patients immediately to treatment after detox or, better still, follow up with opioid substitution to prevent patients' suffering from withdrawal, relapse, and the dangerous loss of tolerance.

Most people know very little about substance use, but many have very strong opinions nonetheless. Among the many people who believe they could resist the compulsive self-administration of a dopamine high, there is incredulity about the behaviour of people who use drugs. Among people who use drugs, there is a feeling of profound fellowship, an understanding of the path that one out of every six people will travel.

A common bias involves the selective use of the term *addiction*. I once spoke to the father of a young man just beginning treatment for opioids under my care.

"I don't understand how my son became an addict," the father complained in a gruff voice.

I looked at the nicotine stains on his wrinkled and callused hands. "Do you have an addiction to smoking?" I asked him.

"I have tried to quit many, many times," the father told me, his eyes softening as he made the connection.

Tobacco is a legal drug, and although it kills one in two long-term users, its use is not linked with the crime or overdoses associated with other drugs. These facts are accidents of neurochemistry and consequences of tobacco's legal and easy availability. In fact, nicotine is nearly as addictive as both heroin and cocaine.

Smoking-cessation programs are usually presented as respiratory- or cardiac-health interventions in hospitals and clinics, but they are, at root, addiction programs. Many health care workers do not realize that they can apply many of the same tools used for smoking cessation to other substance use disorders.

Who becomes addicted in the first place? While Nora Volkow recognized that addiction is a disease of the brain, she pointed out that genes and brain chemicals are not the only agents involved in producing addiction: "Predisposition is not predetermination," she told a congressional subcommittee in 2005. "Environment and other biological factors, including family, culture and community, are of great importance to the development of addiction and are essential to its prevention."[11] In North America, the smoking rate has declined by 1 percent every two years for the last fifty years. Our brains have not changed, but our understanding, our attitudes, and our policies have.

About half the risk for addiction is in our genes. A clear way to demonstrate the role of heredity is through twin studies. The Virginia Twin Study showed that genes and environment play different roles at different points in a person's life. The study suggested that whether or not adolescents began using nicotine, alcohol, or cannabis was strongly determined by social and familial factors. But as these adolescents grew into adults, their social environment became less important and genetic factors became stronger determinants of whether they would abuse substances.[12]

The earliest ingredients of a life are mixed in the womb. Even before that, the ingredients are prepared. Male smokers contribute sperm that has been contaminated by the carcinogenic products of tobacco combustion. When pregnant mothers use substances, babies can be born early, small, with mental impairment, and even dependent on opioids. Opioid use by pregnant women quadrupled in the United States between 1999 and 2014.[13] Illicit opioid use during pregnancy is linked to miscarriage, small babies, infections, postpartum hemorrhages, and fetal death. The fetus is exposed to opioids in the mother's bloodstream and can develop dependence. After the baby is born, they can go into withdrawal, which causes feeding difficulties, failure to thrive, and seizures. The treatment is to give the baby morphine and slowly wean them off it.

The environment a child is born into also plays a very significant role in the development of addiction. There is a spectrum of possibilities, with unconditional love and security on one end and abuse and insecure attachment on the other end. Freedom from hunger or from threats to physical safety does not guarantee sufficient support for a child. A lack of secure attachment or a lack of emotional and intellectual engagement can also put a child on a very dark path. Then there are the stressors, the adverse childhood events — things like abuse, being a victim of bullying, or the loss of a parent through death or divorce. The greater the number of adverse childhood events a person experiences, the greater the likelihood that person will suffer from mental health disorders and substance use disorders. I remember feeling appalled, like I had just learned about some vast, unknown conspiracy against our species, when I first saw a chart showing the strength of that correlation.

Having a bad childhood is not fate, but only the very strong survive a barrage of adverse life conditions. By the time children are in their early teens, they may already have begun to experiment with substances. Addiction is often a pediatric disease. The worst substance use disorders start in childhood; as the brain develops in the presence of substances, it is reshaped and primed to need and want more substances. Adolescents who use alcohol or cannabis in large amounts to cope with the pain of life are often unable to develop healthier coping strategies. Thus, when they are adults facing an angry partner, financial stress, or a rejection, drugs or booze will become their first port of call.

I always ask my patients how old they were when they started using each type of substance — alcohol, tobacco, cannabis, opioids, cocaine, stimulants. Even though it is not uncommon to start at a young age, I am still quietly shocked when I hear how early some began to use. Patients have told me that they started at the age of twelve. I have even heard ages younger than that. Recently, Jeremy and I were reviewing his childhood drug use and he said, "I remember on my thirteenth birthday thinking to myself, *I've become a pothead.* I had been using pot every day for a whole year."

Tobacco and alcohol often come first; these are followed by cannabis, then cocaine and opioids. The concept of *gateway drugs* posits that legal drugs are gateways to the illegal drugs. Not everyone passes through those gateways, but those children with younger and more frequent exposure to alcohol, nicotine, and cannabis are more likely to develop addictions and progress to other drugs.

Genetics and the environment blend together to create differential risks for mental illnesses such as depression, anxiety, bipolar disorder, and schizophrenia. There are many ways for addictions and mental illnesses to overlap. For example, you can develop anxiety as a teen and then take up cannabis or alcohol as a destructive type of self-medication. Or you can start drinking or using cannabis heavily and then develop depression or anxiety. Most people with opioid use disorder have worse moods and more anxiety after long periods of use because of changes in their brain and the chronic cycle of intoxication and withdrawal.

Low socioeconomic status, poor parental support, social isolation, and drug availability all affect rates of drug use. Many of these factors may be linked to the intensity of stress a person experiences and their ability to cope with that stress. The social environment can change the structure and function of the brain; for example, being dominant or feeling dominated can alter dopamine receptors. Studies of mice show that socially dominant animals have more dopamine receptors in their brain and are less likely to self-administer drugs such as cocaine or alcohol. Socially subordinate mice have fewer dopamine receptors and are more likely to use cocaine or alcohol, perhaps because socially subordinate animals feel more stress and are more likely to try to numb those feelings by self-administering drugs.[14]

This pattern of using drugs to self-medicate or to numb or calm emotions is one my patients have described to me many times.

"When I feel down, I crave," Jodie explained to me one afternoon in early spring as she struggled with the early weeks of sobriety. "I've had a lot of thoughts and urges. When I hurt, I remember how drugs relieve that feeling."

Patients like Jodie describe early and powerful feelings of anxiety or depression, which they learn to mask with alcohol or cocaine or opioids. When this pattern of pain followed by relief owing to drugs occurs repeatedly, people learn to associate relief from pain and stress with the use of drugs. It becomes their first, best, and only coping mechanism.

Two weeks later, Jodie told me, "I got a week clean, then I had a fight with my boyfriend and I used. I couldn't stop myself." She linked her relapse to the fight with her boyfriend.

I work with patients and encourage them to speak to their addiction counsellors about developing new and healthier coping skills: simple skills like breathing exercises, talking through their worries with friends and family, or using exercise to burn off their stress.

What does it even mean to become addicted? People may ask themselves whether they have a problem or whether they just like drinking. It can take years and the repeated insistence of partners and children to convince someone they have a problem. Even people who inject heroin will often spin their drug use as a positive choice, a view that is more easily held when all their friends and social contacts also use drugs. At a recent meeting, a young man spoke proudly about his heroin use to a group of addiction physicians. "I'm not sick. I'm not depressed. I like injecting heroin," he said. While this went against the grain of the meeting, it didn't faze many of us.

Some people can use drugs here and there without becoming addicted. Most drinkers do not become alcoholics. About half of people who use heroin during their lifetime develop a heroin addiction.[15] So for that young man, it is a coin toss. He may be able to stop using or he may become addicted. But even if he doesn't become addicted, he is still at risk of contracting HIV and infections from unclean needles, and of overdosing. Even if he doesn't think he is addicted, he could very well be, as people who use drugs can develop elaborate ways to deny the truth about their drug use and obscure it from themselves and those around them.

Although I don't know his experience or his journey, I sympathize with this young man's desire to free himself from the shackles of society's moralizing and ignorance about drug use. *Addiction* is not even a medical term anymore, as it has become too coated in the grime of stigma and prejudice. A few years ago we changed the term to *substance use disorder*, something that sounds as technical and sanitized as possible.

People with opioid use disorders use more and more over longer periods than they intend. They want to control their use, but feel powerless. Driven by powerful cravings, they spend inordinate amounts of time getting drugs, using them, and recovering from drug use. And this pattern of behaviour begins to have consequences in their life. They start to miss work, school, or social activities. They start to have relationship and work problems, either of which can drive them to seek treatment. They develop mental and physical health problems arising from their opioid use. And as they use for longer periods of time, their tolerance goes up and they need to use more. If they can't use, they develop crippling withdrawal symptoms.

To prevent opioid use disorder, and all the chaos that results from addiction, doctors try to determine who will take their opioid prescriptions properly and who will not. Misuse takes many forms. Imagine you have been given a prescription for ninety tablets of Percocet from your doctor. How might you misuse this prescription? You could simply take more than prescribed, so instead of taking one tablet every six hours, you could take ten tablets at once. Or you could alter the route of delivery by crushing or injecting the pills rather than simply swallowing them. If you didn't need all ninety tablets, you could divert them, either for profit or to help out your friends or family. Another form of aberrant use is supplementing the prescription from your doctor with opioids purchased from the street, either the same opioid or another form, such as heroin or powdered fentanyl. When you consider all the ways you could abuse a prescription, it's remarkable how many people manage to take their medication as prescribed.

We know a few important risk factors that make a person more likely to misuse opioids. A big risk is having an addiction to other drugs, such as cocaine or alcohol. Even smokers are at increased risk of abusing opioids, presumably because their brains are already in the business of depending on a drug. If your mother, father, or siblings have had problems with substances, then your risk is increased. But it certainly isn't destiny. I've heard hundreds of family histories that reveal how parents and siblings can have totally different mental health profiles and totally different life trajectories. My patients who struggle with the worst addictions often reflect philosophically on the success of their siblings, who have achieved all the things that addiction can destroy: career, home, family, stability.[16]

Jodie was struggling in her job when I first met her. She worked as a personal trainer but had started cancelling appointments and not showing up on time to the gym, where she also taught spinning. She had been introduced to opioids while recovering from surgery on her hip after a bad biking accident. For years she had been building up to her dream of racing road bikes as a professional, but this injury had killed that ambition. As she recovered from the pain and disappointment, the opioids brought her immense relief. After she left the hospital and thought about how to rebuild her life, she couldn't forget the calm and relief granted by the morphine prescribed by her orthopedic surgeon. She started visiting her family doctor and walk-in clinics and found it was easy to get prescriptions for up to a hundred tablets of morphine or Percocet at a time. She took these pills sparingly at first, but as her tolerance grew, she took more pills, even though she felt less relief.

One day a friend asked Jodie if she'd tried chewing her tablets, saying that it helped to make them act faster. The tablets tasted chalky and stuck between Jodie's teeth; the euphoria was really good, but it didn't last long. She began to read online about other ways to use her pills, and she went from chewing to snorting. Within a year, she had injected for the first time.

"I didn't know what I was doing," she told me. "I was scared of needles, but one of my friends had used needles and she showed me what to do. I was scared, but after that I didn't want to chew or sniff my pills. I only wanted to inject."

She started spending so much on her pills that she was short on her rent and had less food in her fridge. She stopped cleaning her house regularly and eventually quit her job. For a while, she told me she wasn't an addict; she just needed the pills because of her pain. I offered her treatment, but she wasn't ready. One day, a few months after we first met, Jodie was clearly upset.

"Do I look like a junkie?" she asked.

"Why are you asking?" I wondered where her question would lead.

"This guy came up to me and tried to sell me purple fentanyl. I don't even know the guy, but he could see I was a junkie. It made me feel like shit."

Even as she had tried to keep living her life free from labels, others — including me, her family, and drug dealers on the street — had seen signs that she did not have her opioid use under control, that she had an addiction. And as I got to know her better, I learned that the roots of her addiction went deeper than the biking accident she'd had at age twenty-two. As she became more comfortable, she opened up about her parents, her childhood, and the traumas she had lived through. I began to add up the adverse childhood events and I understood that her brain had been moulded by her family history and her childhood into a fertile receptacle for addiction.

One afternoon, Jodie came to the office and I noticed that her left arm hung limply on her thin frame.

"What happened?"

"I overdosed."

"What happened to your arm?"

"I went down and I guess I was lying on my arm for a while. When I woke up I couldn't move it."

She had injected a tiny amount of purple heroin on her own. Her friend had come into her room when she didn't answer the door. She found Jodie slumped on the floor, taking only small breaths, turning blue. She had found the intranasal naloxone kit she knew Jodie kept in her bathroom and squirted it up her nose. Jodie gasped as life returned to her body. Eventually, the paramedics arrived and took her to the hospital, where she was observed for the rest of the day.

Why do so many people overdose? In particular, why do so many men? In Canada, three-quarters of overdose deaths in 2017 were men, while in the United States, two men overdose for every one woman. Why can't people find euphoria without stepping so close to the line where breathing stops? It must have to do with how opioids feel in the brain. The stronger the dose, the better the high, the more likely the user is to overdose. The best high will bring a person close to the edge and then back, but finding that narrow band is so hard because of the unpredictable strength of street opioids, as well as the interactions between contaminants in the product and substances in the person's body, such as alcohol or other sedatives.

More opioid means more intoxication, but because of opioids' action on the brain stem, it also means less will to breathe. By the second century BCE, the Greek physician Nicander of Colophon already recognized the symptoms of an opioid overdose; he described the effects of large amounts of opioid consumption: "Their extremities are chilled; their eyes do not open but are bound quite motionless by their eyelids. With the exhaustion an odorous sweat bathes all the body, turns cheeks pale, and causes the lips to swell; the bonds of the jaw are relaxed, and through the throat the laboured breath passes faint and chill. And often either the livid nail or wrinkled nostril is a harbinger of death; sometimes too the sunken eyes."[17]

Nicander's treatment for an overdose included hot wine, the oil of roses, and slapping the victim on the cheeks, all with the aim of inducing the patient to vomit. Of course, the proper treatment is not hot wine, the oil of roses, or slapping. In the more recent past, a cold shower and ice have also been recommended for those suffering from an overdose, but those are of no help either. Naloxone works. It can be given in the nose or as an injection, but in the emergency room or hospital, it works best when given intravenously. Naloxone is given not simply to wake someone up, but also to get them breathing. Naloxone works for only a short time in the body, however, so further doses may be needed, and patients need to be monitored for at least three hours in the emergency room after an overdose.

If someone is brought back soon enough, an overdose may not

cause permanent harm. This is why safe injection sites work; patients are monitored and treated before permanent damage is done. But an untreated overdose, if it doesn't kill the person, can cause permanent disability. When oxygen stops flowing to the brain, the brain dies. In this way, the effects of an overdose are like those produced by a stroke or a near-drowning. People can end up paralyzed, unable to speak, with cognitive impairment, or in a coma.

Fentanyl overdose may be associated with a condition called acute anterograde amnestic syndrome — people have trouble forming new memories after overdosing on fentanyl. This effect can last for months or longer and may be caused by a lack of oxygen to the hippocampus, the memory centre of the brain.[18]

I knew little about drug overdoses or addiction when I began medical school. Over the next ten years, I learned how drugs work in the brain, about the roots of addiction, and how to diagnose and care for patients with substance use disorders. But there was always more to learn as the ground shifted beneath my feet.

Fentanyl became the biggest cause of overdoses in North America in 2013. In late 2018, an addiction doctor from Canada's Atlantic coast told me they didn't have fentanyl yet in his region.

"It's coming. You'll see it soon," another doctor warned him.

Fentanyl was on the move, as opioids have been on the move for millennia, leaving in their wake profit, crime, intoxication, and death.

CHAPTER 2
The Story of Opium

Tom dropped out of university after opioids took control of his life. He was doing construction work but kept getting hurt. He told me that he really wanted to work in a call centre and have normal friends, friends who didn't use drugs. One hot summer afternoon, he said, "My whole life is consumed with getting that forty bucks I need every day to get high." If there was no work at the site, he would shoplift or panhandle to get the money. He was tall, spoke quietly, and was curious about everything.

"How did this happen?" he asked.

"What do you mean?" I wasn't sure if he was talking about his dropping out of university, his financial strain, or his addiction.

"All these pills and all this purple heroin, all these people dying?"

To appreciate the opioid epidemic in its entirety, you have to understand the deep history of opioids in our world. When Tom asked me that question, I had a vague sense that heroin had been around for a few decades, but as I started to learn more, I had no idea how far back and how deep into the layers of history the journey would take me.

The first thing I learned is that opioids have been with us for millennia. Near the hot, dry Moorish town of Granada in Spain, there is a prehistoric burial site where archeologists uncovered a group of bodies buried six thousand years ago. The site is known as the Cave of the Bats. Those ancient bodies were buried with small woven bags containing wheat, locks of hair, and capsules from the opium poppy plant, *Papaver somniferum*. This is the earliest evidence of the veneration of the opium poppy, one of the first plants domesticated by humans.[1]

One thousand years later, on the island of Crete, the Minoans built a civilization that seemed to be far ahead of its time in terms of art, architecture, and cultural sophistication. The Minoans thrived on Crete and the surrounding islands for one and a half millennia. They flourished contemporaneously with the Egyptians, and their distinctive trade goods have been found throughout the Mediterranean. Like those ancient inhabitants of the Cave of the Bats, they wove opium into the sacred tapestry of their lives. There still exist Minoan jugs decorated with poppy heads. One is decorated with both poppies and a snake, the ancient symbol of healing.

An even more striking artifact is the Poppy Goddess, found in a Minoan cult house in northern Crete. This terracotta statue, which is more than three millennia old, stands two and a half feet tall. The Poppy Goddess wears a kind of hoop skirt, and her hands are raised as if she were hushing a crowd before addressing them. In her hair she wears three poppy hairpins, a holy trinity of narcotics. Her hands and fingers are perfectly formed, and her face has been smoothed by time. Her eyes seem to be closed and she is smiling. Scholars say she appears drugged, in a beatific state induced by opioids. I am not so sure. What is clear to me is that she is a goddess, possibly a deity of sleep or of death, and that she is powerful.

Ancient artifacts from the Minoans' rival kingdom, Mycenae, show goddesses holding poppy capsules. Both the Minoans and the Mycenae smoked opium in pipes. The first known opium pipe was made of ivory and was found on Cyprus in 1929. It still bears burn marks and is as old as the Poppy Goddess, about 3,300 years old.[2]

Homer tells us that Helen of Troy added a drug, probably opium, to wine "to quiet all pain and strife, and to bring forgetfulness of every evil." Greek deities were associated with poppies, including Hypnos, the god of sleep; Morpheus, the god of dreams; and Thanatos, the god of death.

The Greek physician Hippocrates, the father of Western medicine, referenced twenty-five medical uses for opium. Of these, twenty-one are for gynecologic ailments. In *On Sleep and Sleeplessness*, Aristotle observed that opioids make people sleep, noting that poppies, like wine, "produce a heaviness in the head," leaving a user "unable to lift up the head or the eyelids." Roman texts refer to the opposite effect: the insomnia that ensues when opium is withdrawn.[3]

Opium poppies were cultivated from ancient times and throughout history in Europe and Asia. The House of the Golden Bracelet is a breathtaking aristocratic home excavated in Pompeii. A fresco in the house, painted using an array of verdant colours, has survived for two millennia. In the fresco, beautiful birds fly through the blue sky and sit on the branches of trees and bushes, and if you look closely, among lavender and roses you can find opium poppies.

Europe suffered an outbreak of bubonic plague, the Black Death, in the middle of the fourteenth century. At that time, opium was one of the only effective medicines. Plague doctors found it alleviated three of the main symptoms of the disease: joint pain and the pain of the plague sores, coughing, and diarrhea.

The Black Death resulted in more demand for medicine and the services of doctors. Around this time, anesthetics containing opium were developed in Europe and Asia for surgery. Medieval physicians invented a drink "to make a man sleep whilst men cut him."[4] It was called *dwale* and was used for centuries, with a consistent recipe that included pigs' bile, bryony root, lettuce, vinegar, hemlock juice, henbane, and opium poppy latex. All of this was mixed with wine. Patients drank the mixture until they passed out. As it contained a variety of poisons, the death rate from both the anesthetic and the primitive surgeries it facilitated must have been high.

John of Arderne, a famous English surgeon of the 1300s, used *dwale* for his operations, predominantly treating anal fistulas. For anesthesia he recommended "one grain to half a drachm of Theban opium dissolved in a pint or more of wine, according to the strength of the patient, will make him that drinketh it sleep." But he must have seen deaths caused by mixing opioids and wine, for he immediately warned, "And know that it is well to tweak the nose, to pinch the cheeks or to pluck the beard of such a sleeper to quicken his spirits lest he sleep too deeply."[5]

Jerome of Brunswick described the power of opioids in *The Noble Experyence of the Vertuous Handy Warke of Surgeri*, which was translated into English in 1525. He advised that "Whan the payne is grete, then it is nedefull to put thererto a lytell Opium."[6] The Renaissance physician Paracelsus promoted the use of opium and developed an early version of laudanum. Laudanum was a tincture of opioids that was widely promoted by the English physician Thomas Sydenham in his 1676 book, *Medical Observations Concerning the History and Cure of Acute Diseases.* A student of Sydenham named Thomas Dover would go on to create an opioid compound that became known as Dover's powder and remained in use until the twentieth century.

Dover first set down the recipe in his 1732 bestselling medical manual titled *The Ancient Physician's Legacy to His Country*. The recipe to ease gout mixes one ounce of opium with a variety of ingredients, then advises, "Dose from forty to sixty or seventy Grains in a Glass of White-Wine Posset, going to bed. — Covering up warm, and drinking a Quart or three Pints of the Posset-Drink while sweating. In two or three Hours, at farthest, the Patient will be perfectly free from Pain."[7]

Dover's powder and laudanum were two of the most popular medicines until the twentieth century. Dover's powder was found in the medical bags of Italian troops captured during the Second World War and was legal in India until 1994.

Physicians promoted opium for innumerable medical conditions in texts such as George Young's *Treatise on Opium*. The rise of print culture coincided with the rise in the use of laudanum and the increased popularity of products such as Dover's powder, which were advertised and promoted in catalogues and medical textbooks. These compounds were available at apothecary shops without prescription and were found in homes across Europe and the Americas.

Even more potent than laudanum or Dover's powder was an American patent medicine called Mrs. Winslow's Soothing Syrup, which, in addition to alcohol, contained sixty-five milligrams of morphine per ounce. Like other patent medicines, Mrs. Winslow's Soothing Syrup was marketed as safe and family friendly through advertisements featuring smiling mothers and babies. It was first commercially produced in 1849 and was very successful, likely because of extensive advertising in newspapers, on calendars, and on recipe cards. In particular, it was recommended for teething children as it "produce[d] a natural, quiet sleep by removing the child from pain."[8] A faded calendar from 1888 has the following text in English, German, and French: "Advice to Mothers. Mrs. Winslow's Soothing Syrup should always be used for Children Teething. It Soothes the Child, Softens the Gums, Allays all Pain, Cures Wind Colic, and is the Best Remedy for Diarrhoea."[9]

The syrup's fatal concentration of morphine was made even more dangerous by the product's aggressive dosing recommendations, and it quickly became known as "the baby killer." Notwithstanding, the manufacturer reported selling more than 1.5 million bottles annually in the 1860s. Despite medical reports documenting that the syrup was killing children and adults, it was sold in its original form until new laws forced the removal of morphine from the syrup.

The Scientific Revolution led to innovations in medicine that are still with us today. The intravenous use of opioids began in Oxford in 1657. None other than Christopher Wren, architect of St. Paul's Cathedral, was responsible for this new technique to deliver drugs directly into the blood supply of a living creature. Wren was a polymath who made significant contributions as an astronomer, experimentalist, architect, and founding member of the Royal Society. He was friendly with Robert Boyle and Isaac Newton, and it was Boyle who aided Wren in his early experiments on intravenous substances.

Wren recorded his scientific observations of an experiment with alcohol in a letter to an Oxford associate: "Shall I trouble you with what we doe in Anatomy? … the most considerable [Experiment] I have made of late is this. I Have injected Wine and Ale in a liveing Dog into the Mass of Blood by a Veine, in good Quantities, till I have made him extremely drunk, but soon after he Pisseth it out."[10]

At Boyle's apartment in Oxford, the two men and their assistants restrained a large dog by tying its paws to the four corners of a table. Using a lancet and a sharpened goose quill, Wren administered wine and opium into the animal's blood supply. The dog was then released from the table and began to stagger around. As Boyle wished to keep the dog "for further Observation," rather than letting the dog die as so many others had died from similar experiments, Boyle had him whipped around the garden until the effects of the opium wore off.

The intravenous administration of medication rapidly spread throughout Europe after these experiments. Blood transfusions were also attempted. Blood was transfused from one dog to another, then from sheep to horses, goats to dogs, and sheep to humans. Wren moved on to a panoply of other scientific fields, but he and the large dog had made scientific history.[11]

Opium was widely used in the Ottoman Empire and across Asia during this time. Reports filtered back to Europe of the opium use in the "decadent East." In 1546 the French naturalist Pierre Belon described a caravan of fifty camels carrying Turkish opium. But opium was most strongly associated with China. British merchants sold opium to Chinese importers, and the impetus to trade with China was driven further by the growing demand for Chinese tea by the British over the course of the eighteenth century.[12]

Western merchants wanted to sell opium to feed Chinese demand. There were around twelve million heavy opium users in China by the 1830s, providing a huge market for opium merchants. But the Chinese government in Beijing, which appointed Lin Zexu to stop the opium trade, already recognized the social and economic problems of opium use. Lin Zexu wrote a letter to Queen Victoria asking her to stop British merchants participating in the trade of "a drug that is hurtful to men, and [which causes] an unbridled craving … that seems to know no bounds!"[13]

Lin Zexu began to arrest opium smokers and destroy opium pipes on a massive scale. Merchants were required to hand over their opium stocks, which were promptly destroyed and dumped into the sea.

To protect the interests of its opium merchants, Britain engaged first in a variety of political and economic machinations, and later in a number of sea battles against the Chinese. This struggle, the First

Opium War, led to the death of approximately eighteen thousand Chinese troops. The war ended with a treaty signed in August 1842, which required compensation for the destroyed opium, more access and protection for British merchants, and the ceding of Hong Kong to Britain in perpetuity. The unequal situation lasted only another fourteen years, however, before the outbreak of another military conflict. The Second Opium War dragged on until 1860 and resulted in a second catastrophic defeat for China.

The English and French joined forces and together looted and burned the Old Summer Palace of Peking in October 1860. The Chinese Emperor then ratified the Treaty of Tientsin, which again required compensation to Western merchants, allowed missionaries to preach in China, allowed Chinese indentured servants to be sent to America, and fully legalized the opium trade in China. By 1906 one in four Chinese adult males was using opium and people from all social groups in China smoked opium.[14]

At the same time, European physicians had begun to recognize the harm caused by opioids and described opium as a "kind of poison" that created a terrible sickness when withdrawn, leading people to seek out more of the drug.[15] In his 1701 book *The Mysteries of Opium Reveal'd*, the English physician John Jones described the suffering caused by opioid withdrawal. The publication in 1821 of Thomas De Quincey's *Confessions of an English Opium-Eater* brought the issue more vividly into the public domain. Like many people who use opioids, De Quincey could recount the exquisite joy of his first taste: "In an hour, O heavens! What a revulsion! What a resurrection, from the lowest depth, of the inner spirit! What an apocalypse of the world within me. That my pains had vanished was now a trifle in my eyes; this negative effect was swallowed up … in the abyss of divine enjoyment thus suddenly revealed. Here was a panacea … for all human woes; here was the secret of happiness."[16] De Quincey went on to live a long life, albeit one marked by opioid addiction and heavy debts.

In the 1891 Sherlock Holmes story "The Man with the Twisted Lip," Arthur Conan Doyle wrote of a man "much addicted to opium."

The wise and compassionate Dr. Watson describes the man and his addiction:

> The habit grew upon him, as I understand, from some foolish freak when he was at college; for having read De Quincey's description of his dreams and sensations, he had drenched his tobacco with laudanum in an attempt to produce the same effects. He found, as so many more have done, that the practice is easier to attain than to get rid of, and for many years he continued to be a slave to the drug, an object of mingled horror and pity to his friends and relatives. I can see him now, with yellow, pasty face, drooping lids, and pin-point pupils, all huddled in a chair, the wreck and ruin of a noble man.[17]

In the poor and unsanitary conditions of nineteenth-century Europe and North America, opioid use and addiction flourished. As there were few medications available, laudanum and Dover's powder were actually effective treatments for pain, diarrhea, poor sleep, and respiratory diseases.

A German pharmacist isolated morphine in 1804 and named it after the Greek god of dreams. Doctors would make small cuts in the skin and sprinkle morphine powder in them to treat cases of severe pain.[18]

The word *inject* entered English around 1600. It came from a Latin word with the original meaning of "to throw or drive in," and the same borrowing in Dutch was used by physicians to describe their technique for blood transfusions using methods inspired by Christopher Wren. But until the mid-1800s, there were no needles fine or strong enough to inject medicine directly into the body.

In 1853 Alexander Wood invented the hypodermic needle; he may not have been the first to create such a device, but he was the first to publish his results. The injection of morphine to treat pain was quickly taken up and within a decade, hypodermic needles were produced and marketed across Europe and North America.

Patients experienced great relief from the injection of morphine under the skin. Doctors suddenly had a new and powerful weapon against suffering in their small and relatively ineffective arsenal. Because patients liked morphine injections, doctors were generous. An 1869 medical textbook lamented that morphine was overutilized as a treatment. Proponents of injection argued, without any evidence, that using a needle would remove the patient's appetite for morphine as it no longer needed to be swallowed. They actually believed that swallowing opium was more addictive than injecting morphine.

But the warning signs were there from the beginning. Patients began to inject themselves with morphine, despite official medical recommendations never to teach patients how to use hypodermic needles. A medical report from 1870 describes a patient covered in track marks and skin infections from years of injecting morphine. The author wrote of morphine injections: "What wonder that the victim, grateful for his happy deliverance, flies again to the same source for relief, and at last becomes the spell-bound slave of the enchantress!"[19]

The possibility of spreading disease through reusing needles was also recognized, and in fact, reused needles would become a major contributor to the spread of infectious diseases. The death of Alexander Wood's wife was the first recorded instance of a fatal overdose from an injected opioid. A new stage in the history of opioid addiction had begun.[20]

Diacetylmorphine was first marketed as a cough suppressant in 1895 by the German pharmaceutical giant Bayer. It was sold as a less-addictive substitute for morphine, but it was known to be much more potent and thus was given a name reflecting its heroic strength: heroin. In a time when tuberculosis was epidemic, heroin was marketed as a symptomatic treatment for advanced respiratory tuberculosis. Heroin was also available over the counter in packs of hundreds of pills, some which were coated in chocolate or flavoured with rose water. In 1900 anyone with ready money could purchase heroin by mail order from Bayer's American offices.

By 1901, a case of heroin overdose had appeared in the *British Medical Journal*. Opium smokers switched to heroin and other pharmaceutical opioids after the 1909 Opium Smoking Exclusion Act banned opium smoking in the United States. Lawmakers viewed heroin and narcotics with increasing alarm, and heroin itself was banned in 1924. Bayer lost its trademark rights to heroin after Germany's defeat in the First World War, and beginning in the 1920s, production of the drug shifted to makeshift labs located predominantly in China.[21]

By the 1930s, the stereotype of a person who used drugs was a down-and-out urban man of the lower class, a "hustling, poker-dealing junkie."[22] The term *junkie* entered the American lexicon in the 1920s and has never left. Originally, a junkie was a man who scavenged scrap metal from Manhattan and sold it in Brooklyn yards. A junkie did this to make money to buy drugs. After the introduction of new narcotic laws, including the 1914 Harrison Narcotics Tax Act in the United States and the United Kingdom's Dangerous Drugs Act of 1920, the only source of opioids became illegal markets. Thus, a new link was forged between crime and opioids.[23]

The Second World War led to a shift in production to Europe. Poppies from the Far East and Turkey were manufactured into heroin in France and exported to the United States. The Mafia also began to use Sicily as a base to manufacture and distribute heroin to the rest of Europe and on to North America. The Cosa Nostra of New York controlled 90 percent of America's heroin trade at its peak, and the Mafia was still bringing in large amounts through New York in the 1980s.

The jungles of Vietnam provided the setting for the biggest heroin epidemic among America's military members. A report to Congress in 1971 asserted that one in six U.S. soldiers serving in Vietnam was abusing drugs, predominantly heroin. The massive military presence stimulated the production and trafficking of heroin in what was known as the Golden Triangle — the countries Myanmar, Laos, and Thailand. Heroin from the Golden Triangle was smuggled to Europe and the United States through Hong Kong. In the mid-1970s the U.S. heroin industry was so big that if it had been controlled by a single corporation, it would have been the fifteenth biggest in the United States, smaller than Shell Oil but larger than Xerox, Goodyear, and the Campbell Soup Company.[24]

But the pendulum was about to swing once again. Morphine was an ingredient in dozens of over-the-counter patent medicines during the nineteenth century. For most of the twentieth century, opioids were rarely prescribed by physicians and were distributed predominantly as a street drug in the form of heroin. Beginning in the 1970s, the action of doctors, regulators, and pharmaceutical companies were about to, once again, completely transform the opioid landscape.

CHAPTER 3

The Engine of the Epidemic

The desire for profit has propelled the sale of opium for centuries. The Chinese Opium Wars, the blockbuster patent medicines, the murky heroin trade: they were all driven by profit. In modern times, one of the most profitable industries is Big Pharma. Big Pharma has brought life-saving innovations into the world. Big Pharma knows how to make drugs and how to market drugs. And the roots of many of Big Pharma's strategies can be traced back to a New York psychiatrist named Arthur Sackler, who moved into advertising in the 1940s.

Before OxyContin, there was Valium. In 1963 Arthur Sackler acquired the right to import and sell Valium in the United States. The story of the epidemic of addiction and death caused by the sale of Valium and its sister drugs in the class of benzodiazepines is still largely unknown. Many patients have more trouble stopping their use of a benzo like Valium or Xanax than they do stopping their use of heroin. They often use both because benzodiazepines help treat withdrawal symptoms and anxiety. The calming quality of Valium is exactly what Sackler highlighted when he marketed it in the 1960s. It was promoted as a de-stresser, as "Mother's Little Helper." Foreshadowing the marketing campaign that would later sell opioids, this pitch was used to convince doctors and patients that Valium was safe. In fact, patients develop physical dependence on a benzodiazepine, and it can become a lifelong drug, one that is very difficult to stop using because of the terrible effects of withdrawal, such as anxiety, insomnia, and a risk of seizures.

Valium was Big Pharma's first drug to reach one hundred million dollars in sales. Then Valium was the first billion-dollar drug.[1] The use of Valium to relieve stress and improve mood is representative of the kind of learned chemical coping that may have fed the opioid epidemic. People have been encouraged to believe that if you don't like the way you feel, you can change your feelings with chemicals. If you're stressed, take a downer. If you're tired, take an upper. Why should you feel pain when there is a pill for that?

Treating pain was the engine of the modern opioid epidemic. The early twentieth century saw a tightening of legal restrictions on opioids and the stigmatization and even criminalization of opioid prescribers. For the next fifty years, opioids were dispensed with great parsimony, and pain was poorly controlled. The first major change to this situation arose as a result of a shift in the way of thinking in the British palliative care community in the 1970s. Nurses and doctors advocated for the use of morphine to soothe patients dying with painful cancers in the finals days of life.

A Swedish oncologist named Jan Stjernswärd brought this philosophy to his new role as the chief of the WHO's cancer program. In a medieval castle in Milan, he convened a group of sixteen pain specialists to develop a rational approach to pain management. In 1986 the WHO published its pain ladder, which laid out the approach to pain management I learned in medical school twenty years later: start with acetaminophen and anti-inflammatories, then work up to progressively stronger opioids with the goal of granting the patient freedom from pain.

The WHO pain ladder embodied a new type of patient-centred health care, which valorized the patient's reported pain and the patient's freedom from pain. Morphine became an essential drug for treating cancer-related pain. The WHO then planted the poisoned seed: freedom from pain is a universal human right. This eventually led to the idea that denying a patient opioids or an increased dose of opioids violated that right. A central tenet of palliative care was that there is no ceiling dose — keep increasing the opioid dose until either the pain is quelled or the patient experiences intolerable side effects. The opioid tap was opened all the way. Morphine consumption around the world rose by thirty times between 1980 and 2011.[2]

The ideas of European palliative care and the WHO pain ladder spread to North America. Cancer physicians and pain physicians began to use more morphine to soothe dying patients. Anesthesiologists became more comfortable with using opioids during and after surgery, and the idea spread further. This new-found comfort with prescribing opioids and this aggressive attitude toward treating pain spread from the cancer wards and the operating rooms and was applied to other types of pain and other types of patients until it enveloped every level of clinical care. In 1984 Purdue Pharma created MS Contin, a time-released morphine pill that I would see prescribed in escalating doses as a medical student and then as a junior doctor.

Like any revolution, the revolution in pain medicine met hostile and ferocious resistance. The palliative care physicians at the vanguard were accused of misunderstanding the nature of pain and the addictive nature of opioids. Fears about addiction and about the potential for opioid abuse never completely faded, but the voices warning of the dangers of opioid use were drowned out by louder calls to manage pain and by the marketing campaigns of Big Pharma, which was interested in selling new, more powerful, and putatively safer opioids.

But to convince the scientists that opioid use should be liberalized, its proponents needed science. One unassuming paper became a critical piece of evidence for the pro-opioid lobby. In a brief letter to the editor published in the January 10, 1980, issue of the *New England Journal of Medicine*, Hershel Jick and Jane Porter from the Boston University Medical Center described a review of the charts of 11,882 hospitalized medical patients who had received at least one dose of opioids. Jick and Porter looked to see how many of those patients, who didn't already have addiction issues, developed well-documented addiction during their hospital stay. They stated that they found only four cases.[3]

This was a flawed and tiny letter, not even a study in the scientific sense of the word.

For a case of addiction to be well documented, it would have to be actively screened for and then accurately documented by clinicians in a way that would allow a researcher searching through more than eleven thousand charts to find it easily. Furthermore, the time frame used to support their claim was inadequate. A chart review of hospitalized patients does not capture what happens after those patients leave the hospital — all eleven thousand could have gone to their nearest heroin dealer, but there is no way to know. Flawed as its claims are, this little letter was used to justify the massive increase in opioid prescribing that was to come.

As of 2017, the letter had been cited six hundred and eight times, whereas the average letter from the January 10, 1980, edition had been cited only eleven times.[4] For a letter to be cited at all is a big deal, and the frequent citation of this letter is a testament, at least in part, to the awe the medical community holds for the *New England Journal of Medicine*. No medical journal has more credibility, which must be one of the reasons the popular media have hyped the letter so much. *Scientific American* called it an "extensive study" in a 1990 article, and in 2001 *Time* magazine described the paper as a "landmark study" demonstrating that the "exaggerated fear that patients would become addicted" to opiates was "basically unwarranted."[5]

That little letter, the "fact" that less than 1 percent of patients treated with opioids develop addictions, is the foundation of the argument for the liberal use of opioids. This number was slipped into the training manuals of Purdue drug reps to be repeated to physicians and then to patients and concerned policy-makers again and again. Don't worry, a landmark study in the *New England Journal of Medicine* shows the risk of addiction to opioids is negligible. The American Pain Society translated the paper into a statement on its website, declaring that the risk of addiction to opioids was low when opioids were used to treat pain.

The final catalyst added to this explosive formula was the concept of pain as the fifth vital sign. The president of the American Pain Society said in a 1996 speech, "We need to train doctors and nurses to treat pain as a vital sign."[6] And that is exactly what happened. Accreditation organizations across North America began to use a patient's satisfaction with pain management as an important metric for judging the quality of medical care. As society became more focused on individual rights and as medicine became more focused on patient autonomy, the patient experience became central to people's interactions with the machinery of health care. In almost every way, this has led to better, safer, and more humane care. Opioids were supposed to be part of this revolution in the quality of care.

Considered from another perspective, however, the opioid revolution and the change in attitudes that accompanied it are illustrative of darker aspects of human psychology, and point to problems in health care systems straining under rising demands and exploding costs. The change in attitudes resulted in a belief that pills are the solution to all our ills. First there was the phenomenal success of Valium, the first billion-dollar drug. In many ways, Valium is the worst solution to stress, anxiety, and insomnia. But this and other products were aggressively marketed by the pharmaceutical companies and eventually came to appeal to both patients and doctors alike. Pills, powders, patches, and needles have become essential for modern medicine. For many patients, leaving a medical visit with a prescription in hand feels like an accomplishment. Leaving a visit with a list of physiotherapists or psychologists may feel less satisfying. As for doctors, prescribing pills takes less time than does deciding on alternative treatment methods, and there are many incentives at play in health care systems in North America that push doctors to spend less time with more patients.

It was Arthur Sackler's company, Purdue Pharma, that would go on to develop and market the bestselling opioids. The benefits of opioids were sold, while the risks were undersold. Billions of dollars were at stake. Physicians took up the call to treat pain. Percocet and Vicodin became household names. Pain control became a criterion by which doctors and hospitals were judged. Whereas in the past, patients were prepared to bear their suffering, patients now came to expect and demand never to suffer. In this new world, prescribing opioids was normal; denying opioids was abnormal, cruel, and malicious.

OxyContin entered the world in 1996. It came at the perfect time. Just as fear of addiction was being squashed and pain as a vital sign was entering medical discourse, Purdue sold OxyContin as a smooth-acting, time-released, low-risk, high-efficacy pain pill. OxyContin was designed to be taken twice a day to smooth out the unpleasant cycle of relief and withdrawal associated with short-acting opioids like morphine and oxycodone. The time-released action was also purported to take away the rush, the high, the euphoria that users got after taking those short-acting doses. In fact, after the U.S. Food and Drug Administration (FDA) approved OxyContin, it also permitted a unique label stating that OxyContin had lower abuse potential than other oxycodone products because of its delivery system. It was the first time a controlled opioid had been granted such a label, and it was another weapon in Purdue's marketing armamentarium.[7]

The marketing war broke through to every type of pain and every type of patient. This campaign met virtually no resistance. Purdue worked to insert OxyContin as the opioid of choice in the pain ladder. *Less than 1 percent addictive* was the mantra repeated by salespeople over and over again: Don't let patients suffer needlessly with chronic back pain; improve their quality of life; let them regain control; let them live pain free. The message was hammered home relentlessly to physicians and nurses across North America.

I still get slick pamphlets in my inbox and requests to meet with drug reps selling newer and, again, putatively safer opioids, but these marketing efforts are nothing like those made during the first years after the introduction of OxyContin. The number of pharmaceutical sales reps in the United States rocketed from 35,000 in 1995 to 110,000 ten years later. The boots on the ground, or feet on the street, would regularly ply doctors with food, gifts, trips — and the assurance that OxyContin was safe and effective. In 2001 alone, Purdue spent two hundred million dollars on the marketing and promotion of OxyContin, and sales reps received big bonuses linked to increased sales of the drug.[8]

The marketing worked. OxyContin prescriptions in the United States rose to 6.2 million doses per year by 2002. Sales of OxyContin exceeded one billion dollars in 2001 and 2002. That single drug made up 90 percent of Purdue's annual revenue. As doctors became comfortable with prescribing opioids and patients came to expect them, prescriptions for all opioids grew. Over the same time period, prescriptions for fentanyl patches, morphine, and oxycodone also grew.[9]

This binge on opioids was coupled to an enormous increase in opioid-related harm. By 2004, OxyContin was the most commonly abused prescription opioid in America. Emergency room visits for opioid-related complications were up; overdoses were slowly but steadily rising. In July 2001, the FDA revised OxyContin's label by removing the optimistic statement that the formulation was less addictive. They also stated that data were not available to determine the rate of addiction in patients with chronic pain. People were being introduced to drug abuse more often by prescription opioids than by marijuana, and most opioids were coming not from illegal sources but from prescriptions, friends, or the family medicine cabinet.[10]

In her 2018 book *Dopesick: Dealers, Doctors, and the Drug Company That Addicted America*, journalist Beth Macy said that OxyContin was the "new moonshine" in rural America.[11] She described the nexus of poverty, hopelessness, and access to OxyContin that made Appalachia the epicentre of America's epidemic, with West Virginia as the state with the highest overdose rate in the nation. OxyContin fuelled wave upon wave of crime across the region. Every store, every home became a target. People bartered stolen merchandise for Oxy tablets. They paid in pills for transportation to clinics known to prescribe opioids in high numbers. Pills begot more pills; OxyContin prescriptions created more demand for OxyContin.[12]

The idea at the time was that patients needed what they needed and clinicians should keep increasing their doses until they were no longer in pain. Patients would enter the pharmacy with a handwritten prescription and leave with their bags bursting with opioids. As patients were given higher doses, many found they did not need all their pills and so would share extras with others. Opioids became a new currency. The ecosystem was awash in pills. In every type of practice, from the emergency room to gynecology clinics, opioids were handed over with great abandon. Consider how an ordinary visit would have gone at that time.

Doctor: How is your pain?

Patient: Bad.

Doctor: Are you taking your OxyContin?

Patient: Yes, but it only lasts for half the day. The rest of the time I'm suffering. I'm running out early. I need more.

Doctor: Okay, let's raise your dose by ten percent.

Doses only ever went in one direction: up. A 10 percent increase every month for a few years led to astronomical doses in the hundreds of milligrams. Each of those dose increases might have seemed reasonable; however, by taking a step back and looking at the overall trajectory of doses over a period of years, we can see the dangers. Deaths from prescription-opioid overdose quadrupled in the United States over the first fifteen years of the new millennium.[13]

This was happening on every hospital ward and in every type of clinic across North America. Pain clinics began to sprout up all over the United States, and they got very good at prescribing pills and patches. At the vanguard were physicians tempted to compromise quality of care to gain financial rewards. In a two-minute, two-hundred-dollar visit, they would ask a patient if they had pain and then prescribe opioids. But for every unscrupulous prescriber, there were many doctors who were just trying to treat pain in what they thought, and were told, was the best way.

As the new millennium began, the use of prescription opioids was normalized and celebrated across North America. Tremendously successful marketing campaigns of companies like Purdue had helped change attitudes among medical practitioners and patients about pain and the use of opioids to treat pain. When I entered medical school in 2005, however, the tide was starting to turn. A rise in overdose deaths had been detected; some cautious voices were raised, urging the judicious use of opioids. But the belief in the efficacy of opioids remained and continued to spread. In fact, the principle of palliative care doctors that there was no upper limit for the dose of opioids was still being taught in medical schools across Canada and the United States.

Writing in December 2018, the physician Abigail Zuger lamented, "It is impossible to overstate how difficult it was a dozen years ago to ignore the resounding calls for effective pain control by any means possible, narcotic dependency be damned. Our leaders, our teachers, our regulatory agencies, and our patients demanded no less."[14]

When I was a medical resident, my supervisors would shake their heads and tell me, "Whenever we refer someone to the chronic-pain clinic, they come back on high doses of opioids. Then we have to take over the prescription." Paramedics or family members or the police would bring patients into emergency rooms after an overdose or a car crash or a fall. I would see reports time and time again with the discharge diagnosis scrawled in the bottom right-hand corner of the page: "Opioid overdose" or "Opioid withdrawal," or the more nebulous "Drug addiction."

Studies began to show that older doctors with higher volumes of patients were more likely to prescribe higher doses of opioids. We started talking about avoiding the "pill mills" and trying to get our patients into the multidisciplinary pain clinics where there was more focus on exercise, counselling, weight loss, and non-opioid medications.

We came to realize that all the opioids being marketed were as addictive as heroin. As many as one in five patients receiving opioids in outpatient clinics became addicted to them, and even more were misusing their opioids in some way, such as taking more than prescribed.[15] This was a lot more than 1 percent. Between 2004 and 2011, emergency room visits in the United States related to the misuse of prescription opioids increased by 153 percent.[16]

Purdue was chastised for its role in the opioid epidemic. The first criminal charges and fines came in May 2007, when Purdue was accused of misbranding OxyContin by claiming it was less addictive and less liable to abuse than other opioids. Dozens of other suits brought by U.S. states and Canadian provinces against Purdue and other drug companies followed, and many are still snaking through the legal system.

Despite the legal action, Purdue continued to aggressively market OxyContin. In 2010 it released a gel form designed to be tamper-resistant. But within a few weeks there were recipes online describing how to break down the pills to better abuse the drug. Purdue had been punished, blamed, and excoriated, but the evil had not been exorcised.

* * *

As the epidemic of prescription opioids spread, a new threat emerged. This was the growing supply of heroin from Mexico. In *Dreamland,* Quinones followed the dealers of black tar heroin from Mexico as they broke into previously untapped regions of the United States. This arrival of cheap and abundant heroin coincided with and fed off the surge in prescription-opioid abuse. He showed how dealers from a small area of Mexico called Xalisco developed a new delivery system: young men, carrying small quantities of heroin stored in balloons in their mouths, would drive to meet customers. They didn't carry weapons and, for the most part, they were non-violent. The efficiency of their system, their use of free samples and credit, and their focus on customer service fed the churning storm of the epidemic.[17] Between 2007 and 2015, the number of Americans who had used heroin within the previous year more than doubled, to eight hundred thousand people.[18]

At that same time, global poppy production was increasing and political groups such as ISIS earned much of their revenue from heroin. Heroin from Afghanistan travelled through Iran and Pakistan, then across the Arabian Sea to Somalia, and then overland to Uganda and Kenya. The Kenyan city of Mombasa became a major hub for heroin, with rising levels of addiction and crime in its wake. In 2015 more than a ton of heroin was found in a dhow off Mombasa. Thirty-one nations have brought naval forces together to create the Combined Maritime Forces to reduce piracy and drug trafficking around the Red Sea and Arabian Gulf. In 2014, more than 90 percent of the heroin whose origin could be traced that was seized in Canada came from Afghanistan. Most of that was shipped through Pakistan, India, or Iran.[19]

The story doesn't end with heroin, because in 2013, something changed again. Opioids were still being prescribed, although perhaps with more care than previously. Heroin was easily available, and heroin deaths were climbing slowly. But just as a forest fire can suddenly shift with the winds and rapidly threaten vast stretches of land, so the opioid epidemic shifted with the arrival of mass-produced illicit fentanyl.

CHAPTER 4
Fentanyl Arrives

The bus pulled into the Vancouver station late on a summer night in August after a ten-hour trip from the Rocky Mountain resort of Jasper. It was 1994 and my dad had taken my brother and me on our first trip to western Canada. We checked into a hotel with a rowdy bar on the ground floor. The hotel was in Gastown, the historic neighbourhood that borders Vancouver's Downtown Eastside. Five years later I'd come back with my family and we would live in the centre of Vancouver, just as the year 2000 was about to dawn. I'd come to know the city well. But only now, as I try to understand the opioid epidemic, have I started to ask the question *why*. Why does Vancouver have such a bad drug problem? Why is it ground zero for Canada's opioid epidemic?

I'm not the first to ask this question, and when I surveyed other addiction doctors, they answered that Vancouver is a port city and its nice climate may attract people who use drugs. A *Vice* article in 2017 asked the same question and suggested that the city, in fact, has two distinct reputations with regard to drugs: "On one hand, the city's known to be ahead of the curve on progressive drug policy — always adopting the latest harm-reduction practices and testing new addiction treatments. On the other hand, it's suffered more drug panics than any other Canadian city, and has a reputation for higher-than-average drug use and addiction rates. Vancouver is simultaneously a place the globe looks to for drug policy guidance, and a cautionary tale of recurring out-of-control epidemics."[1]

Vancouver's situation seems paradoxical, but once you look at the history of drug use in the city and the criminal and financial systems it supports, the reason for the epidemic is no longer mysterious. It all starts with the ocean.

The Port of Vancouver is one of the busiest in the world; it is the third busiest in North America. In 2017, more than three thousand vessels brought over 3.2 million containers, over 420,000 vehicles, and countless other products, together worth more than two hundred billion dollars. But that's not all they brought. Hidden in the containers and the vehicles and smuggled in by the crews of those three thousand ships were drugs. Port cities like Vancouver serve as hubs for the drug trade. In them can be found the greatest quantity of drugs and drugs of the highest purity.

Port cities like Vancouver see large population influxes, including sailors with cash to spend, and there are red-light districts to soak up that cash. Transient workers used to live in the inexpensive rooms and hotels along East Hastings, which have morphed into mixing places for the chronically homeless and people looking to buy drugs. Aggressive policing has led to exponential rates of drug convictions. In the decades after the Second World War, more than half of Canadian drug convictions occurred in Vancouver, and most of those convictions were in the Downtown Eastside, where up to five thousand people who used drugs lived within a few blocks from each other. In the 1990s, the Downtown Eastside became the epicentre of the Canadian HIV epidemic, experiencing rates of the disease among the highest in the developed world.

Soon after I left Vancouver in 2002, the city pivoted from primarily fighting the war on drugs toward serving at the vanguard of harm reduction. The provincial government of British Columbia and the public health authorities supported innovative safe injection sites and new forms of treatment and pushed existing treatment and addiction training for health care providers. It was just in time, because as the supply of prescribed opioids fell, a new drug began to flow across the ocean to fill the void. That drug was fentanyl. The number of overdose deaths in British Columbia rose from 211 in 2010 to 1,450 in 2017. Fentanyl was responsible for more and more of those overdose deaths, and by 2014 it was the leading cause of opioid overdose in Canada.[2]

Fentanyl had arrived in North America.

In mid-2016, as the scale of the rising death rate in British Columbia became clear, the government declared a state of emergency. A few months later, the provincial coroners created what was called the Drug-Death Investigation Team. The team investigated every suspected overdose from illegal drugs. They found fentanyl in 76 percent of the cases. They also found high levels of cocaine, alcohol, and stimulants like crystal meth and speed. In the youngest group of victims, made up of people from fifteen to twenty-nine years old, fentanyl was found in 85 percent of the deaths.[3]

In May 2018, the CBC ran the headline "High Levels of Fentanyl — and Deceit — Detected in Vancouver Street-Drug Supply." The story described something I had been seeing around the same time on the other side of the country. Most of the powder sold on the street as heroin was actually something else; the only sure thing was that it contained fentanyl. According to the CBC article, the Vancouver tests showed fentanyl in 88 percent of all the street opioids tested.[4] In the first three months of 2018, Vancouver had an overdose rate of 59.6 per 100,000, which was perhaps the highest rate in North America.[5]

Labs in China were alleged to be the source of this death. Seeking to confirm this, journalists and investigators emailed chemists who claimed to be based in Guangzhou and who promised to send tiny but extremely potent quantities of fentanyl powder through the mail. My own patients told me they had ordered small quantities of fentanyl or heroin on the dark web from dealers in China. Large-scale dealers ordered powder from China and then pressed the fentanyl with other fillers into pills, which they would then smuggle all over North America. One of the first busts of such dealers came in 2013, when Montreal police arrested two men on their way to a UPS store. They were planning "to ship a microwave oven containing 10,180 fentanyl tablets to New Jersey."[6]

* * *

Again, the story comes back to Vancouver as a port city, because in addition to expensive real estate and skiing at Whistler, Vancouver is becoming known for a uniquely potent form of drug-related crime and money laundering known as the Vancouver model. And it turns out this might have something to do with the expensive real estate. Drawing on a government report obtained through a freedom-of-information request, journalists outlined how organized crime syndicates called triads, based in China's Guangdong province, manufacture fentanyl and other drugs, ship the drugs through Vancouver, and then use casinos and high-priced real estate to launder the money. The clean money is then returned to China, and the cycle is repeated. As the cultural historian Lucy Inglis observed with reference to the Opium Wars, "The Chinese are making up for the addiction once thrust upon them."[7]

In a video interview, David Eby, the attorney general of British Columbia, said, "Vancouver is now recognized internationally as a hub of transnational money laundering," and admitted that he was shocked by the scope and scale of the crimes conducted by Chinese organized crime. He said that this was not the reputation he wanted for Vancouver and added, "We pay for this in different ways, and one of them is the opioid crisis we face in British Columbia."

Nor is this a new phenomenon. Former RCMP superintendent Garry Clement said he believed the reports of massive money laundering and had seen it before: "Sadly, it's the truth. The triads were a multinational crime syndicate back in the '90s, and we have allowed them to expand, using Canada as a base.... It is phenomenal what the triads can do."[8]

The triads are also linked to wildlife smuggling, selling forged products, and human trafficking. Drug money mixes with money from other criminal activities and is then used to buy legitimate businesses and real estate. More than half of Vancouver's most expensive properties are owned not by individuals, but rather by legal entities like trusts and shell companies that conceal ownership. With the help of lawyers and bankers in Hong Kong, Macau, Australia, and Vancouver, the triads take advantage of weaknesses and loopholes in the financial and legal systems.

After 2010, fentanyl swept east across the continent, first to Alberta, then across the Prairies to Quebec and Ontario. The chief coroner of Ontario reported in May 2018 that overdose deaths had doubled in Ontario between 2010 and 2017 and that most of the increase was due to fentanyl. In 2010 just over one hundred deaths in Ontario were attributed to fentanyl; by 2017, that number had reached 752. Law enforcement had come down hard on those distributing fentanyl, but it was still getting onto the street. Calgary saw zero deaths from fentanyl in 2011, but only four years later, there were ninety deaths from fentanyl. A warning from the local police read, "In 2015, more Calgarians have died from fentanyl use than traffic collisions and homicides combined. Your next dose of fentanyl may be your last."[9]

Fentanyl entered the United States through both China and Mexico. A review of data from ten American states showed that half of those who died from opioid overdoses in the United States in the second half of 2016 tested positive for fentanyl.[10] New Hampshire had the highest rate of fentanyl deaths in the United States and the second highest rate of overdose deaths after West Virginia. A graph of overdose deaths in New Hampshire shows almost no deaths from fentanyl between 2010 and 2013, then a jump to 145 in 2014, then another jump to 283 in 2015, when two out of every three drug deaths were caused by fentanyl.[11] The chief of Manchester's fire department, Daniel Goonan, told a journalist in 2017, "We don't have a heroin problem here; we have a fentanyl problem." He said that at least half his job was responding to overdoses with first aid and naloxone.[12]

My patient Nathan was looking at the computer screen in my office as I showed him a graph of the precipitous rise in fentanyl overdoses in Canada in recent years.

"Everything has an unintended side effect," he mused, shaking his head slowly. "They got pills off the street, then all of a sudden, everyone was using fentanyl."

I looked at his urine test, which was positive for fentanyl.

"I used a point of that fake heroin with fentanyl in it," he told me.

The more fentanyl took over the drug scene, the more I wanted to understand where it had come from. Like so many things in medicine, fentanyl's power for good also contains the secret to its destructive force. In 2017 the WHO listed 433 medications essential for a well-functioning health care system, and fentanyl patches made the list.

I learned that fentanyl's story began in Belgium, with the birth of Paul Janssen on September 12, 1926. That day marked the beginning of the life of perhaps the single most inventive and prolific drug designer in history. By the end of his life in 2003, Paul Janssen had developed more than eighty compounds that changed medicine fundamentally.[13]

Paul's father was himself a physician. He had started as a rural general practitioner, and then began to develop and sell tonics and vitamins. Paul gravitated to the twin worlds of medicine and chemistry and went to medical school at the Catholic University of Leuven. Already passionate about chemistry and pharmacology from his early years, Paul decided during his second year of medical school to travel to the United States to learn about the science and business of pharmacology. While in the United States, he visited Columbia, Harvard, Chicago, Caltech, and a number of pharmaceutical companies.

He completed medical school in 1951, and in 1953 founded his own research company, Janssen Pharmaceutica. The small company began to apply modern scientific ideas to drug development; researchers worked to understand how the chemical structure of molecules affected their role in the body and then tried to manipulate those structures to enhance or modify their effect.

Paul and his team turned their gaze to morphine and the other opioids available at the time. They believed that the ring of piperidine, an organic compound on the morphine molecule, was the key to its analgesic, or pain-relieving, properties. They wanted to modify the molecule to build better and safer forms of opioids. In particular, they wanted something better than meperidine, another opioid available at the time, which was ten times weaker than morphine. They thought meperidine was too water soluble and tried to make their compound more fat soluble, to let it soak deep into the body and give it a greater analgesic effect.

Their work paid off in 1957, only one year after Paul had completed his PhD at Ghent University. They created phenoperidine. This new drug was twenty-five times more potent than morphine. It became the new king, the most potent opioid in the world at the time. It was marketed for anesthetic use and is still available today.

But they were not done. For another three years, they worked and reworked the molecule, trying new combinations, changing the properties of the basic piperidine structure. On December 8, 1960, they built something radically more powerful. The chemical name for the compound was N-(1-phenethyl-4-piperidyl) propionanilide — they shortened it to fentanyl. This was the new emperor. It was one hundred times more potent than morphine and was the fastest-acting opioid ever seen: the perfect anesthetic.

Janssen brought fentanyl to market in 1963 in Europe, but the FDA would not approve the drug in the United States. A key barrier to getting fentanyl approved in the United States was the opposition of Robert Dripps, a professor of anesthesiology at the University of Pennsylvania. He believed fentanyl was too potent. Ultimately, the FDA relented, but they allowed fentanyl to be introduced only in a very low concentration, combined with another Janssen drug.

Over the coming decades, fentanyl was found to be an ideal drug for surgery. It worked so fast; within one minute of being given fentanyl intravenously, a patient felt a dramatic release from pain. The side effects of fentanyl were similar to those of other opioids: nausea, vomiting, dizziness, respiratory depression, reduced heart rate, and, finally, sedation and unconsciousness at higher doses.

And then came the patch.

From the beginning, fentanyl was dismissed as an oral medication because of the body's low absorption of the drug when it was swallowed. But fentanyl could get through the skin. In the mid-1980s a small company in Northern California called Alza Corporation developed a patch to deliver fentanyl. The patch provided a steady release of fentanyl over seventy-two hours. Alza then partnered with Janssen to market the patch.

Like other opioids at the time, it was initially marketed to treat severe cancer pain. It was approved by the FDA on August 7, 1990, under the brand name Duragesic. The drug was a huge commercial success. The patent on Duragesic lasted until 2004, and during that year it had more than $2.4 billion in sales. After the patent expired, generic drug companies rushed to produce their own fentanyl patches. Along with the patch, every imaginable variation of delivery system for the drug was developed, including the fentanyl lollipop, which was called Oralet and used as a pre-surgery anesthetic agent.

After the drug's approval, the use of fentanyl spread from operating rooms in Europe and North America to those around the world. Today, fentanyl is the preferred opioid for pain relief during surgery. It is the drug of choice because it has little effect on the cardiovascular system during surgery and it is short acting. But there is something more basic and more prosaic about fentanyl that helps to explain its success in the marketplace of drugs: it is easy to make. It can be made inexpensively, just as it was made with simple tools in December 1960. This simplicity is also its greatest weakness.

Someone once said that civilization would be easily destroyed if all it took to build a nuclear bomb was to put some sand in the microwave. Building fentanyl from raw ingredients in the lab is not as simple as microwaving sand, but it's not as complex as enriching uranium. As early as 1979, clandestine labs were producing and selling fentanyl for the illicit market.[14]

In 1980 fifteen people in California overdosed on what was believed to be heroin, but post-mortem analyses showed no regular opioids. Only when toxicologists broadened their search to look for fentanyl and its analogues (very similar molecules) did they realize that what had taken those fifteen lives was not heroin but rather illicitly produced fentanyl analogues sold on the street as heroin. In 1984 a lab in California identified fifty overdose deaths attributed to illicit fentanyl.[15]

Those early illicit labs were shut down and the chemists responsible were arrested, and for several years illicit fentanyl faded from the scene. Then a new drug hit the streets of the United States in 1991. It was called Tango and Cash, and it was a mixture of heroin and 12 percent fentanyl. Tango and Cash resulted in 126 overdose deaths and was traced to two labs in Wichita, Kansas, where investigators seized eighteen kilograms of fentanyl. Fentanyl did not really catch on in the 1990s, however, perhaps because there were so many prescription opioids around and China was not yet providing cheap and easy supplies. But between 2005 and 2007, more than a thousand fentanyl deaths were identified by the Drug Enforcement Administration (DEA). The drug was traced to a fentanyl lab in Toluca, Mexico.[16]

In the early years of my medical practice, most of the fentanyl abuse I saw involved prescribed patches. Patches were highly coveted on the street because of their potency. They were purchased from people with prescriptions or were stolen from pharmacies. It seemed that everyone knew how to extract the drug from the patch so that it could be smoked or injected. Research papers listed the many ways patches could be misused: application of more patches, changing the patch more frequently, injecting, smoking, chewing, swallowing, inserting the patches into the rectum or vagina, or even diluting the patch in tea.[17] Many young patients I met who had no interest in needles had escalated from sniffing Percocet and OxyContin to smoking fentanyl patches. By heating the patch and inhaling the fumes, they could achieve a powerful and instant high.

Patients with prescriptions for fentanyl patches also learned to abuse them. The medical literature began to show flashes of this danger. In 2013 an oncologist from the Mayo Clinic published a case report of a sixty-year-old man being treated for a blood cancer.[18] Two years earlier, he had been started on a fentanyl patch after getting hit by a car. When he came in for his second cycle of chemotherapy, he was not himself and complained of shortness of breath. His oxygen level was slightly low, and his doctors worried he had a pulmonary embolism, a blood clot in the lungs — a relatively common occurrence in patients with cancer. But no clot could be found. Then his blood pressure began to fall. Then he had a seizure. His doctors decided to intubate him to give them time to stabilize him and figure out what was causing his rapid decline.

That was when they found the fentanyl patch. A folded, clear, plastic patch was stuck just above his glottis. He was given two doses of intravenous naloxone and he woke up. The cause of his symptoms had been found, but there was another mystery that they would never answer: how did the patch get there? Psychiatrists at the Mayo Clinic evaluated the man, but he said he didn't know what had happened and told them he was not trying to kill himself. I believe that he had discovered that chewing or putting patches against his inner cheek led to euphoria or maybe just better pain relief. He then became unconscious and lost track of the patch. The authors of the case study concluded by warning, "Inappropriate use of transdermal fentanyl patches may be more common than currently recognized and should be considered in fentanyl-treated patients who present with signs of narcotic toxicity."[19]

In recent years, more and more people who use drugs have begun to use powder fentanyl without realizing it. In the last three months of 2015, the San Francisco division of the California Poison Control System identified eight patients poisoned by counterfeit alprazolam tablets that were later found to contain fentanyl. One of the incidents described in the report involved a man in his late twenties and a woman in her late thirties who were found unconscious next to another person, who was already dead. For the two survivors, sedation lasted longer than normal, and when they woke up, they were found to have injuries caused by the compression of nerves and their tissues had started breaking down, suggesting they had been down for a long time. The person who had died was examined by the coroner, and fentanyl was detected in their urine and blood. The authors concluded with the following observation: "It is unclear how these alprazolam tablets were manufactured; however, pill press molds with the characteristics seen on the recovered tablets are available for purchase online."[20]

Before the spread of fentanyl, it was legal to buy a pill press. In North America, most illegal pill manufacturing happens in private homes. In one rental in Calgary, a landlord who went to his property to collect rent was met at the door by his tenant wearing a face mask covered in white powder. The landlord called the police, who discovered a large-scale pill production operation. The public health authorities deemed the house uninhabitable, and the owner had to hire a crew to rebuild the interior of the house.

Fears about the increasing number of fatal overdoses caused by fentanyl-contaminated drugs spread from the drug-using community to treatment agencies to first responders. In early 2017 the media reported that a policeman in Ohio searched a suspicious car for drugs using latex gloves but fell unconscious hours later, after brushing some white powder off his uniform with his bare hand. It is very unlikely that briefly touching a small amount of fentanyl powder could cause unconsciousness, but the story was out.

In June of 2017, the DEA released a twenty-page document titled *Fentanyl: A Briefing Guide for First Responders*. Agents identifying unknown powders were advised to have naloxone kits on hand and to use "nitrile gloves, N-95 dust mask, eye protection, disposable paper suit, or paper coveralls, and shoe covers."[21] A photo of a one-cent coin showed the face of Abraham Lincoln beside a tiny dot of white powder. The text warned that only two to three milligrams of fentanyl can "induce respiratory depression, arrest and possible death."[22] Two to three milligrams is equivalent to five to seven grains of table salt.

Drug control agencies began to fight back against the illegal production of fentanyl by trying to clamp down on the supply of the materials used to make the drug. In March 2017, the United Nations' drug agency placed restrictions on the fentanyl precursors 4-ANPP and NPP, as well as on the fentanyl analogue butyrfentanyl. China added these same precursors to its list of controlled substances in February 2018. Border and drug officials in the United States and Canada worked to improve their methods of intercepting parcels containing both fentanyl and fentanyl precursors entering the country. This is challenging, as it takes only microscopic amounts of precursors to make a huge number of fentanyl doses. For example, you need only 450 grams of 4-ANPP to make almost half a million doses of fentanyl. The DEA has estimated that one kilogram of fentanyl can produce one million counterfeit one-milligram pills, whose sale would bring in millions of dollars of revenue.[23]

Another challenge is that a lot of parcels enter Canada and the United States every day and very little is known about where they come from or what they contain. A highly publicized U.S. government review of opioids smuggled through the U.S. postal system found that 319 million packages arrived in the United States in 2017 with no data. Investigators posed as buyers and were offered fentanyl and precursors by Chinese labs, which requested payment in bitcoin. Suppliers preferred to use the U.S. postal service because FedEx and UPS require more information when delivering packages.

All this increased supply changed the face of North America's opioid epidemic. In 2016, my patients and I were alarmed when, more and more frequently, their urine drug screens showed the presence of fentanyl.

"But my guy told me his heroin was straight," they would protest, genuinely afraid.

By 2018 they didn't blink when I asked them about fentanyl. The only heroin around — the purple stuff — was crammed full of fentanyl, and everybody knew it. Fentanyl had gone from something exotic and uniquely terrifying to something many people who had used drugs for a long time had come to know and like.

"The city isn't interested in pills anymore; everyone wants that purple heroin, with fentanyl in it," Lacey told me one afternoon in the summer of 2018. She paused for a moment, waiting for me to say something, but I just waited, and she continued. "I'm so hooked on fentanyl. All day long I just crave it. I've never felt like this before. I can't believe where I'm at. I'm sad, I'm more depressed. I've never, ever felt like my life is controlled. I get up and all I think about is drugs."

Lacey had been using opioids for two decades, but she felt instinctively, as we all did, that this was something new. Fentanyl gives you a shorter but more intense high.

A young man with pink cheeks, a boyish face, and brown curls told a documentary crew in Calgary in 2016, "It doesn't last long so you're sick again; heroin you can do in the morning and you can be all good until tomorrow, [but with] fentanyl you can withdraw three times a day."

When I asked my patient Steve about his cravings, he told me they were bad. He said, "The fentanyl gets to you. You always want more."

He thought for a moment, then added, "You can give me two hundred milligrams of morphine and I'd be fine, but I just used a tiny piece of purple and I died — only five bucks' worth put me out. They had to naloxone me twice."

Fentanyl was no longer a warning light, a message to others to stay away. Fentanyl was a flashing light luring in users with its quiet potency. When users brought in their white, blue, purple, and pink powders to be tested, they were no longer surprised when the machine flashed the word *fentanyl.*

Steve told me he couldn't understand what was happening around him. "They OD, they nearly die, then a week or two later they go back to using again. I don't understand why people are selling this shit that is killing people."

He told me he was trying to come to terms with his opioid addiction and with the epidemic around him. As he stood up to leave, his black baseball cap pulled down, his tall frame looming over me, he surprised me.

"I'm reading everything I can about opioids, about where all the pills came from. It's been a real eye-opener for me. It's so fucked up. All this is so fucked up."

If Steve — broke, homeless, addicted to fentanyl — was reading about the epidemic, there was hope. He wanted to understand it; he wanted to hear the stories and read the evidence. Awareness about the epidemic was rising. The media was filled with stories about it, and there was a new consensus that radical measures were needed.

Just as the size and nature of the opioid epidemic kept changing, so too did the type of drugs available. Even the type of fentanyl entering the market was not stable. While most commentators use the singular term *fentanyl* to describe the cause of so many overdose deaths, what we are actually describing is a multitude of closely related fentanyls, in the plural. When fentanyl is made in drug labs, the process is messy and ends up making many forms of fentanyl, some of which are stronger, some of which are longer acting. For example, I began to see the analogue acrylfentanyl show up on drug-testing equipment in 2018 and to hear from patients that the fentanyl on the street was becoming longer acting. Acrylfentanyl is both stronger and longer acting than regular fentanyl, and it represents just one of the many subtypes my patients use.

Because of the rising contamination rates and the proliferation of the types of drugs being used, the safe injection site at our clinic began to use a sophisticated drug-testing device that could run tests on the drugs people were bringing in to use. The machine cost $130,000. It was so sophisticated we needed the support of a university chemistry department to test it and review the data it was generating, and update its software as new drugs came into the ecosystem.

I was talking with our manager when one of the safe injection site workers walked quickly down the hallway. "We found carfentanil in crack cocaine," he said in an alarmed tone. An hour later, the clinic sent out an email with an advisory that we had detected carfentanil in a white creamy substance thought to be crack cocaine. I immediately started talking about this with my patients, and by the next week they all knew about it.

"I used crack and I was out for eight hours," Melanie told me. "It was definitely carfentanil."

The same day, I heard rumours about a death at another clinic in town. Shirley had used drugs for years, but she had gone down so fast after using crack cocaine, it could only have been carfentanil.

Where did carfentanil come from? The story of fentanyl's discovery did not end in 1960. The explorers at Janssen's labs were not done. They continued to probe the chemistry of the fentanyl family, finding a number of new relatives, including a successful analogue called alfentanil. Within fourteen years, they had figured out how to make a drug at least twenty times more potent than fentanyl itself. Instead of giving it a flashy name, they simply called it carfentanil.

Researchers then looked for a use for their super-weapon. They decided to try it on the biggest animals they could find. It was tested in a dart to subdue wild animals. In one experiment, carfentanil was fed in a variety of doses to rhesus monkeys and dogs to see how little of the drug was needed to knock them out. The study concluded, "There are obvious differences in the dose of carfentanil necessary to produce anesthesia in the dog and in the rhesus monkey. Primates appear to become much more profoundly anesthetized with carfentanil and sustain greater levels of respiratory depression relative to dogs."[24]

In September 2017, the upstairs tenant of a rental unit on Liatris Drive, in a quiet suburb east of Toronto, called the fire department because of an alarm coming from the downstairs unit. The firemen entered the house, climbed down to the basement, and came across the largest quantity of carfentanil ever seized in Canada — forty-two kilograms — along with thirty-three handguns, ammunition, and cutting agents. A few months before, the tenant of the lower unit, a young man, had suffered a drug overdose and gone into a coma. Two men were charged in relation to the weapons and the drugs. The police calculated that if the powder were divided into points (0.1-gram doses), it would yield 420,000 doses, worth more than ten million dollars on the street.

The story didn't end there, because in July 2018 a twenty-nine-year-old man named Faisal Hussain killed two people and injured thirteen in a shooting rampage on Danforth Avenue in Toronto. As the police and media raced to understand who he was and find a motive, they discovered that his brother, Farad Hussain, had been the tenant in the downstairs unit of the house on Liatris Drive. Farad had a criminal record including possession of weapons, ammunition, and drugs. It was part of his bail conditions that he stay in the house on Liatris Drive. We will never know what connected Faisal's violent rampage and Farad's opioid overdose, but the secret web linking carfentanil, weapons, and violence is yet another manifestation of the opioid epidemic.

Carfentanil is a powerful weapon, and has been used as such. On October 23, 2002, Chechen separatists captured more than eight hundred hostages in a theatre in Moscow. They strapped explosives to themselves and wired up more explosives around the building. After a three-day standoff, Russian special forces pumped an unidentified substance into the ventilation system, then stormed the building. The Chechens were found unconscious. They were shot, and the explosives were removed from their bodies. More than 120 hostages died from the effects of the chemicals that were later analyzed by scientists at the U.K. Defence Science and Technology Laboratory. Using clothing and urine samples from survivors, the lab identified the chemicals as an aerosol version of carfentanil mixed with a similar drug, remifentanil. One survivor, an engineer named Olga Dolotova, later described seeing white plumes descending before she lost consciousness. She woke to find herself on a bus full of bodies.[25]

By late 2018 and throughout 2019, almost every urine drug test I ordered was positive for fentanyl, while carfentanil was being found in overdose victims in alarming rates across North America. The staff at safe injection sites throughout Canada found they needed more naloxone to bring patients back from overdose. We began to talk about "the kind of fentanyl you can't come back from." Shifts of nurses worked twenty-four hours a day in a safe injection site called The Trailer next to the Shepherds of Good Hope on Ottawa's King Edward Avenue. They were seeing far more people and far more overdoses, which were far more difficult to treat, than they had predicted when The Trailer opened a year before — up to 180 people a day, twice as many as they had anticipated.[26]

The Calgary addiction doctor Hakique Virani said in the documentary *Dopesick: Fentanyl's Deadly Grip* that the worst we expected when OxyContin was phased out was the return of heroin; no one expected bootleg fentanyl. No one was prepared. More and more patients were telling me that things were different with fentanyl. Doctors and advocates called for more liberalized drug policies and more prescription opioids, blaming restrictive policies for the rise of fentanyl. Everyone was trying to explain the epidemic: blaming doctors, pharmaceutical companies, the economy, the regulators, the dealers. But to defeat the epidemic, we first have to understand why it happened.

CHAPTER 5

Explaining the Epidemic

Steven Pinker, a Harvard psychologist, immediately recognizable by his fulsome silver curls, stood in front of a packed church just a few blocks from my house. He spoke about his new book, *Enlightenment Now: The Case for Reason, Science, Humanism, and Progress*. It aimed to demonstrate, with the aid of dozens of meticulous and detailed graphs, that the lives of humans today, when compared with the past, are better, safer, easier, longer, and richer across the world. He showed that worldwide, life expectancy has risen from the mid-thirties in pre-modern times to more than seventy years, and that the chance of dying in a plane crash or car accident has plummeted over the past fifty years. But one graph seemed to be going in the wrong direction. The trend for accidental poisoning deaths was climbing straight up.

"I was puzzled when I first saw this," he told us that night. "But when I looked into the data, I realized that this category of deaths includes drug overdoses. What you are seeing here is the effect of the North American opioid epidemic."

After I left the church that evening, I thought about how addiction is fighting progress. I thought about the deep history of epidemics and our collective response over the centuries. Daniel Defoe wrote an account of London's outbreak of plague in the late seventeenth century. In it he compared the plague to the Great Fire of London, which struck in 1666: "The violence of the distemper, when it came to its extremity, was like the fire the next year. The fire, which consumed what the plague could not touch, defied all the application of remedies; the fire-engines were broken, the buckets thrown away, and the power of man was baffled and brought to an end. So the plague defied all medicines; the very physicians were seized with it, with their preservatives in their mouths; and men went about prescribing to others and telling them what to do till the tokens were upon them, and they dropped down dead, destroyed by that very enemy they directed others to oppose."[1]

The early stage of the plague was marked by the twin perils of rising numbers of victims and collective denial. Defoe wrote, "From the first week in June the infection spread in a dreadful manner, and the bills rose high; the articles of the fever, spotted-fever, and teeth began to swell; for all that could conceal their distempers did it, to prevent their neighbours shunning and refusing to converse with them, and also to prevent authority shutting up their houses; which, though it was not yet practised, yet was threatened, and people were extremely terrified at the thoughts of it."[2]

As the denial became untenable, panic and superstition took hold. Fear saturated every sight and every encounter. People began to hear "voices warning them to be gone, for that there would be such a plague in London, so that the living would not be able to bury the dead."[3] Everywhere, omens warned of disaster; reports spread of clouds shaped like a flaming sword hanging over the city, of hearses and coffins, and of heaps of dead bodies lying unburied.

We can explain the Great Fire of London: houses made of straw and wood and heated by open fires were built too close together. When a fire started, there was no effective fire service to extinguish it and contain its spread. We can explain the Black Death of the Middle Ages and the subsequent outbreak of bubonic plague in London from 1665 to 1666: rats infected with fleas, which were in turn infected with the bacteria *Yersinia pestis*, ran amok in the city. Explaining the modern plague of opioids is complex, but it is vital if we want to counter it and prevent future outbreaks. To do this, we need to explore the minor and the major causes of the epidemic.

As Steven Pinker pointed out that night, human well-being has, in many ways, improved in the past couple of centuries. But many social commentators claim that people are becoming lonelier, more depressed, more anxious, and more drug addicted, even as we, on the whole, become wealthier and better educated. Mental health conditions and addictions are linked to other "diseases of modernity" such as obesity and type 2 diabetes. Declining social cohesion, greater inequality, social media, and the internet are all blamed for the apparent rise of these conditions.[4] Certainly people are using more opioids, but is that part of a larger crisis in mental health?

One in six people around the world has a mental health or substance use disorder. The majority of those people suffer from depression and anxiety. In the United States, however, the rates of anxiety and depression have been relatively stable since at least 1990.[5] Similarly, the frequency rates for depression in Canada have been relatively stable for the past generation.[6, 7]

On the other hand, more children are now diagnosed with attention deficit hyperactivity disorder (ADHD) than ever before.[8] Is that because the condition is becoming more common, because doctors are getting better at recognizing it, or because it is being overdiagnosed and overtreated?

Although it's not clear what is driving this increase, it is clear that the condition is becoming more prevalent. This rise has been observed in the United States. Australia has similar rates and is showing a similar increasing trend. The rates are lower in Canada and Europe but are also on the rise. ADHD is prevalent in all ethnic groups, but some populations have seen significant growth in the number of individuals affected. For example, the prevalence of the condition has doubled among girls.

ADHD is not a benign condition. Kids with ADHD are more likely to have oppositional defiant disorder, conduct disorder, anxiety, depression, and learning disorders, and they are more likely to go on to have substance use disorders.

As more kids receive diagnoses of psychiatric conditions, more of them are given pills. Rates of prescription of ADHD medications, antidepressants, and even antipsychotics are increasing for kids in Canada and the United States. Allen Frances is an articulate and formidable opponent of the over-medicalization of mental health. He was chair of Duke's psychiatry department and led the fourth revision of the

Diagnostic and Statistical Manual of Mental Disorders, the classification of psychiatric conditions. He told an interviewer that Big Pharma is behind rising prescriptions rates for children: "Having saturated the adult market, pharma has turned its attention to aggressively marketing pills for children who are, in some ways, their perfect customers — because once pills solutions become the norm, the kid may become a customer for life."[9]

Many problems of modernity can be linked to the success of unbridled capitalism. Two Dutch researchers compared the European and North American situations and blamed the higher rates of opioid use and misuse in North America on the "commodification of health care," that has created a "a culture of consumerism" in medicine. They identified two key factors in the United States that are absent in Europe and that have contributed to this culture: direct-to-consumer advertising and private health care systems that incentivize quick ways to increase patient satisfaction. For many years, this has resulted in the increasing prescription of opioids. As a consequence of these shifts, they argued, "North American patients anticipate a quick solution for a complex problem such as pain."[10]

We saw in the last chapter that there was a cultural shift in North America from an acceptance that it is necessary to bear pain to an expectation that opioids should be used to eliminate all pain. When I see graphs showing the year-upon-year increase in opioid users and opioid deaths, I see the infectious spread of addictive medications and the terrible consequences of their overuse; I also see the spread of a dangerous idea about how to achieve bliss, euphoria, and freedom from pain.

For an idea to spread, it must find receptive minds. It's clear that we, as a society, have become very receptive to the idea of using opioids. The reasons for this are numerous, but the central reason is that we have become conditioned to using chemicals to change how we feel. Cat Marnell, the flamboyant beauty editor who wrote the addiction memoir *How to Murder Your Life*, told an interviewer, "People think of addicts as being out of control, and they really are. But I'm also a control freak. I want to control everything with a pill, from my appetite to sleeping."[11]

This attitude has contributed to the opioid epidemic to the extent that kids are growing into adults who cannot tolerate natural feelings, and so they reflexively reach for a chemical to turn off bad feelings. A culture of sharing and misusing other drugs, such as stimulants and benzodiazepines, may also be feeding the culture of misusing opioids. So, while the underlying mental health of society may not be changing fundamentally, the way doctors and Big Pharma have responded to these conditions has changed in North America, as have societal expectations regarding managing pain, behaviour, and mood.

Another thing that has changed is technology. The history of the late twentieth and early twenty-first centuries demonstrates how the screaming progress in computer power has been the catalyst that accelerated many parts of our world. The use of the internet and the dark web has fed into the epidemic, as dealers and consumers have learned how to order, tamper with, abuse, and divert drugs online.

According to the U.S. Federal Bureau of Investigation (FBI), there were more than 1.2 million transactions on Silk Road, a website that trafficked in drugs and other illegal products, between February 2011 and July 2013. Its founder may have made around eighty million dollars in a single year from commissions on those transactions. Silk Road was shut down in 2013, but new sites have blossomed on the dark web, including the popular AlphaBay, which allowed anonymous customers to pay in bitcoin for fentanyl. Law enforcement agents track large purchases, but small orders in benign-looking envelopes slip through every day.[12]

Cellphones have catalyzed the opioid epidemic in a way that is rarely discussed. In 1993 almost no one in North America had a cellphone; by 2011 almost everyone did, regardless of income. Cellphones are now a basic necessity of life, used and cherished even by my homeless and my most unstable patients. In 2012, Beth Macy interviewed Brian, a young opioid user in recovery. He told her, "The cellphone is the glue that holds it all together for the modern drug user."[13] The opioid epidemic has occurred alongside the development of almost universal access to cellphones and the ability to text and make calls from anywhere. With a text message, the pickup point for a drug deal can change, information can be passed at the last moment, and a high-schooler can step out of his home to meet his dealer and be back in a few moments without his parents noticing. Heroin was a lot harder to access before the internet and cellphones. The prevalence of these technologies explains, to a significant degree, the severity of the current epidemic.

In my clinic one afternoon, Marco sat down across from me, looking sheepish. "I relapsed, Doc. It was bad, but it was because of the booze."

Macro had struggled with cocaine and opioid use for thirty years, but I hadn't heard him mention a drinking problem before.

"I didn't know you were a drinker," I replied.

"I'm not — it's not my thing. But now you can buy it at the grocery store across from my place."

The laws in Ontario had just changed so that alcohol was available in grocery stores. Previously, it was available only at government liquor stores known as the LCBO, run by the Liquor Control Board of Ontario.

"I bought some booze, then I got on the cocaine, then the fentanyl. I spent like six hundred bucks in three days. Now I'm broke. They wanted to kick me out of my housing, but they said they'd give me another chance."

The effect of the increased availability of alcohol in Ontario is, I believe, a perfect example of the effect of availability on drug-use patterns. People with alcohol problems began to tell me that while they had learned to avoid the LCBO, they were now coming across big new wine and beer sections while buying their groceries; they were even being offered free samples on their way out of the store. And the more they were seeing alcohol, the more they were using it.

When a substance is very rare, few people are exposed to it, and thus few people are likely to become addicted to it. When a substance is abundant, the opposite is true. Take the example of food. In 2016, Nora Volkow spoke to a group of addiction doctors in Montreal about food addiction. She told us that the pleasure derived from food releases dopamine, which runs through the same addiction pathways as those affected by drugs. "Addiction doctors should be involved in the obesity epidemic; this is an addiction problem," she proclaimed.

It is the availability, marketing, and promotion of junk food that has turned our love and obsession with finding and consuming food into a public health crisis. Similarly, it was the mass production of cigarettes that led to the tobacco epidemic. Restricting access to harmful substances, by contrast, reduces consumption. During the Prohibition era, for example, legal alcohol vanished for thirteen long years in the United States. This absence resulted in much lower rates of alcohol use and less cirrhosis of the liver.

So, exposure is a problem.

While addiction cuts across all strata of society, there is only one thing that unites every person who has become addicted to opioids: exposure to opioids. This is why the exposure theory makes sense. Americans had been getting richer, safer, and smarter for decades. But as things got better, their access to opioids also began to increase, first through prescriptions and then through illicit sources. I have met addicted homeless men and women, students, nurses, paramedics, doctors, accountants, professors, and government workers who were prescribed opioids in the late 1990s or the early years of the new millennium, when it was still believed the risk of addiction was less than 1 percent.

In *Dark Paradise: A History of Opiate Addiction in America*, historian David Courtwright argued that the present opioid crisis is the product, to a significant degree, of the same forces that have produced opioid crises in the past. He traced the rise of opioid addiction over the nineteenth century. It peaked in the 1890s, and Courtwright notes that this rise was the result of doctors liberally prescribing their well-heeled patients opium and morphine for a wide range of ailments. This changed at the beginning of the twentieth century as medical attitudes toward opioids became more conservative and laws began to restrict physicians from prescribing opioids in most cases.

After reviewing the history of opioid use in the nineteenth and twentieth centuries, Courtwright concluded that availability is a key factor, echoing the observation of William S. Burroughs, author of *Naked Lunch*, who wrote, "Addiction is an illness of exposure. By and large those who have access to junk become addicts." In a similar vein, Courtwright wrote, "Over and over again the epidemiologic data affirm a simple truth: those groups who, for whatever reasons, have had the greatest exposure to opiates have the highest rates of opiate addiction. This is as true of doctors and their patients in the nineteenth century as it is of delinquents and slum dwellers in our own day."[14]

One generation ago, heroin was the opioid of choice for its relatively few users, because it was virtually the only opioid in town. In the 1960s, more than 80 percent of opioid users started out with heroin.[15] Heroin was the opioid that could be purchased from gangsters; it was the opioid people discussed in hushed tones in dark alleys. But supply was low. In 1982, one gram of pure heroin cost $2,690. By 2012 that price had come down to $465 per gram.[16] Any economist can tell you that lower prices result in more demand, and addictive drugs such as heroin have followed this pattern.

Heroin also used to be exclusive to the big cities of North America. With the current epidemic, however, every small town in rural America and even the remotest communities in northern Canada have supplies of opioids. When heroin dealers moved into new towns and small cities that previously had only a trickle of diverted prescription opioids, addiction blossomed. As heroin use increased, so did crime. Overdoses went up, and so did death rates. Opioid users are not born; they are made and sustained by exposure to the drugs.

Even cheaper than heroin in the 1990s were prescription drugs paid for by insurance plans, which is why three-quarters of opioid users started with prescription opioids.[17] The U.S. state with the highest overdose rate is West Virginia, which, beginning in the 1990s, experienced an explosion in the number of prescriptions written for opioids. Investigators looked into what was happening; they discovered that in two well-publicized cases in Williamson, a town of just over three thousand residents, two pharmacies just four blocks from each other dispensed more than twenty million prescription opioids between 2006 and 2016.[18]

The over-prescription of opioids then fed into the next waves of heroin and fentanyl use. People who have abused prescription opioids are forty times more likely to develop a heroin addiction than people who haven't.

Monique was thirty-nine when I met her. Wearing a suit jacket and long skirt and with her blond hair pulled back in a ponytail, she looked like a banker. She actually did work in a bank, and she made a good income. She was divorced and had no kids. As a teen growing up outside of Montreal, she drank a little and tried smoking cigarettes a few times, but never got into drugs. She had had a good childhood, and she was healthy until she turned twenty-five. A few weeks after her birthday, she started to feel pain in her abdomen, especially after a big meal. She ignored her symptoms until one night she was in so much pain she started to vomit and experienced chills and hot sweats. Her friend took her to the emergency room, where a doctor told her she had stones in her gallbladder.

That was the night she first felt the touch of opioids.

She got better quickly and in a couple of days was sent home with fifty tablets of Percocet. Even though her pain was gone, she kept taking the Percocet — it gave her so much energy, and she was doing so well at work. When the prescription ran out, she didn't think much of it; she just thought the good times were over, but she'd get back to living like before. A day later, she felt terrible. She was sweaty and nauseous, her back hurt, her legs hurt, and she couldn't work, so she went to her clinic and told them she thought her infection was back. Monique mentioned that Percocet had really helped the last time, and her doctor gave her another prescription.

From there, her story took on a familiar pattern: longer courses of Percocet, more hospital and clinic visits, increased doses, starting to crush and snort her Percocet after she found it wasn't giving her that feeling she remembered from the first few weeks. Then she got into a discussion about her pain and her Percocet with a neighbour, who mentioned that he had some strong pills called Oxys. Soon she was spending more of her salary from the bank to buy the Oxys from her neighbour.

Although Monique was still working when she came to see me, things weren't easy. She was constantly in pain and she was depressed. In addition to her neighbour, she had developed a network of people who supplied her with pills. She was a good customer; she always had money. She told me that at first she would give pills to her girlfriends when they asked, but recently she had tried to stop doing that, not wanting to spread the addiction.

"If I had known this would happen, I would never have taken those fucking Percocets when I had my gallstones," she told me.

Imagine if, like Monique that night at the hospital, you are experiencing physical and mental anguish, something that we all suffer from during our lives. You are struggling to sleep because your back pain won't relent, and on top of that your work is making you so stressed you dread going to the office. Your friend suggests you try a Percocet. At first it makes you nauseated, but soon afterward you don't notice your back pain and you can't remember why you were so stressed. You start to believe.

Soon you are taking Percocet and sleeping better and functioning better at work — everything is better. You tell others about how you feel, and you share some Percocets with them. In a form of social contagion, all your friends are introduced to the joys of opioids, then all their friends in turn, and so on. Through exponentially increasing social networks, the epidemic spreads. Some people will try the opioid and feel worse or feel nothing. But enough people will feel good for long enough that they become converts and help spread the idea that this pill or that one can solve all your problems. And just like an infectious disease, once the harmful effects of opioids have begun to set in, it is too late to stop the spread.

When I graduated from medical school in 2009, the voices expressing caution were growing louder still. Older physicians continued to prescribe high doses, but the next generation was trained to use as few opioids as possible. The problem was getting patients off them. To put a patient on three hundred milligrams of OxyContin over a period of years is the easiest thing in the world; to get that patient off completely is the hardest. Each dose decrease results in real withdrawal symptoms, more pain, more suffering; these drugs are so pernicious. Switching to another opioid only puts off the problem for another day.

In 2012 Anna Lembke, a Stanford psychiatrist, wrote an impassioned article titled "Why Doctors Prescribe Opioids to Known Opioid Abusers." Lembke wrote, "In many instances, doctors are fully aware that their patients are abusing these medications or diverting them to others for nonmedical use, but they prescribe them anyway. Why?"[19] She traced it to the impetus to treat pain regardless of other considerations, arguing that "self-reports of pain are above question, and the treatment of pain is held up as the holy grail of compassionate medical care."[20] Patient satisfaction surveys included pain management ratings, and physicians who were reluctant to give opioids would receive poor ratings that could affect their income and job security. The rise of online ratings has made things even worse. A patient who has been refused an increase or has been made to decrease their opioids will express their frustration by anonymously berating their physicians on websites that are unaccountable.

A problem here is that pain comes in many forms. Monique's first experience of pain was due to her gallstones; that could have been treated with anti-inflammatories or a very short course of opioids. Her subsequent episodes of pain were probably all related to opioid withdrawal, not another attack of gallstones. The longer a person takes opioids, the more pain they experience, especially when the opioids are stopped or reduced.

Lembke predicted that opioid prescribing would come under control only once the costs of irresponsible prescribing outweighed the costs of patient frustration and complaints. During my first five years working on the front lines, I saw the tide turn. As the legal and regulatory environment changed, patients came to realize that prescriptions were harder to get, and it was harder to complain if you didn't go home with pills. Patients in Europe had been living in such a world for years.

Europe, for the most part, has not experienced an opioid epidemic. Yes, people die from opioids in Europe, but in 2015 the rate of death was about one-seventh of that in the United States: fifteen deaths per million people in Europe compared with about 104 deaths per million in the United States.[21] And heroin has been the biggest source of overdose in Europe; prescription opioids have not been a driver of death as they have in North America. Lower rates of opioid prescribing and better drug policies explain this substantial difference. The countries with the lowest overdose rates in Europe — Portugal, France, and Italy — have among the lowest rates of opioid prescribing in Europe. They also have robust harm-reduction policies and excellent access to treatment, something I will explore later.

Some have attributed the North American opioid epidemic to economic decline. Although it's true that more economically marginalized areas of the United States have had worse problems with opioids, economic decline alone is not sufficient to cause an opioid epidemic.[22] Economic decline certainly doesn't explain Canada's opioid problem. And European countries, in particular southern countries like Greece and Portugal, have suffered huge economic shocks in recent decades without a resulting opioid epidemic. A key difference between these countries and North America is that opioids have been used less in Europe. European doctors did not face the onslaught of OxyContin marketing, opioid prescribing has been more tightly controlled, and the culture has not demanded the elimination of all pain and has not treated pain as the fifth vital sign.[23]

Another useful comparison is with Japan, a country that has endured prolonged economic stagnation, but that may have the lowest rate of opioid addiction among the industrialized nations. Japan ran an opium and narcotics monopoly in Manchuria, one of its Chinese territories, from the 1930s until the end of the Second World War. But Japan restricted opium use among its own citizens as early as the nineteenth century. Opioid prescribing is much less common in Japan than in North America, and the use of potent opioids is twenty-six times less per capita in Japan than in the United States. Japanese physicians, rather than prescribing opioids, turn to anti-inflammatories and non-pharmacologic treatments such as acupressure and massage.[24]

Rates of opioid addiction are likely under-reported in Japan owing to a strong cultural aversion to drug use, but they are certainly far lower than in North America. Opioid overdoses do not register on official statistics; most overdoses are attributed to benzodiazepines and psychiatric medications. Amphetamines are the drug of choice in Japan, where long work hours and high productivity are demanded. The business press has reported, however, that since 2017, Big Pharma has been promoting the sale of prescription opioids in Japan and that sales are increasing, so overdose rates may rise if the lessons from North America are not heeded.[25]

Thus, it was exposure to prescription opioids that drove the first wave of the epidemic in North America. The question is why it is still growing. After 2010, the supply of prescription opioids began to dry up, but by no means did it stop. Heroin and then fentanyl began to fill that vacuum. In the United States, Mexican heroin dealers had been bringing better and cheaper heroin to more parts of the country for years as demand increased.

Was the rise in the use of heroin and then heroin-tainted fentanyl, pure fentanyl, and carfentanil caused by a decline in opioid prescriptions? Researchers and advocates have made that argument, blaming, for example, the introduction of tamper-resistant OxyContin for the rise in the use of heroin after 2010.[26]

Supply affects demand. For example, opioid use was at its low for the twentieth century during the Second World War, when shipping was disrupted and there was a shortage of many goods, including heroin.

But then the supply comes back.

I've seen this phenomenon myself. When the police in Ottawa were particularly successful at temporarily clamping down on the drug supply, consumption necessarily declined. Long-term addiction patients like Jessica would come in with negative urine drug screens and explain to me, "There's nothing out there; it's all garbage." As a substance becomes less available, fewer people use it.

When the supply of opioids in Ottawa rose again, my patients once again began to use. "I ran into my dealer outside my building, and by the time I was inside, I had two points of purple heroin," Jessica told me a few weeks after her last visit.

When we look at what happened during those tumultuous years, however, the link between reduced prescribing and increases in heroin and then fentanyl use is not as clear as it may seem at first. When people have an opioid addiction, they will progress to cheaper and stronger opioids as their disease progresses and when the opportunity arises. As the heroin market expanded, prices went down, quality went up, and people began to make the switch. Prescription opioids were the gateway for the vast majority of users, but heroin was the destination.

The switch from prescription opioids to fentanyl fits the same pattern. Fentanyl is stronger, cheaper, and even more addictive than heroin, so it is a logical next step for a person with a long-term addiction. But in most cases, people who use drugs do not choose what they buy; they buy what is available. Similarly, new users entering the drug world will try what is on the market, and these days what's on the market is fentanyl.

There is a logical reason that fentanyl dominates the illegal opioid market today: it is the most potent drug available, so less of it, compared with other drugs, is required to produce a high. This makes it attractive to suppliers; relatively small amounts of the drug are necessary to satisfy a market. The small amounts can be easily shipped, and because of the drug's potency, it can be easily "stepped on" (cut down with fillers such as caffeine and other white powders). So, for suppliers, it offers the twin benefits of portability and profitability.

One of the harms of addiction treatment that I worry about is the geographic overlap between people recovering from drug use and people trying to sell drugs. Often, these are the same people, just at different stages of treatment, because the best way to pay for a drug habit is to sell drugs. In practice, it means there is a concentration of drugs around addiction clinics and pharmacies. A simple solution would be to provide addiction treatment at every level of the health care system, so addiction care is not concentrated in one clinic or one wing of the hospital.

A big difference between Europe, Canada, and the United States is the availability of treatment. Access to basic health care is universal in Canada and Europe. Access to effective medications to treat opioid addiction is excellent in Europe, with very high levels in France, the Netherlands, and Portugal, and good but patchy access in Canada.[27] While some provinces, such as British Columbia, have excellent access to treatment, others, such as Alberta, have much less. In the United States, only about one in five patients has easy access to effective treatment.[28] Even inside the addiction treatment world, however, there is often a lack of understanding about what works. The focus on expensive, private, abstinence-based residential treatment centres in the United States is one reason that outcomes are worse in the United States relative to those in Canada and Europe. I explore the issues of access to treatment later in the book.

An instructive analogy can be drawn between the opioid epidemic and a little-known episode in twentieth-century drug history. This is the story of amphetamine sales and use between the 1940s and the 1960s. Amphetamine molecules resemble adrenalin and act like an extra-strength version of caffeine. People using an amphetamine feel more energetic, more alert, and less hungry.

Amphetamines were initially marketed in America as a medication for colds. During the Second World War, they were issued in huge numbers to bomber crews and soldiers to keep them awake during combat. By 1946 they were prescribed by physicians for many reasons, including to aid in weight loss.

Amphetamine use and abuse spread in the 1940 and 1950s, in part owing to the enthusiasm of physicians who were convinced this was a new wonder drug, and in part to the promotional efforts of pharmaceutical companies. The sale and use of amphetamines rose and continued, largely unchecked, until the beginning of the 1970s. Finally, in 1971, the U.S. federal government, having noticed the increased production of amphetamines and the spreading epidemic of methamphetamine injection, dramatically reduced the quotas given to pharmaceutical companies that produced and sold them. Over the next few decades, amphetamine use declined, although it did not disappear.

Reflecting on the history of the amphetamine boom, drug historian David Courtwright makes an observation that looks remarkably prescient:

> When doctors treat a host of vague complaints by handing out powerful drugs flying the false colors of safety, they act as the sorcerer's apprentices. Some patients, invariably a minority, decide they can continue taking the medicine for other purposes. After all, it can't do any harm. They urge it on their friends. It helped my blues, my hangover, my fatigue, my weight problem, my sex life; it will help yours. Those who continue using get their supplies from physicians, concocting various stories to obtain prescriptions, or purchase directly from profiteering pharmacists and other illegal suppliers. Extramedical use evolves out of authorized medical use in a process of parallel chain reactions. The more pharmaceutical companies promote a drug and the more physicians prescribe it, the more parallel chains are set in motion and the sooner the drug is democratized.[29]

That these words were written in 2001, before the opioid epidemic had become "democratized," is remarkable, as it shows that what happened with Purdue was not an isolated exception, but rather part of a pattern, a known risk of the way profits and medical practice can mix with psychoactive substances to breed addiction.

In summary, the major cause of the current North American opioid epidemic was a permissive environment that increased exposure to opioids for people from all walks of life. Initially, these were prescription opioids, which either were directly prescribed to a patient or were shared or taken from a medicine cabinet. The increased number of prescriptions normalized the use of opioids and created a culture in which patients expected opioids. This was worsened by the belief that taking pills to change how you feel is normal and that any physical or mental suffering should be addressed by pills.

When the supply of prescription opioids became more difficult to access, the supply of heroin and then fentanyl increased to fill the demand from those addicted to prescription opioids. The potency of fentanyl makes it an ideal drug for users and dealers, and this has been driving up the number of overdose deaths in recent years. Other factors that have driven the epidemic are improved communications technology — the internet and cellphones — and poor access to effective addiction treatment.

But understanding the epidemic, like acknowledging that you are powerless to stop drinking or using drugs, is only the first step. To end this epidemic, we need to know how to treat the disease.

CHAPTER 6

Treating Addiction

Ernst von Fleischl-Marxow was a handsome and charismatic physician, much admired by Sigmund Freud. He was a professor at the University of Vienna and a member of the Austrian Academy of Sciences. He researched the electrical impulses of the central and peripheral nervous system. While dissecting a cadaver one day, he badly injured his thumb. The wound became infected, leading him to suffer from chronic pain. To cope, he began to use morphine, which was easily available and frequently administered by injection in the late nineteenth century. His habit developed into a full addiction, his mood and function worsened, and soon he felt hopeless and suicidal. One night in April 1884, Freud stayed up with him through the night, caring for him. Freud later described Fleischl-Marxow's condition as so bad that "every note of the profoundest despair was sounded."[1]

Freud's medical opinion was that cocaine could help his friend to stop using opioids. The novel treatment worked. Fleischl-Marxow stopped using opioids, and Freud promoted cocaine as a treatment for opioid addiction, as well as for alcoholism and depression. Very quickly, Fleischl-Marxow developed a cocaine addiction, and before long, his opioid use returned, resulting in his compulsive use of two drugs. In fact, he would mix cocaine and morphine together and inject the combination. This lasted for another six years, until Fleischl-Marxow died at the age of forty-five.

Even though treatment has improved since Freud's day, today only one in six patients with an addiction seeks treatment. Denial and the desire to continue using, driven by the machinery of dopamine, push most people who use drugs toward increased consumption and away from abstinence. Being conditioned to hate and fear withdrawal, being unwilling to enter a room of strangers and commit to a higher power, and believing that there are no effective treatments all play a role.

To defeat any epidemic, you have to discover the cause, educate the public, and stop it from spreading. But you must also treat those already infected.

Despite its fifty years of honourable work as a cornerstone of addiction treatment, methadone has a bad reputation. Many people equate the use of methadone with the use of heroin. Historically, a lot of the opposition to methadone has come from within the addiction community. The focus on abstinence in the twelve-step model encourages people from that tradition to see methadone as another type of addiction, as a crutch and not a cure.

Methadone is, to be sure, a blunt instrument. It is a powerful medicine that fills a person's opioid receptors so their urge to use other opioids is sated. It is a crutch in the same sense that any medication for a chronic disease is a crutch. Like many medications, it works when you take it and it stops working when you stop taking it.

We often look for the magic-bullet treatment for a disease. For most infections, the magic bullet is a short course of antibiotics. A single dose may be enough to cure even a potentially serious infectious disease such as syphilis; an infection that wreaked havoc on our ancestors for centuries can now be cured with a single dose of penicillin. But this is a glorious exception.

The medicine cabinets of many elderly people becomes increasingly stuffed with pills over the years. One medication for every decade of life is typical, so that adds up to eight medications a day for an eighty-year-old. With the state of medicine today, this is normal. In the future, I don't doubt that taking medications by mouth once a day for years at a time will seem quaint and primitive, like bloodletting and leeches. But that time has not yet arrived. Thus, for methadone and its newer cousin, buprenorphine, daily doses remain the norm. The impact of methadone is usually minimal. Patients taking it should be able to go to school, to work, to drive, to look after their families. The whole point of methadone, like most interventions in medicine, is to give the patient the best quality of life possible.

Before I made the decision to become a methadone prescriber, I had to overcome significant doubts about the drug. I knew enough about the history of the opioid epidemic and the treatments used to contain it to be skeptical about whether methadone, too, would ultimately be seen as a good idea gone bad, something promoted because of ignorance or because it offered someone a profit. I did not want to be complicit in the use of another drug that would end up hurting my patients. I didn't want to have my medical work footnoted with the sentence, "He did harm, but he thought he was doing good." So, like doubters before me, I went in search of the truth.

I started with the history. I went back to the beginning of addiction treatment and learned that in the early twentieth century, narcotic clinics in the United States legally provided heroin or morphine to patients. New York City's Bellevue Hospital admitted the first case of heroin dependence in 1910. But the 1914 Harrison Act was interpreted as prohibiting maintenance opioids, and law enforcement went after the physicians running these clinics. Around twenty-five thousand physicians were indicted under the act, and about one in ten was imprisoned. The law was challenged before the Supreme Court, but the medical profession had been burned. By 1923, all narcotic clinics were closed.[2]

Within a few years, researchers were trying to change things. In 1928 Charles Terry and Mildred Pellens wrote a report advocating for opioid maintenance as the best treatment for long-term opioids users. This view was anathema to puritanical American policy-makers but the practice was more widely accepted in Europe. In the late 1930s, scientists at Bayer in Germany developed methadone, which was used by the German army during the Second World War as a painkiller. After the war, the rights to methadone were passed to the American company Eli Lilly. Methadone was marketed for pain relief for decades.

In the postwar years, there was a limited amount of methadone available for pain relief, but there were no addiction treatments. By the 1960s, "treatment was scarce, prison common, and relapse likely," according to the addiction psychiatrist Herbert Kleber.[3] Then came a husband-and-wife team who changed addiction treatment as we know it. Vincent Dole, a Stanford- and Harvard-educated internist who became interested in addiction medicine, and his wife, the psychiatrist Marie Nyswander, undertook a study using methadone as a medical treatment for heroin addiction. The study was published in the *Journal of the American Medical Association* on August 23, 1965.[4]

The study described a group of twenty-two patients with heroin addiction who were "stabilized on methadone hydrochloride." It suggested that methadone has "two useful effects: (1) relief of narcotic hunger; and (2) induction of sufficient tolerance to block the euphoric effect of an average illegal dose of diacetylmorphine." Dole and Nyswander defined success in terms of overall function: "With this medication, and a comprehensive program of rehabilitation, patients have shown marked improvement; they have returned to school, obtained jobs, and have reconciled with their families."

The methadone era had begun. Researchers designed new trials for methadone, and the FDA approved methadone use in research programs. Initially in New York, then across the United States, doctors and government agencies shifted toward providing methadone maintenance for heroin users. This early development of methadone treatment occurred against the backdrop of the Vietnam War, which saw rising heroin use among soldiers. At the same time, in the 1970s, urban heroin use and associated crime levels also rose. In Canada, methadone treatment was started in Vancouver in 1963 and was selectively used across the country during the 1960s and 1970s.

The pushback from law enforcement agencies and abstinence-based addiction treatment organizations was immediate and is ongoing. In the early days of methadone maintenance treatment, a director of a therapeutic community observed, "I think methadone is a great idea. We should give money to bank robbers, women to rapists, and methadone to addicts."[5]

The HIV epidemic of the 1980s and 1990s changed the landscape of addiction treatment, as evidence emerged that methadone patients were less likely to contract HIV. A 1993 study in Philadelphia found HIV infection rates were one-quarter as high for patients receiving methadone compared with those for patients who used street heroin.[6]

After looking at the history of methadone, I scoured medical databases and journals, and at first I was disturbed by the drug's dangers. I learned that the risk of death goes up seriously in the first few weeks of treatment. Because methadone is such a strong opioid, it can cause fatal toxicity if the dose is increased too quickly. This alarmed me, but I read on. I discovered that the risk then goes down, and over time patients on methadone have a 50 percent lower risk of dying than patients who do not take opioid substitution. There are few medications that reduce the risk of death to such an extent. I also read that patients were less likely to overdose, to inject, to share needles, and to contract HIV and hepatitis. They were less likely to be hospitalized, and they committed fewer crimes.

I learned that it's hard to get on methadone and hard to stay in the program for months and years at a time. The reason people are willing to put up with all the appointments, all the urine drug tests, and all the pharmacy visits is because receiving methadone treatments is much less trouble than feeding an opioid addiction — and because it works.

Early in medical school, I trained with an addiction doctor who had a reputation for guerrilla-style activism to promote change. He told his students stories about his days in the trenches fighting for HIV and addiction treatment at a time when little was known about these conditions and less was done to treat them. One day, as I sat in his clinic, he mentioned that he was suing the provincial college of physicians because of its methadone program.

"All the rules violate people's human rights. They rob them of their dignity," he explained.

He told us that he thought the rules created too many barriers, and he wanted them changed to promote trust and dignity. He was not the only one thinking along these lines. A decade before, a review of methadone treatment by the U.S. Institute of Medicine had argued that "current policy puts too much emphasis on protecting society from methadone, and not enough on protecting society from the epidemic of addiction, violence, and infections that methadone can help reduce."[7]

"You might not want to get involved in the case, because you're still a student," the doctor suggested gently.

This conversation echoed in my mind as I started to learn the guidelines and to train as a methadone prescriber. The guidelines are very restrictive. Patients need to come to the clinic once or twice a week for several months; they need to provide monitored urine drug screens at every visit. Most cumbersome of all, they need to go to the pharmacy or clinic every day to have their methadone measured out, after which they need to drink their dose in front of a pharmacist. This can go one for months, years, and decades. As patients stop using opioids or other drugs, they are trusted with more doses to take home, which provides an added incentive to abstain.

Once, after I had given a lecture on opioids to a group of junior doctors, one of them raised his hand and asked, "Why do patients need to stay on methadone for the long term? Isn't that just substituting one addiction for another? Why not get them off and let them get on with their lives?"

His skepticism hit me from across the hall, but it was not the first time I'd been confronted with such misgivings. I told him that patients could come off methadone as quickly as they desired, but the problem they faced was a high risk of relapse. There's an old adage among smokers: "It's easy to quit; it's hard to stay quit." For smokers, relapsing is frustrating, but they can always try again. For opioid users, relapsing is very often fatal. As soon as a long-time user stops, they lose the tolerance they earned through repeated exposure to high doses. But they don't necessarily know they've lost it. So, when that fateful day of relapse comes, if they use anything close to the same dose they had been using before treatment, they overdose. This is known as "death by rehab" because many traditional rehab programs that emphasize abstinence instead of opioid substitution send patients back into the world with brains ripe for relapse and without the protective layer of tolerance to opioids.

Knowing all this gave me confidence to answer my skeptical student. The evidence favours long-term methadone treatment. One of the early methadone studies found that 82 percent of patients who quit methadone treatment relapsed after twelve months out of treatment. Death rates for people who prematurely drop out of treatment skyrocket in the first few weeks after stopping their medication. That's why it is called methadone *maintenance* treatment. It allows users to maintain a stable quality of life while continuing to pay down their opioid debt with a daily dose of methadone. I tell patients that they will be ready to come off methadone once their life is dramatically different in terms of their schooling, their work, their social circle, their coping skills, their mental health conditions, and their cravings to use drugs.

Herbert Kleber argued, "Ultimately, the problem of interminable maintenance vs relapse may require learning how to reverse the brain changes associated with addiction. Until then, long-term agonist treatment remains a reasonable alternative."[8] Reversing the brain changes associated with addiction is a lofty goal, but until we have the scientific know-how to do that, the need for maintenance treatment will persist. It's likely, too, that the stigma against methadone as a medication and against methadone users will also persist. Because methadone treatment has been relegated to the fringes of medicine, there are no endowed halls of addiction treatment like there are for cardiology and cancer care. Addiction care lurks in the shadows, treating ghosts who hide their medication just as they hid their drugs.

Jennifer had been on methadone for about six months and had gone from using OxyContin every day to total abstinence from it. One day she showed up at the clinic in a panic. After she calmed down, I asked her what had happened.

"Nothing happened," she reassured me. "I'm doing really good, but my mom keeps asking where I'm going, and I don't want her to know about my methadone."

She needed me to change her pharmacy and give her more doses to take home because she didn't want her mother to find out that she was on treatment for opioid addiction. As I called her pharmacy to figure out what we could do to help her, I reflected on how sad it was that even her recovery from drugs had to be a secret.

Despite the stigma attached to its use and the social problems connected to the clinics from where it is dispensed, the evidence is that methadone works. This truth is increasingly accepted internationally. In response to rising rates of HIV among its population of people who inject drugs, China changed its drug laws, shifting in 2008 from a strict, punitive system involving hard labour and forced rehabilitation toward one in which users could avoid charges if they went to treatment. A 2012 article in the *Economist* quoted one official explaining the shift: "Our new approach towards ordinary users is that they are victims and patients who need help."[9] In 2011, police in Guizhou province launched the Sunshine Project, which provided drug treatments, including methadone. People with a known opioid addiction were hired by private enterprises. They were permitted to receive methadone while at work, from a pharmacy at their workplace. Officials claimed they have seen reductions in crime, in new HIV infections, and in relapse rates from the program.[10]

Methadone programs in Africa also focus on treating addiction and preventing HIV. Half a million people use opioids in East Africa alone. I lived in Tanzania when I was growing up and witnessed the country's HIV epidemic in the early 1990s. At that time, there was very little access to addiction treatment. It wasn't until 2011 that the first large methadone program was opened in Dar es Salaam, the country's capital. As was the case in China, it was the overlap of HIV and injection drug use that convinced officials to start the program, as up to half of people who inject drugs in Tanzania are HIV positive. The program has worked at reducing drug use and linking addiction treatment to HIV care.[11]

While methadone is often served in orange juice, another flavour of addiction treatment is available. Very soon after I started working in addictions, buprenorphine (Suboxone) became a star in the addiction treatment world. I learned that buprenorphine was safer and possibly just as effective as methadone at reducing risky behaviours, HIV transmission, crime, and overdoses. Guidelines now recommend buprenorphine as the preferred medication for opioid use disorder because the overdose risk is about six times less with buprenorphine than with methadone. Because it is safer, the rules are more relaxed for buprenorphine. For example, fewer pharmacy visits are required, which makes it easier for patients to get on with their lives.

In the United States, buprenorphine is available as a film that you put inside your cheek so it rapidly dissolves. In Canada, we still use small tablets that patients place under their tongue. Patients have told me the tablets taste like lime or spearmint; I've even heard them compared with asparagus. But the important thing about the buprenorphine used to treat addiction is that it is mixed with naloxone. The naloxone passes right through the body if the tablet is used properly, but if someone tries to inject it, the naloxone is activated and puts them into immediate withdrawal. It's an effective deterrent strategy that is now being tried with pain medicines, such as Targin, which combines oxycodone and naloxone.

And buprenorphine works. Michael had been taking buprenorphine for a few months when he realized that opioids no longer held any power over him. He was packing his small apartment to move in with his boyfriend when he found a bottle. His heart jolted in his chest, and he picked the bottle up and shook it gently, listening to the sound of tablets striking the side. He opened it and saw ten white tablets, which he immediately recognized as OxyContin. He was alone and could have easily swallowed, snorted, or even injected them; perhaps no one else would have ever known. But instead, as he described to me later, he felt revulsion.

"I looked at those pills and thought about how they had fucking controlled my life. Every day they were the first thing I thought of when I woke up. I was so angry. I hated those pills, what they did to me, and what they made me do."

He flushed them down the toilet and went on with his work, feeling that somehow he had just passed an important test.

On the other hand, when Nathan showed up after a six-month absence, he told me, "I've been using whatever I can get my hands on."

He had come off buprenorphine after his family gave him a hard time about his "dependence" on a medicine. He tried to prove he could abstain without substitution treatment, and it worked for a few months. Then he swallowed a few Percocets after a day at his construction job. Soon he started crushing pills and snorting heroin and thinking about going back to his habit of injecting.

"I feel like I'm ready to use needles again. I came in today to stop using."

We restarted buprenorphine later that day, and Nathan was able to stop the Percocet and heroin use within a few weeks.

As I reflected on Nathan's success, I came across a Swedish study from the early days of buprenorphine treatment that reinforced for me the power of the medicine. It was a year-long placebo-controlled study, which means that patients were given either buprenorphine or a sugar pill and did not find out which they had received until the end of the study. During that year, all patients were given cognitive behavioural group therapy to prevent relapse and weekly individual counselling. They also gave supervised urine drug screens three times per week. At the end of year, 75 percent of the patients who had received buprenorphine were still in treatment, but all patients taking the placebo had dropped out of treatment, despite the groups and the counselling.[12]

But there are barriers that prevent buprenorphine from reaching more opioid users. One barrier is a lack of knowledge among primary-care providers about the medication and how to use it. This makes them uncomfortable and thus less likely to prescribe or administer the drug. Another barrier is that most guidelines require patients to take their first dose of buprenorphine in an office with a clinician monitoring them. This restriction is in place to prevent a nasty risk of buprenorphine known as precipitated withdrawal — an innocuous-sounding term that actually speaks to a world of pain.

Sherry looked at me with a strained expression. Her brown hair was oily and her T-shirt hung loosely at her neck. It was early in my training as an addiction doctor, and this would be the first time I would start the therapy on my own, without the comforting presence of a more experienced physician to guide me. I thought of all the ways things could go wrong; I imagined her writhing in pain, covered in sweat as she vomited on the office floor. I had never seen precipitated withdrawal, but that is how I feared it would play out with Sherry if things went bad.

To make myself feel better, I explained the science in meticulous detail. "Sherry, buprenorphine is not like other opioids," I said. "It latches on to the same opioid receptors in your brain as the heroin you are using now, but it only partially stimulates them. That is why it is safer and less sedating than other opioids. But while it only partially stimulates receptors, it has a really strong binding affinity. That means if there are any other opioids in your brain, the buprenorphine will push them off the receptors and take their place. But then, instead of a full opioid pushing on those receptors, you will have only a partial opioid and that can make you feel pretty bad. It can put you into precipitated withdrawal."

Sherry nodded slowly, not fully understanding, as many patients and even other doctors don't fully understand at first. I explained that precipitated withdrawal feels like the worst opioid withdrawal, the worst dope sickness you can experience.

"The way we get around this," I continued, "is to make sure all the heroin is out of your brain when we start the buprenorphine. So you should go about twelve to twenty-four hours without using before you come in on Monday morning, and then it will be safe to take the buprenorphine."

Two days later, a cool morning in April, I saw Sherry sitting in the waiting room, clutching her white paper bag from the pharmacy. She sat down in my office and put the paper bag on the chair beside her, and I assessed the severity of her withdrawal. It was bad; she was clearly suffering, which meant it was safe to start. So I asked her to put the first tablet under her tongue. She did not hesitate. After a few minutes, nothing dramatic had happened.

She went back to the waiting room and returned three hours later. "I think it's working. I feel almost normal. I had to go get a piece of pizza, I was so hungry."

We breathed a sigh of relief.

Office-based inductions are safe, but the process of administering them is time consuming — certainly more time consuming than writing a prescription for a medication a patient takes at home before returning to the clinic a few days later.

In the summer of 2018, rumours of a new way of getting patients on buprenorphine began to filter through the addiction community. One morning in August, I got an email from a former student, with the subject line "Suboxone microdosing." She wrote that she had heard about a new way of starting patients on buprenorphine, a method that did not require them to go through withdrawal. It was called the Bernese method, after the Swiss city of Bern. She sent a protocol that had been developed in Vancouver and a case report from Switzerland describing two patients who had been started using this new microdosing method.

The first case described a woman in her thirties who was sniffing three grams of heroin daily. She had been on and off buprenorphine in the past and was motivated to restart treatment. The barrier she faced, which is the same barrier I hear from so many patients, was fear of withdrawal. In particular, she feared that the withdrawal associated with induction would trigger her post-traumatic stress disorder (PTSD), something she had experienced with previous inductions. Her PTSD stemmed from sexual abuse at the age of twelve. At fifteen, she started experimenting with hallucinogens, cannabis, cocaine, and heroin. At eighteen, she became bulimic, fell into a severe depression, and attempted suicide. Her doctors wanted to start buprenorphine without disrupting her fragile mental health, and she agreed to use the Bernese method.[13]

The simplicity of this method is that it does not require patients to go into withdrawal or stop using drugs immediately. The woman was initially given a tiny dose, one-tenth of the usual starting dose, and the medical staff then slowly increased her dose while she continued to use heroin. After only five days, she had stopped heroin, and her buprenorphine dose was rapidly increased. And she did this with no diarrhea, no drenching sweats, no sleepless nights. When I read about this five-day period of her life, I realized that, if the treatment worked as advertised, microdosing could be the biggest innovation in addiction medicine in years. All this time, we could have been sparing patients the suffering of being in withdrawal in order to start buprenorphine.

I once read that if you delay the discovery of a treatment that could save one hundred thousand lives, say by blocking the funding request or banning certain types of research, you are, in a very real sense, responsible for those lost lives. Every day we delay getting a treatment into widespread use is another day with preventable suffering. Buprenorphine microdosing may be such a treatment. Even as I write this, I am thinking about my patient Rachel, who failed to start buprenorphine just two weeks before I learned about microdosing.

Rachel had struggled to stay on methadone for several years. She often missed doses at the pharmacy and had trouble showing up for regular appointments. She wanted to change to buprenorphine. Over the years I had known her, her name came into my head many days as I walked to the clinic. *Will Rachel still be alive?* I would ask myself. Several times she did not return to the clinic for a week or two, and that question would grow and grow. When I did finally see her next, I would sigh in relief and we would try again. When I learned about microdosing, I felt that if I had known about it earlier, I could have started treating her with it and been confident that she would be safe. As it was, I hadn't seen her since her failed induction to buprenorphine using the traditional method. I worried that it was too late for her.

For one of my patients, a young woman named Darla, around the same age as Rachel, it was too late. Before I share her story, I will explain why a different form of buprenorphine treatment might have saved her life.

One night in early September, just as the summer heat was beginning to fade, I went to a lecture by Mark Greenwald, a neuropharmacologist from Wayne State University, who had come to Ottawa to preach about injectable forms of buprenorphine. In a dimly lit Italian restaurant, he described his research on long-standing heroin users a world away in Detroit. He explained that his lab had top clearance and was able to give people who use drugs tiny doses of radioactive-labelled carfentanil and then image their brains using PET scanners. He reassured us that using carfentanil in this way is standard in research settings and the doses used were so small that the volunteers weren't knocked out by the drug. Researchers then gave the patients various doses of buprenorphine by mouth and took more PET scans to determine how much buprenorphine was needed to block the carfentanil from attaching to the brain. It turned out the dose was around sixteen milligrams, which correlates to around two to three nanolitres of buprenorphine per millilitre of blood.

That target of at least 2 to 3 nanolitres in the blood was then set as the target for the buprenorphine treatments. Dr. Greenwald showed us three different products. Two involved injections that were administered monthly; the third was an implant made from four matchstick-sized rods that released buprenorphine over a six-month period. A challenge with this last product is that a hole must be cut in the patient's arm so that the implant can be buried in the tissue below the skin. Although this mode of treatment is more intrusive than the injections, its benefits can be immense.

"Think about the time horizon of most people who use drugs," Dr. Greenwald said in a quiet and serious tone. "They need to use heroin about four times a day. When they start oral buprenorphine or methadone, they need to take their medicine once daily, so their horizon stretches to a day. But imagine they take one dose a month of injectable buprenorphine. They need to make only twelve decisions a year about whether to take their medicine. If they are on the six-month implant, they need to make only two decisions, down from three hundred and sixty-five."

As I listened to him, I thought of Darla. She had been on buprenorphine tablets for only a few months this time around. A few years earlier, she had started on the treatment, but right away she'd been in a hurry to get off. She hated being on meds; she did not want to be reminded of her addiction every day. She moved away to New York, stopped her buprenorphine, and quickly relapsed back to smoking fentanyl patches. When she came back to Ottawa, she showed up at the clinic, and I restarted her on buprenorphine that afternoon. Within a few months, things had turned around for her. She had stopped using, and she told me she had no cravings or withdrawal. She was going to meetings and getting counselling, and she had found a job working as a hairdresser. She was even able to see her daughter, who had been living with Darla's mother for the past few years. I was so happy that the treatment was working for Darla and her family, whom I had gotten to know when they accompanied her to visits.

But again, Darla was in a hurry. She wanted to come down on her dose. She told me she didn't need it, she had no cravings, she would never go back to using. I reminded her of what had happened a few years before when she had come off too soon and relapsed. She heard me out, but was insistent that this time was different. I did as she asked, hoping that the lower dose would still hold her. But as I sat in Greenwald's lecture looking at pictures of brains lit up by radioactive carfentanil, I understood why she had died. Her dose was too low to block the fentanyl powder she had injected.

Darla had to make a decision every day about how much buprenorphine to take, and every day she decided to take less and less. What if I could have made the choice easier for her by taking away her choice? By giving her the chance to make only two decisions a year? What if I could have given her the implant or the injection, neither of which were yet available in Canada? Would this technology have saved her? She probably would have refused. She might have skipped her appointment to get her injection, or maybe not.

I suddenly felt impatient. I thought, *We need more treatments now, not when the FDA or Health Canada says we can use them; we need to start giving our patients more options so they can make fewer bad choices.*

Treatment for addiction should be easier to access than heroin or fentanyl is, but in many places in the United States and Canada, this is not the case. For one thing, there has been almost no increase in the number of patients receiving methadone in the United States over the past ten years. And while there was initial enthusiasm among some providers for buprenorphine, there hasn't been much expansion of care since 2011, even as the death rate continues to rise.

A series of articles in mid-2018 laid out the challenge and benefits of bringing opioid substitution into mainstream care. The authors asserted that "the overdose crisis is an epidemic of poor access to care."[14] As we have seen, methadone and buprenorphine work. But almost four out of five Americans with opioid use disorder don't get these treatments. And even when patients do get into care, it is often "fragmented and difficult to navigate."[15] These issues are particularly bad in the United States because of the way health care is funded, the marginalization of addiction care, and the severity of the opioid epidemic.[16]

Long wait-lists are the norm for opioid substitution treatment across North America. One of my patients moved to Montreal recently and was told she would have to wait six months to start methadone. In most provinces in Canada and in states across the United States, people have either delayed access or no access to opioid substitution in their hometowns. In a 2016 CBC interview, Edmonton-based addiction physician Dr. Hakique Virani stated, "Unfortunately, the availability and accessibility of methadone and Suboxone programs in Alberta and many other places in Canada is extremely poor. And to me, that's a head-scratcher, because really, detox beds are quite expensive, and we cannot begin to touch the demand for treatment that exists in the population. On the other hand, maintenance medication therapy with methadone and Suboxone is remarkably cheap. So not only are we talking about more effective treatment with pharmacotherapy, we're also talking about safer treatment."[17]

And we know that waiting is dangerous. A study from Israel showed that patients have high death rates while waiting to get into methadone programs.[18] In Europe, treatment rates for patients with opioid addiction are much higher: 63 percent in the United Kingdom and 75 percent in the Netherlands.[19] Even when patients get on to buprenorphine in the United States, they often struggle to stay in treatment because of insurance and cost barriers.

A long-touted approach to removing barriers to access is to bring opioid substitution into primary care. One of the reasons for this is that there are a lot of primary-care providers in the United States — at least 320,000, compared with only about three thousand physicians who have been certified by the American Board of Addiction Medicine.[20] Breaking down regulatory and insurance barriers to allow more people to get on and stay on opioid substitution is a critical part of breaking the back of the opioid epidemic. If treatment levels could rise from one in five to three out of four, as is the case in the Netherlands, thousands of lives would be saved every year.

But asking overburdened primary-care providers to do one more thing means they will have to do less of something else. There are only so many minutes in an hour and seconds in a minute. In a deeply personal article about coming to terms with treating opioid use disorder, American internist Audrey Provenzano wrote, "The reason I didn't have a waiver to prescribe buprenorphine was that I didn't want one. As a new primary-care physician, I spent every evening finishing notes and preparing for the next day. Every Friday I left the office utterly depleted, devoid of the energy or motivation it would take to spend a weekend clicking through the required online training."[21]

There was the burden of one more course, one more certificate, one more set of guidelines to learn and then follow, but it was more than that. She continued, "But more than not wanting to take on the extra work of prescribing a medication for OUD [opioid use disorder], I did not want to deal with patients who needed it.... Already overwhelmed, I did not want to take on patients with needs that I did not know how to meet."[22]

I believe Dr. Provenzano spoke for a large majority of front-line health care workers when she unpacked her biases and internal barriers to treating addiction. The slow growth of buprenorphine treatment is evidence that the early adopters have taken up the mantle, but getting other parts of the health care system to change will be a long battle. If a small number of providers take on a large number of patients, this can dramatically increase access. In the United States, federal limits on the number of buprenorphine patients per provider continues to limit access without good scientific rationale.

As I've gained experience prescribing methadone and buprenorphine, I've become comfortable. But as science continues to search for new treatments, we have fresh evidence supporting neglected medications. An important treatment used in the United States but unavailable in Canada is injectable naltrexone. Naltrexone is the long-acting version of the opioid blocker used in overdose rescue kits, naloxone. Strong and growing evidence supports injectable naltrexone to help patients abstain from opioids. A challenge with injectable naltrexone is the cost, but it should be covered by insurance because it can save lives.

When new evidence or new treatments become available, I am interested but cautious. The first time my mind opened to injectable heroin, a treatment used for patients who fail to recover on methadone or buprenorphine, I was at an opioid conference held in a beautiful converted factory in Toronto. Scott MacDonald, the only doctor in Canada to run an injectable heroin program at the time, spoke clearly and convincingly before showing a video outlining the program. In the video, nurses drew up sterile syringes of the clear medication, a pharmaceutical-grade heroin manufactured in Switzerland with controlled dosing and free of the contaminants found in street drugs. Everything in the clinic was stainless steel and glass. Patients lined up calmly, received their medication, were monitored for about twenty minutes, and then were free to leave the clinic and return later for more medication. It looked and operated like an ordinary clinic administering flu shots or chemotherapy, except that the medication being dispensed was a good deal safer than chemotherapy. As I saw those sterile syringes filled with clear heroin, I realized that for these patients with severe addiction, for whom other treatments had failed, heroin is a medicine like any other medicine. My mind had opened.

"Injectable heroin is a safe and effective treatment. It is associated with reduced death rates, with reduced crime, and with reduced relapse to street opioids," Dr. MacDonald repeated after the video. I could see now that this was the truth. Injectable heroin did everything the ideal medication for opioid addiction should do. It was safe and it worked. True, patients had to come back several times a day for additional doses, but that kept them more engaged in treatment and more able to get care for other medical conditions as they came up.

After the talk, I left the conference and went for a run along the shores of Lake Ontario. As the wind whipped up huge waves against the concrete breakers and I felt the endorphins of exercise start to suffuse my brain, I thought about Scott MacDonald and his clinic, with its neatly ordered syringes of injectable heroin. It was a safe and effective treatment. It had been used in England for a hundred years; it was a standard treatment in Germany, the Netherlands, and Switzerland. Were we failing our patients in North America by not offering this treatment? We had to be.

A few months later, I sat down in an empty seat at a meeting on tobacco addiction and saw that to my right was none other than Scott MacDonald himself. In the minutes before the session began, I told Scott the impact he had made on me with his simple message, powerfully repeated, at that big hall in Toronto. He smiled; he was pleased, flattered, but also happy that his message was getting out. He told me that he had trained in Ottawa before going to work as an addiction doctor for the navy, treating sailors with drinking problems in a twenty-eight-day detox program. He had gone on to practise HIV medicine in Toronto, and then in the early 2000s he had moved to Vancouver, where he had been a lead doctor in the two major trials proving the effectiveness of injectable opioids in patients with the most severe opioid addictions.

I told Scott that I had doubts about injectable treatment. I worried that the option of injecting prescribed opioids would change the ecosystem of drug use. I worried people would abandon their stable life on methadone because of the temptation of free and safe injectable heroin. He put my mind at rest, reminding me that injectables are the most intensive step on the treatment ladder. This means two things. First, only the patients who have continued to relapse while on every other type of treatment will need injectables. Second, the time and inconvenience of having to make multiple visits to a clinic every day means that many people will choose to simplify their treatment over time. This has been borne out in European countries like Switzerland, where many people drop out of injectable treatment and return to the relatively simple treatment of methadone over the long term.

I had similar discussions with staff at my clinic and with patients who were curious or concerned about the effects of introducing this treatment option. In fact, injectables may make drug use less appealing both to users and to young people attracted by the thrill and dangers of heroin use. When they see people calmly lining up in a mundane-looking clinic to pick up their sterile needle full of clear fluid, the allure of the drug disappears. Using heroin acquires all the thrill of getting a flu shot. For those not dissuaded, such clinics have the benefit of ensuring that they use much more safely.

When we rolled out a program in Ottawa, we started to see good results. Ronda was one of our patients who had struggled for a long time with opioid use but was now an active participant in an injectable program offered down the street. A peer worker came to tell me about it.

"The injectable program is a miracle. Have you seen Ronda? She's a healthy weight; she's got an apartment. I never expected to see that."

Soon afterward, I went to Vancouver to see for myself how Scott MacDonald's program worked. He gave me and a group of addiction providers a tour of the Crosstown Clinic. The clinic is located in a former bank at the corner of West Hastings and Abbott Street. As it's an old bank and it houses large amounts of injectable opioids, the clinic has formidable security. There is a series of time-delayed locked doors. The old vault is used to store the drugs. When I was buzzed through the front door, I came into the main clinic area, which was decorated with witches and ghosts for Halloween, signs advertising women's clinic day, overdose alerts, and reminders for everyone to wash their hands.

Scott stood in front of the group and told us the history of the two major studies that proved the safety and efficacy of injectable heroin as well as injectable hydromorphone. Although it was a year after I had first heard him advocating for the program in Toronto, and although the opioid epidemic had only intensified during those twelve months, the North American addiction treatment landscape had not changed to widely provide injectable treatments.

"If [injectable therapy] is to have an impact on population health, it needs to be massively scaled up, and we're nowhere near that," Scott said. "Our waitlist is more than four hundred people. Fentanyl is making everything worse. Don't wait until fentanyl comes to your community to start a program like this."

As the latecomers from the group crowded in, Scott took us across the clinic to the injecting room. It looked like the inner sanctum of a temple, with old stone walls painted white, a white ceiling, bright fluorescent lights, and a stainless steel table lining the wall, flanked by a long low mirror. The room smelled of alcohol swabs. Across from the stainless steel table, there was a hole in the wall. A sign above it read, "Deposit all rigs in slot below." Diagrams on the wall showing the safe locations to inject in the body were placed next to yet more signs reminding everyone to wash their hands.

Scott explained that each patient had up to seven minutes to inject their dose, but many could do so in less than one minute. We talked about how patients could access HIV treatment, hepatitis C treatment, and basic health support. Just as I was beginning to feel claustrophobic in the highly secure room, a nurse opened the door and loudly informed us that we had four minutes until the clinic reopened and asked us to please wrap up. We all shuffled through the time-locked doors, and as I stepped outside and back onto West Hastings Street, I breathed in the crisp fall air.

We need innovative addiction care of the type that Scott MacDonald is offering at Crosstown, but we also need to fix our foundation by using fewer opioids and by educating the next generation of health care providers to avoid the mistakes we have already made. We need to rethink our relationship with prescription opioids and, ultimately, with Big Pharma.

CHAPTER 7

Rethinking Our Relationship with Opioids and Big Pharma

When Marcia Angell's father was eighty-one years old, he shot himself. He lived with his wife outside of Orlando, Florida. On March 15, 1988, as his wife lay sleeping in the next room, he took a pistol from the bedside table, turned his head to ensure the bullet would not harm her, and ended his life. Marcia Angell, a physician trained as a pathologist who rose through the ranks to become editor-in-chief of the *New England Journal of Medicine* and a professor at Harvard Medical School, shared this tragic story in an editorial supporting physician-assisted suicide in a January 1997 issue of the journal.[1]

She said later that her father was a Republican who was protective of his family and believed in patriotism and the right to self-determination. He was a civil engineer and had worked with the Tennessee Valley Authority, the Army Corps of Engineers, and "as chief design engineer of the St. Lawrence Seaway." He served in the South Pacific during the Second World War and "became a lieutenant colonel in the Army Reserve."[2]

At the time of his death, he was not depressed or in extreme pain. He had metastatic prostate cancer, and earlier that day he had fallen while walking back to his bed from the bathroom. His wife could not lift him, so she called the paramedics. They helped him into bed and said they would be back the next day to take him to the hospital. He must have thought it was his last night of independence, his last opportunity to end the suffering when and how he chose.

Marcia Angell does not look like a revolutionary; nor does she make a habit of sharing personal stories. In interviews, in media appearances, and in lectures spanning the past two decades, she speaks in a calm tone and with a measured cadence; she speaks without anger or condescension. But she does not soften her message by using meek words, either. She is a pathologist who cuts through the unyielding connective tissue of lies and greed to get to the soft layer of truth underneath.

She is the enemy of any agent in America's health care system that places profit over health. She has a lot of enemies. To America's pharmaceutical industry, she is a dangerous, outspoken radical. She is a skeptic, asking tough questions, challenging conventional wisdom. She says skepticism is an essential quality of a scientist, a quality that is often forgotten in the face of profit.

In its April 21, 1997, issue, *Time* listed the twenty-five most influential Americans. A number of the names are still familiar today; some have fallen out of the media limelight; others have fallen into disgrace. First on the list was Tiger Woods. Other names on the list included Harvey Weinstein, Madeleine Albright, Colin Powell, and one fictional figure, Dilbert, the comic strip anti-personality. In the middle of the list, surrounded by tech billionaires and politicians, was Marcia Angell, cited for her clear and rational voice on all medical issues from her perch at the *New England Journal of Medicine*.

Seven years after that list came out, just as I was beginning my master's degree, Dr. Angell published a book that sizzled with conspiratorial suggestion and subversion, from its title to its last line. It was *The Truth About the Drug Companies: How They Deceive Us and What to Do About It.* Just as the opioid epidemic was about to peak, she promised that her book would "expose the real pharmaceutical industry — an industry that over the past two decades has moved very far from its original high purpose of discovering and producing useful new drugs," to become an industry that she saw as "primarily a marketing machine to sell drugs of dubious benefit," one that "uses its wealth and power to co-opt every institution that might stand in its way, including the U.S. Congress, the Food and Drug Administration, academic medical centers, and the medical profession itself."[3]

Over her twenty years working at the *New England Journal of Medicine* and during her time at Harvard, she witnessed first-hand the gravitational pull of industry influence on medical research. She saw drug companies put twice as much money into marketing as into research and drug development, focus on small tweaks to existing medicines, and fight price regulation on the one hand while encouraging stronger government protection of their patent rights on the other. To her, Big Pharma was the Wizard of Oz, "full of bluster," but in reality much different from the image it presented to the world: "Instead of being an engine of innovation, it is a vast marketing machine. Instead of being a free market success story, it lives off government-funded research and monopoly rights."[4]

The industry justifies high prices by citing high drug development costs. Dr. Angell blasted this as sheer fantasy, saying that "nothing could be further from the truth," that this is their nerve, their public relations pitch.[5]

In her view, Big Pharma is a parasitic industry that feeds off publicly funded research. She told an interviewer in 2003, "If you look at where the original research comes from on which new drugs are based, it tends to be from the NIH [National Institutes of Health], from the academic medical centers, and from foreign academic medical centers. Studies of this, looking at the seminal research on which drug patents are based, have found that about 15 percent of the basic research papers, reporting the basic research, came from industry. That's just 15 percent."[6]

After a drug is developed through publicly funded research, Big Pharma sells the drug back to the public at extortionate prices, making it consistently among the ten most profitable industries. While drug companies make good profits in Canada and Europe, the United States is the ultimate market, as it is the only advanced economy that allows companies to charge what the market will bear.

I looked for the most recent data I could find and discovered that in 2016, Big Pharma had profits of more than 25 percent. Inflation-adjusted spending on prescription drugs per person in the United States increased from $90 in 1960 to $1,025 in 2017. Between

2008 and 2014 alone, the prices of the top-selling brand-name medications increased by 127 percent as the prices of generic drugs declined. In 2017, prescription drugs represented 10 percent of expenditure on health care in the United States.[7]

Dr. Angell follows the billions of dollars that Big Pharma spends to influence lawmakers, regulators, physicians, and, ultimately, the public. In the early years of the millennium, she was already speaking out about the distorting influence of Big Pharma's money on medical trainees, on academic medicine, on physicians' prescribing patterns, and on patients' patterns of medication use, the very phenomenon that we now know fed into the rampant opioid prescribing that jump-started this epidemic. For while Purdue is a relatively small figure in the pantheon of Big Pharma, which is dominated by five American giants and five European ones, Purdue plays by the same rule book.

But to Dr Angell, the problems are deeper than pill pushing and Big Pharma. Dr. Angell lashes out against a health care model that she has called "a dreadfully inefficient expensive system that leaves too many people out."[8] In an interview to mark the two-hundredth anniversary of the *New England Journal of Medicine*, she reflected on a critical piece of wisdom she took from her time as an editor: "The essential question is: is health care a commodity that should be delivered according to the ability to pay … or is it a social good that everyone should have, that should be distributed not according to the ability to pay but according to medical need? I came down in that second school very very firmly and more firmly as I went along, and I favour a single-payer system, a non-profit single-payer system, essentially medicare for all in a non-profit delivery system."[9]

In June 2009 Dr. Angell testified to a House of Representatives subcommittee that examined the single-payer health care option. She sat in front of a thin black microphone, a scrum of reporters and television crew crowded behind her. She began, "Chairman Andrews, members of the subcommittee, thank you for inviting me and for your leadership on this important issue." She paused and looked down at her notes, before continuing. "The reason our health system is in such trouble is that it is set up to generate profits, not to provide care."

She laid out the costs of the U.S. system and the profit margins for insurance companies, health care facilities, and specialists. She spoke for a few moments before concluding that health care in the United States "is directed towards maximizing income, not maximizing health."

The vagaries of the U.S. health care system, and comparisons with those of every other industrialized nation, show that the profit motive is not a good basis on which to design a health care system. Similarly, the free market is not the right system to distribute addictive substances. This has been shown time and again over the past two centuries, with a variety of substances.

In the nineteenth century, when patent medicines contained opioids, adults and children overdosed regularly, with little consequence to manufacturers. This situation was changed in the United Kingdom with the Medical Reform Act in 1858 and the Pharmacy Act in 1868. These laws regulated the practice of medicine, required prescriptions for the purchase of controlled medicines, and mandated the removal of opiates from patent medicines. The deaths from morphine began to fall among both adults and children in the United Kingdom. Similar laws across Europe and North America increased medical professionalism and restricted access to opiates.

The regulators and the medical profession failed to anticipate the harms of prescription opioids, but a huge step forward came in 2016 when the U.S. Centers for Disease Control (CDC) released new opioid guidelines. In an article published in the *New England Journal of Medicine*, the heads of the CDC and the FDA wrote, "We know of no other medication routinely used for a nonfatal condition that kills patients so frequently."[10] The guidelines turned opioid prescribing on its head. First, they urged doctors to use non-medication treatments and non-opioid medication as much as possible. This may sound cruel, like abandoning patients to suffer, but as we began to look for flaws in opioids, we found them everywhere. The veil was lifted.

The evidence showed that acetaminophen and ibuprofen are as effective as opioids in the short term and that almost everything is better in the long run than opioids, once we take into account tolerance and the harms caused by chronic opioid use. A study from emergency rooms in New York City further blew apart our conception of opioids. Patients with acute pain were chosen randomly to get either acetaminophen plus ibuprofen, which don't contain opioids, or a Percocet, Tylenol 3, or Vicodin tablet, which do. They didn't know what they were given. Two hours later, they were asked about their pain. All the patients had experienced considerable and almost identical improvements in their pain.[11] No one would have done such a study ten years earlier because no one would have believed the results.

The CDC guidelines sought to ensure that doctors provided the lowest doses of opioids for the shortest time period. The supply of prescription opioids did not stop abruptly, but it began to slow. Between 2012 and 2016, the number of opioid doses prescribed per thousand people in Canada fell by about 9 percent, but the number of opioid prescriptions rose slightly. The change in the United States was more dramatic. There, opioid prescriptions peaked in 2012, with 81.3 prescriptions per 100 people. By 2016 this had fallen to 58.7, a decline of over a quarter and the lowest rate in more than a decade.[12]

If opioids were absolutely necessary, the CDC now suggested giving as few pills as possible. One of the biggest reasons for the increased exposure to opioids, as was explored in the last chapter, is that patients were given a large supply of opioids when they needed only enough for a few days. The extra pills were then either given away or stolen, which widened the circle of exposure and increased the odds that someone along the way would be ensnared in the net of addiction. To combat this problem, the CDC advised clinicians to give the lowest dose for the shortest duration; instead of thirty days, they recommended three days, with prescriptions for more than seven days to be given only rarely.

As epidemiologists and pain doctors began to dig through the data surrounding the rising overdose rates, a pattern emerged. It seems so obvious now, but it needed to be set out in black and white to be believed at the time: high doses lead to increased risk of death. So someone on a dose of fifty to ninety-nine milligrams of morphine has double the risk of someone on a dose of less than twenty milligrams of morphine, while people on more than one hundred milligrams have nine times the risk of overdose death.[13] Based on this evidence, the 2016 CDC guidelines also suggested keeping the dose to less than fifty milligrams or at most ninety milligrams of morphine per day. They also advised using urine testing to check that patients were doing two things: taking the prescribed drugs and not taking illicit drugs.

The guidelines also warned against prescribing opioids with benzodiazepines. This point had been drilled into me during my training, and I've never been able to forget the vivid picture my supervisor painted: "The last thing you want is for your patient to be found dead holding a prescription from you for opioids in one hand and a prescription for benzos in the other."

Finally, and in another dramatic break with the past, the CDC guidelines recommended that doctors arrange for their patients who had developed opioid use disorder to be transferred to methadone or buprenorphine treatment. I find these treatments are also useful exit strategies for patients on high doses of opioids. Instead of rapidly tapering or discontinuing these opioids, which does lead to real suffering, clinicians should switch them to buprenorphine. Because buprenorphine is long acting and safe, it avoids many of the problems of the traditional opioids prescribed for pain.

At first, the response to the CDC guidelines was skeptical. Defenders of the old idea of treating pain first and foremost mounted a counterattack. Critics demanded, "But how will we treat pain?" Patients with chronic pain feared, and still fear, abandonment. The important point here is that the idea that long-term, high-dose opioids are the salvation for chronic pain turns out to have been built on, if not a lie, then a catastrophic misconception. The CDC tried to puncture this misconception, arguing there was no good scientific evidence that using opioids for longer than six weeks actually helps with pain. In fact, "several studies have showed that use of opioids for chronic pain may actually worsen pain and functioning, possibly by potentiating pain perception."[14]

The authors of the CDC guidelines, in conjunction with Nora Volkow, then responded by releasing more guidance on how to manage pain in a world with fewer opioids.[15] Their alternative treatments for chronic pain included cognitive behavioural therapy, exercise, and yoga, as well as acetaminophen, ibuprofen, and other classes of medication. They pointed out that anti-inflammatory drugs such as ibuprofen and naproxen are first-line medications for both osteoarthritis and low back pain, two of the most common reasons for opioid prescriptions in recent decades.

In Canada, a new guideline came out in 2017. It was much more liberal than those set forward by the CDC and did not discourage long-term opioid use. It made no mention of managing opioid addiction. I asked Jason Busse, the lead author of the Canadian guideline, about this soon after it came out, and he was very dismissive of the CDC recommendations. He told me he thought that the CDC panel had been biased against opioids and did not give them a fair hearing. When I asked why the Canadian guideline didn't discuss opioid addiction or treatment, he said that these topics were outside the scope of what the authors had aimed to accomplish. I was shocked. Opioid addiction was outside the scope of the Canadian opioid guideline at the time of the worst opioid epidemic, and possibly the worst medically induced epidemic in history?

The CDC guideline process was independent of Big Pharma, but the Canadian guideline was contaminated by industry. Seven out of thirteen non-voting experts declared that they had in the past been paid by Purdue or other opioid manufacturers; one member of the four-person steering committee declared funding from Purdue; and one member of the voting guideline panel was even paid by Purdue while the guideline was under development, even though this was against the guideline process. Despite the tepid quality of the Canadian recommendations, there was still industry-led pushback against that guideline. In a 2018 debate in a Canadian medical journal, two physicians with industry links argued that guidelines aimed at reducing the prescribing of opioids would lead to increased mental and physical suffering with little impact on overdose deaths.[16]

On the other side of the debate, an infuriated doctor pointed out that "denying that physician prescribing of opioids has caused the opioid crisis keeps us in it, just as denying that human activity has caused climate change keeps it going."[17] The doctor concluded that "when the opioid crisis is over, we will wonder why it took so long to reduce opioid prescribing."[18]

Marcia Angell has continued to write and speak truth to the power of drug companies. In a conversation at Harvard's Center for Bioethics in 2015, she lamented the fact that more than ten years after she had published her book on Big Pharma, things were not getting better. "I think it is getting worse," she said. "The pharmaceutical industry is now seeing faculty at prestigious medical centers as their salespeople."

She attributed this to the fundamental mismatch between the goals of Big Pharma and the goals of academic medicine: "They are investor-owned companies whose mission is to increase the value of their shareholders' stock; that is their mission, to sell drugs any way that is legal; many of them have done it in illegal ways as well."

The influence of Big Pharma on doctors has become the target of ridicule in popular culture, most memorably with comedian John Oliver's 2015 tirade on the subject, which explained how money from Big Pharma "combines with cash receptors in your doctor's wallet to create fast-acting financial relief, so your doctor can rest easy and enjoy life," but side effects can include "chronic over-prescription" and a host of other bad things. The president of the American Medical Association responded to articles about Oliver's monologue by asserting that the association supports transparency about payments to physicians on publicly accessible databases, but that "appropriate interactions between physicians and industry can often drive innovation, discovery and changes in medical practice that may promote better patient outcomes."[19]

I agree that appropriate interactions are fruitful for science and patient care — the rapid growth in the number of new treatments for HIV, cancer, and diabetes is a testament to the undeniable good that the pharmaceutical industry can shepherd into the hands of sick patients. But it is very hard to find the perfect balance between improved health, justifiable financial reward, and profiteering.

Some clinicians say that the financial force of Big Pharma is too great to escape, that everyone has a conflict of interest, but psychiatrist

Daniel Gorman is skeptical: "Is it hard to avoid getting into relationships where they're actually paying you to do research or give talks?" Dr. Gorman said to an interviewer in 2017. "That's not difficult. You just say no."[20]

It is possible for regulators to build a system that keeps the profit motive, as much as possible, away from day-to-day clinical decisions. For example, we need to reduce prescribing. But if we had a safe, non-addictive, non-abusable opioid, the impetus to prescribe today's popular opioids would be much less. We are looking for that miracle drug, one that academia can discover and Big Pharma can market. In 2016 I thought we had found the perfect opioid. A group of drug designers announced that they had looked at three million compounds, each of which could bind to the opioid receptor in more than a million configurations, with the goal of finding a drug that relieved pain without causing overdose and addiction. They found PZM21.[21] It was exciting. I thought this could be the answer, but a wiser colleague cautioned me, saying that we'd been down this road before — the road that seemed to promise safer and less addictive opioids; the road paved by millions of tablets of heroin and OxyContin. She was probably right, because two years later, a follow-up study announced that PZM21 causes respiratory sedation in lab mice and isn't particularly effective at killing pain.[22] We had not found soma, the wonder drug in Aldous Huxley's novel *Brave New World*, and perhaps that was for the best.

Our old-fashioned, pre-PZM21 opioids still have a place in medicine; we must not create a world with more suffering by throwing them out completely. Opioids have a vital role in operating rooms, on hospital wards, and for the short-term treatment of severe pain. It is the long-term use of high-dose opioids that we need to reconsider. Three conditions should be met before such long-term therapy is embarked upon: alternatives must fail; the pain must be causing a real impact on the patient's quality of life; and the benefits of using chronic opioids must outweigh the risks. Once started, treatment should be regularly reassessed. Doses should be kept to a minimum and the goals of patients and their providers should be realistic: a reduction in pain, not a life completely free of pain.[23]

Perhaps one day there will be a new PZM21, one that no researcher will be able to fault, one that will not put any lab mice to sleep or into the throes of addiction or withdrawal. Analgesia — the reduction of pain — is not itself addictive; acetaminophen and ibuprofen kill pain without causing addiction.

As we have set our sights on responsible prescribing, addiction leaders have dared to take one more step and involve primary-care providers in substance use screening and treatment. Changes in medical practice need to start with changes in training, but clinicians still get too little training in addiction. This leaves health care workers feeling ill equipped to deal with substance abuse, although they are capable of handling much more immediate, life-threatening problems like seizures, heart attacks, and major traumas. A lack of comfort makes them more likely to respond negatively or dismissively when patients ask for pain medicine, which in turn can lead people with substance use disorders to learn that clinics and hospitals are not friendly places and not sources of treatment. It can make them see such locations as yet more minefields of stigma and discrimination in an indifferent universe. Staying away from health care leads them to neglect their mental and physical health.

Shifting the skills, knowledge, and attitudes of health professionals toward concern for and competence in substance use disorders could reverse this negative cycle. People with addictions would be more likely to engage in care and more likely to have their health conditions managed, leading to improved health and reduced costs for society, as HIV and hepatitis C transmission is reduced and emergency room visits decline.

Small groups of clinicians stretching their scope of practice and taking a lead can make a big difference. In response to the opioid epidemic, the infectious-disease service at Boston's Beth Israel Deaconess Medical Center began to offer addiction care alongside its more customary care for infectious conditions. It now offers buprenorphine induction and counsel patients on naloxone use. Building on the social justice approach and holistic mentality of infectious-disease physicians fighting the HIV epidemic in the 1980s and 1990s, staff at the centre have chosen to make addiction care part of their repertoire.[24]

Thousands of nurses, nurse practitioners, and doctors across the continent have gone out of their way to learn about addiction so that they can prescribe effective treatments, connect patients to care, and become better stewards of addictive medications. We need more addiction treatment and better stewardship of opioids, but we also need to make changes outside the clinics and hospitals. We need to keep searching for solutions.

CHAPTER 8

Searching for Solutions

The search for solutions to the opioid epidemic has been as frantic as the nurses ripping open a naloxone kit in a futile effort to save that girl in the clinic bathroom. In *A Journal of the Plague Year*, Defoe told how fear led Londoners to desperately seek remedies as the "terrors and apprehensions of the people led them into a thousand weak, foolish and wicked things." Fortune tellers and astrologers aggressively plied their trade; dozens of remedies were sold, each promising to protect against or cure the plague. Defoe observed that "it is incredible and scarce to be imagined how the posts of houses and corners of streets were plastered over with doctors' bills and papers of ignorant fellows, quacking and tampering in physic."

The quackery was countered by the lord mayor, who "ordered the College of Physicians to publish directions for cheap remedies for the poor," which, Defoe noted, "was one of the most charitable and judicious things that could be done at that time, for this drove the people from haunting the doors of every disperser of bills, and from taking down blindly and without consideration poison for physic and death instead of life."

Across North America, all levels of government and an array of medical and addiction organizations have been searching for solutions. Addictions are expensive; they cost the United States seven hundred billion dollars each year. The costs come from medical bills, crime, and lost work productivity. A relatively inexpensive solution is harm *reduction*: policies and practices that make drug use safer without insisting on abstinence. Because harm reduction does not preach abstinence, it has powerful opponents. To some, it is a licence to continue drug use. Critics see providing needle exchanges and safe injection sites as a self-defeating strategy that renders drug use cheaper and safer and thereby feeds addiction without addressing its root causes. Harm-reduction advocates counter that they are preventing unsafe injections and overdoses and are ultimately saving lives. They argue that by getting users connected with care, they can start them on treatment for their physical problems, psychiatric diseases, and substance use disorders as well.

Harm reduction should be offered to everyone engaged in treatment for opioid use disorder. There are four main forms of harm reduction: first, education about the safe use of needles and crack pipes; second, access to sterile syringes, needles, and other supplies; third, access to take-home naloxone kits; and finally, access to supervised injection sites.

The first time I walked into a needle and syringe service at the downtown public health clinic in Ottawa, it was like entering a secret world. With calm efficiency, one of the centre's nurses, Judy, showed me the works.

"This is the vitamin C packet to dissolve the drug, this is sterile water, this is a clean spoon to heat the drugs, and these are the needles and syringes," she said as she laid them all out. "People come here and we collect some basic information and give them the gear they need."

I asked Judy what happened after business hours and on the weekend.

"They call the van," she said.

The van, it turned out, was a roving harm-reduction office filled with needles and naloxone kits. The van also offered health services like HIV tests. The van (and similar vans from other community health centres) drove all over the city. Once I learned about it, I began to see the van on the road late at night and even, on occasion, parked a few streets from my house. The van featured in many stories from my patients: the van had brought them to their visit with me or they had had to call the van to get a new naloxone kit after their own kit had been used to rescue someone who had overdosed.

Mobile health care plays an even more proactive role in European countries like Portugal, where mobile health units drive around, delivering doses of methadone to patients who are too unstable to regularly or punctually attend a clinic or pharmacy.

Even today, when I see a young man or an older woman walk out of the needle exchange office at my clinic with a brown paper bag, which I know is full of sterile needles, syringes, and other tools of drug use, it takes a moment for me to register what I am witnessing. I feel like I should look away. I think about the process. Someone walks into the office and leaves a few minutes later, with no money exchanging hands, with new, sterile medical equipment, which they will use to inject drugs. And this happens hundreds of times a day in hundreds of towns and cities across the world. But like many aspects of drug use and even drug treatment, it is happening in secret and still retains a hint of the illicit.

We carry deep-seated preconceptions about drug use, about wrong and right, preconceptions that can be difficult to change. It is because of these preconceptions that so many countries do not provide needle exchanges. It remains illegal to carry syringes in many countries, as they are considered drug paraphernalia. In the United States, most states have different rules, and local health authorities have to declare emergencies to justify such programs. As of 2016, there was no penalty for carrying marijuana paraphernalia in Washington, DC, but possessing a syringe could lead to a misdemeanour conviction and a sentence of six months of jail time. In Arizona, simple possession of paraphernalia was considered a felony punishable by up to two years in jail. In Alabama, simple possession was only a misdemeanour, but if the paraphernalia was used, it could become a felony charge with a maximum sentence of ten years. Such zero-tolerance drug-paraphernalia laws can lead people who inject drugs to fear carrying syringes and force them to share equipment or dispose of it unsafely.[1]

Australia shows that although needle exchange programs cost money, they can be extremely cost effective. Data from Australian programs have revealed that for every dollar spent on needle exchanges, four dollars are gained in short-term health care cost savings, twelve dollars gained in health care costs over ten years, and an impressive twenty-seven dollars are saved if the economic benefits of avoiding disease are taken into account. A 2015 review of global needle exchange programs deemed them "one of the most cost-effective interventions ever funded."[2]

One of the key health and economic benefits of needle exchange programs is in preventing the spread of HIV. There are around twelve million people who inject drugs in the world, and about 1.6 million are HIV positive. About one in ten new HIV infections in the United States is related to injection drug use. In Southeast Asia, the Middle East, and Eastern Europe, HIV is largely spread by sharing injection equipment. People who use injection drugs who become infected with HIV can then spread HIV to their sexual partners. A meta-analysis showed that needle exchanges can reduce the spread of HIV infections by 58 percent. To reduce the spread of disease, Asian countries with large numbers of people who use injection drugs, such as China and Vietnam, have introduced needle exchange programs.[3]

The naloxone kit was not part of the gear given out in the clinic or from the van when I first started in addiction medicine. Over the past decade, it has gone from being unimaginable to being widely disseminated and generally accepted as a key component of the harm-reduction tool kit in Canada. In areas of Massachusetts where large numbers of naloxone kits were distributed, overdose deaths were reduced by 46 percent compared with areas of the state that did not introduce naloxone. And yet in thirty-six U.S. states, carrying naloxone without a prescription was illegal in 2017, which shows how little science is incorporated into many drug laws.[4]

To help convince skeptics of the potential benefits of naloxone kits, advocates tell a story with two alternative endings. Imagine Cheryl, a thirty-five-year-old woman with an opioid use problem, a five-year-old daughter in foster care, and a boyfriend — let's call him Jack — who also uses opioids. Cheryl and Jack are getting their lives back on track. They have an apartment and both work part-time. Cheryl gets to see her daughter on weekends and may be able to regain custody if she stays off opioids for a year. They are both six months into recovery, but one night Jack relapses and overdoses on heroin. In the universe without naloxone, Cheryl tries to save him with the only tools at hand. She slaps him hard, yelling his name. She pours cold water on him. She calls 911, but before the paramedics arrive, he is dead. Her morale is sapped by grief, and she relapses to opioids herself, quits her work, and loses her apartment and the hope of ever regaining custody of her daughter.

But there is an alternative ending to the story, one that has become more common in the real world. When Jack overdoses, instead of slapping him and dumping cold water on him, Cheryl opens the bathroom cabinet, takes out the naloxone kit she picked up a few months earlier, and injects the medication into his thigh. She calls 911, and the paramedics arrive to find Jack shaken and afraid, but alive. They take him to the hospital, where he is observed for a few hours before returning home. This experience redoubles Cheryl's and Jack's motivation to leave opioids behind, and they return to slowly rebuilding their lives.

Such a story could be told for many treatments in addiction medicine and in medicine more broadly. While medicines alone are not enough to end all disease, because there will always be barriers to access and problems with adherence and tolerance, when they are available and are used at the right time, they can make a world of difference.

After 2013, naloxone went from being something new to a normal part of the drug ecosystem in the regions of Canada and the United States where it was rolled out. The introduction of the intranasal formulation has made its administration even easier and quicker. Users are trained to administer naloxone and then call 911 because naloxone is shorter acting than most opioids. This means that while someone may wake up from a naloxone dose, if they have a big enough dose of long-acting opioids in their body, they may fall back into respiratory depression after the naloxone wears off. But although people are trained to call 911 to ensure patients are properly monitored after an overdose, this doesn't always happen.

Joel shared his experience with me. "I had to use the naloxone on my girlfriend last week," he said. "I shot her with the nose one and she came back in five minutes. I didn't call the ambulance — I just took care of her."

I asked why he hadn't called the paramedics. He told me he didn't want them around; he wanted to take care of his girlfriend himself. But after thinking for a moment, he gave me a more complete explanation.

"You know, Doc, people are scared of calling nine-one-one after someone overdoses because they've been victimized by the cops for so long, so they just give the naloxone and deal with the shit. They have drug paraphernalia around and they're worried about getting arrested," he said.

I was actually surprised that in 2019, this was still happening. But it is really no surprise that criminalization remains a barrier to progress, that even as an effective antidote is being rolled out, it is coming up against the old issues of stigma and fear.

Another life-saving form of harm reduction has met obstacles in North America for years. Until very recently, only one example has operated on the continent. As with naloxone, critics say it leads to the normalization of drug use. I'm talking about safe injection sites, which are also called supervised injection sites. In these sites, drugs can be injected or smoked, which is important because many overdoses are caused by inhaling drugs.

The manager of one clinic in Ontario told me that he had spent years working to open a safe injection site, encountering barrier after barrier, and then all of a sudden, so many opened at the same time that there was a shortage of qualified staff to operate them. It is an idea whose time arrived in a big way, sometime between 2017 and 2018.

On February 24, 2018, the *New York Times* editorial board proclaimed, "Let cities open safe injection sites."[5] They declared that "most of America's past policies have failed catastrophically" and they laid out the case for safe injection sites, contending that "all evidence so far shows these facilities have proved incredibly effective at slashing overdose deaths in every country that has welcomed them. If lawmakers are serious about ending the opioid crisis, American cities and states should follow their lead." They reported that Seattle and San Francisco were on track to open sites and that many other cities were on the same path.

A few weeks after I saw this article, Rachel walked unsteadily into my office. "You can tell I used heroin, right?" she asked.

I looked at her pupils, which were small and dark. I watched her sway in her chair, looking around the room, confused. I asked her when she had last used.

"Like, three minutes ago in the bathroom," she told me.

Even though a young woman had died in the bathroom a few months earlier, Rachel had still walked into the very same room, locked the door, and injected herself with heroin. Our own safe injection site was set to open in the coming weeks, and I silently hoped that Rachel would make it. I reminded her not to use alone, but I feared she couldn't hear me through her opioid haze.

In late 2017, the Canadian government made it even easier to open safe injection sites, and by early 2018 Ontario was starting a process of opening temporary safe injection facilities linked to organizations or health centres that already had drug-user services, such as needle exchanges or addiction treatment, in place. Applications poured in from around the province, and more than twenty sites were up and running within a matter of months.

In mid-2018, a new government took over in Ontario and the premier said that while he personally opposed the sites, he would have his health minister review the evidence before making a final decision. Everything was paused for a few months and we all waited, fearing the worst. Then on a Monday in late October, Ontario's health minister announced that "the evidence clearly demonstrated these sites were necessary" and that the government would spend more than thirty million dollars a year to keep twenty-one sites open across the province. As there were only around one hundred and twenty safe injection sites in the whole world, this represented a huge commitment by the provincial government.

Seattle, San Francisco, New York, and Philadelphia, by contrast, continued to face hostility from the U.S. federal government about their plans to open safe injection sites. Rod Rosenstein, the deputy attorney general, argued in August 2018 that "Americans struggling with addiction need treatment and reduced access to deadly drugs. They do not need a taxpayer-sponsored haven to shoot up." He pointed out that "one obvious problem with injection sites is that they are illegal." He stated that "it is a federal felony to maintain any location for the purpose of facilitating illicit drug use" and that violations can be punished "by up to twenty years in prison," among other penalties. These are not hypothetical punishments, according to Mr. Rosenstein, who asserted that "cities and counties should expect the Department of Justice to meet the opening of any injection site with swift and aggressive action."[6]

Critics fear that safe injection sites will encourage people who use drugs to flock to certain neighbourhoods and cities and will lead to rising, not falling, crime and overdose deaths. So far, however, the evidence has not shown an increase in overdoses. This will be easier to study as some regions introduce safe injection sites and others do not. The impact of a successful safe injection site will go beyond the reversal of overdoses. A vital component of making a safe injection site really work is the link to other forms of harm reduction, to case management, and to treatment.

A trove of evidence related to safe injection sites comes from Vancouver's Insite, the first such program in North America, which opened in 2003. A 2011 study showed that overdoses declined around a third in the area around Insite. People are less likely to overdose, less likely to need paramedic care, less likely to contract HIV, and less likely to die when they have access to a safe injection site.[7]

I visited the neighbourhood around Insite on an unusually warm fall day. Actually, I walked right by the clinic on my first pass, as there was no sign apart from discreet white etching on the glass door and adjacent window, which read

> Welcome to Insite
> Open Daily
> 9:00 AM to 4:00 AM

There was no other indication that this place is part of North America's addiction history. Next door is the boarded-up Balmoral Hotel, formerly a low-income housing building that was so neglected and abused it was closed down by the city in June 2017 after it was deemed in imminent danger of collapse.

Insite is in the heart of Vancouver's Downtown Eastside. When I lived in Vancouver in the first few years of the millennium, I would take the bus west on Hastings and watch as the streetscape shifted from suburban to inner city to affluence. Fifteen years later, when I visited the area again, I was struck by how little things had changed. As in the past, when I walked east from downtown, the city started to become transfigured somewhere around Homer Street. By the time I reached Main and Hastings, wealthy Vancouver, the city of luxury cars, high-end jewellery stores, and hipster coffee shops, had been replaced by an area full of boarded-up storefronts, pawnshops, people bartering sticks of deodorants and bottles of shampoo, and, in one case, a man selling chicken and rice from a small cooler perched on top of a fold-out table. The wet fall leaves covering the sidewalk were mulched together with cardboard, plastic wrappings, Styrofoam cups, and cigarette butts. I watched a few people with shopping carts overflowing with belongings covered in orange tarps, cruising or sitting on the sidewalk, eating burgers, and feeding scraps to their dogs.

Since Insite opened in 2003, it has been used for injecting drugs more than three and a half million times. No one has died. In 2017 there were more than 175,000 visits by 7,300 patients. People used the injection room 415 times per day. Nurses had to intervene to prevent a fatal overdose more than two thousand times that year. Upstairs at Insite is a detox centre called Onsite, where users can stay for a week or two to detox off drugs. A block down from Insite, on the other side of East Hastings, is another safe injection site called the Overdose Prevention Society. It opened illegally in 2016 in a tent but now operates as a legal safe injection site and has hosted more than 100,000 injections, also with zero deaths.

When the safe injection site opened at my clinic in Ottawa in the spring of 2018, there was little fanfare. Our attitude was that there was nothing to celebrate. Too many people had died while we waited for approval, then funding, and finally construction. Now it was finally open. Nurses and outreach workers were trained in the use of oxygen and naloxone, and in the art and science of assessing who was sedated and who was dying.

Because the entry to our opioid substitution clinic was shared with the safe injection site, opponents had predicted that there would be hordes of dealers and users loitering and crowding into our clinic. Rod Rosenstein has stated that another problem with safe injection sites is that they "destroy the surrounding community. When drug users flock to a site, drug dealers follow, bringing with them violence and despair, posing a danger to neighbors and law-abiding visitors."[8]

In fact, after the safe injection site opened at our clinic, nothing changed. One day there was no site; the next day there was a site. A steady flow of people now show up and ask, "Can I use the SIS?" They walk in, sit at a stainless steel table, use sterile equipment to inject drugs they bring with them from outside, talk to workers, get monitored and assessed, and when they are able to get up and walk out, they leave.

Within a few weeks, the perceptions about a safe injection site were transformed from a frightening and unpredictable new entity in our clinic's ecosystem to an unremarkable and ordinary part of life. I started to routinely ask my patients who were still using opioids if they were using a safe injection site, and most said yes. The bathrooms of our clinic and the surrounding businesses are no longer battlefields littered with used syringes or crime scenes choked with dead bodies; they have become, once again, just bathrooms.

Living through this transition reminded me that many of the horrors of drugs flow from criminalization and prohibition. Prohibition has turned people who use drugs into what public health officials call "vectors of infectious disease," as the use of unclean needles in unsafe settings can lead to the transmission of HIV and hepatitis C. Gangs and organized crime are drawn to the lucrative drug trade, and users commit property crimes to acquire funds to pay for drugs at prices that are inflated by scarcity and risk. Approximately one in five inmates in U.S. prisons is inside for one or more drug-related crimes.[9]

While drug dealing is one way to pay for drugs, it is by no means the only crime that feeds the river of money and goods flowing from people who use drugs to drug suppliers. I have heard stories of most types of crime: shoplifting, bank robberies, pharmacy break-ins, and various flavours of fraud — prescription, credit card, forgery.

When Bill came back to see me after a year away, I asked him where he had been.

"I owed a lot of people money. The bills were piling up and I was using drugs. Even though I knew it was a bad idea, I tried robbing a pharmacy. I got caught."

He smiled ruefully as he told me the story, but as I looked at his massive frame, I could only imagine the terror he must have inspired in the staff and customers of whatever local pharmacy he had set upon.

Crime and addiction interact in part because drugs are illegal and in part because of the vast quantity of money required to feed a habit. Criminologists have been exploring the links between addiction and crime for decades. As substance use disorders worsen, people often lose their jobs. They then burn through their assets, sell their house and cars, and end up with very little. At this point, they might have a heroin habit and a crack habit costing them several hundred dollars per day. Let's say it's only two hundred dollars per day. That's six thousand dollars per month and seventy-two thousand dollars a year for drugs alone.

It makes sense to me that drug treatment reduces crime, and the evidence supports this hunch. One study from the United Kingdom showed that drug dealing in particular was reduced to less than one-fifth and overall crime declined to less than two-thirds one year after dealers attended drug treatment, whether it was residential treatment or a methadone program.[10] The authors of that report followed up on this group of treated patients five years later and found fewer convictions for stealing, dealing, and violent crimes.[11] Studies of methadone, buprenorphine, and injectable opioids similarly show that people on treatment commit fewer crimes.

North America's hunger for opioids fuels a vast network of smuggling, fraud, theft, and violence. While I may feel safe in my sterile office, with the door closed in an effort to shut out that world, the consequences still seep in through the cracks, carried in by my patients, by their lawyers, and by the police.

"My rent was seven hundred dollars a month and I wasn't making enough money, so I started dealing cocaine again," one young man told me. I hadn't asked if he was involved in crime — in fact, I never ask about crime — but he needed to tell me, to get it out, to explain himself to someone who would listen.

A few months later, I got called to the front reception desk to speak to a uniformed police officer. He smiled politely.

"Doc, I know you can't tell me anything about this patient's health, but he said he had a gun and was going to shoot up a store. I just wanted to know what you thought."

What did I think about making threats?

A week later, the same patient came to the clinic, asking for a letter for court. He wanted me to tell the judge that he was taking his buprenorphine and was no longer using drugs. I asked him about the gun and the threats.

"They just pissed me off. You know I wouldn't hurt anyone, Doc. I don't do that anymore."

That is a phrase I hear often: *I don't do that anymore.*

Crime and violence are a way of life for some young men caught in a particular neighbourhood, raised in an environment where such activities are tolerated and even celebrated. Stimulants like cocaine fuel robberies and assaults, while opioids drive people to do anything, commit any crime, to avoid the crushing withdrawal symptoms. But when the addiction is quelled, subdued by opioid substitution, and when men pass through their violence-prone twenties and early thirties, they come out the other side chastened and softened. They don't need or want to do *that* anymore.

These experiences have given me a small window through which to view the much larger war on drugs taking place across the globe. In 2006 the Mexican government intensified its domestic war against drugs by bringing the military into the fight, even in civilian areas. The following decade saw a huge rise in homicide rates and an epidemic of violence that brought down Mexico's life expectancy and also affected neighbouring countries in Central America. The United States puts a significant emphasis on law enforcement and the use of courts and prison to deal with both drug dealers and people who use drugs.[12]

There really is a revolving door connecting jail with drug-using communities and the homeless. I spent only a few weeks working as a medical resident in the Ottawa jail, but as I waited for prison guards to let me through a series of checkpoints, I reflected that what most inmates require is health care, housing, income support, and connection to ongoing treatment. Studies have shown that treating prisoners for their substance use disorders and keeping them engaged in treatment after they leave prison reduces both their rate of relapse and their rate of reincarceration.[13] Prisoners can still get drugs in jail, but there's relatively little supply compared with the outside. At our clinic, we work hard to make sure people stay on their opioid substitution while in jail and get seen right after their release. The case managers will often let me know who is being released on a Friday and who needs doses at the pharmacy for the weekend.

In 2014, opioid substitution was available in fewer than half the countries in the world. Of those countries with opioid substitution, only half again had the treatment available in prisons. Opioid substitution is generally absent from U.S. prisons but is available in most Canadian ones. European countries like Spain and Scotland have been able to reduce overdoses and the spread of HIV in prisons by introducing treatment and harm-reduction policies. Spain had a real problem with injection drug use in the correctional system in the 1990s. The Spanish government introduced HIV treatment, opioid substitution, and needle exchanges, and by 2012, the rate of new HIV infections among Spanish prisoners fell from seven per thousand to almost zero.[14]

The first few days and weeks after release from prison are a critical period for a prisoner with a history of substance problems. So much can go wrong. First of all, they can relapse. If they are on opioid substitution, they can lose their connection to their clinic or pharmacy and drop out of treatment. If any of these things happen, people are much more likely to overdose. In the first two weeks after their release from prison, men are twenty-nine times and women are sixty-nine times more likely to die than the general population. A program in Scotland to distribute naloxone kits to prisoners at the time of their release prevented more than five hundred overdose deaths from 2011 to 2014.[15]

A different and uniquely successful model is drug court. Drug courts allow people with criminal charges stemming from drug use to attend drug treatment instead of jail. There are more than 2,800 drug treatment courts in the United States, and the model is widely used in Canada. The logic is impeccable: why overwhelm the judicial and prison system with non-violent people who use drugs and would benefit from treatment? It is the embodiment of the notion that what people who use drugs need is treatment, not punishment. The evidence suggests it works, and my patients tell me proudly of the stability they achieve when they are in drug court.[16]

"I've been going to treatment every day and my urines are clean. My drug-court officer tells me she didn't expect me to do so good," Ian told me when I asked about his experience with the program. "We have to go to groups and meetings every day for seven hours, and we have to do two urine drug tests a week," he explained. "I really like the groups. I'm learning interesting stuff like dealing with cravings and how to feel less stressed."

This is an impressive model, and it could be one of the solutions to the war on drugs. It represents a step toward Portuguese-style decriminalization, which is celebrated in the harm-reduction and addiction medicine community. Recently, my colleague hung a poster on her door that puts it simply: "Portugal prevented drug overdoses by treating addiction as a public health issue." A number of media stories in 2017 reflected on the decade-and-a-half experience of decriminalization in Portugal. The most telling statistic is the drug overdose rate per million people, which in 2016 was 6 in Portugal, 80 in Canada and 198 in the United States.

In 2001 Portugal's government turned away from using hard power with a new law that changed the possession of up to a ten-day supply of a drug from a criminal to an administrative issue. This change occurred in the context of the highest rate of HIV infection in Europe, largely attributed to injection drug use. Individuals with small amounts of drugs are referred to a committee made up of a social worker, a psychiatrist, and a lawyer. The committee has considerable powers to fine, to ban travel to certain neighbourhoods or even abroad, and to restrict a person's ability to work if they are in a position to harm the public. As in North American drug courts, the committee can also mandate drug treatment.

In some ways, Portugal's brand of decriminalization is actually quite tame. Distributing and selling drugs are still crimes, and the police and courts go after dealers. There are no outlets selling legal drugs; there is no legal marijuana. More than just the law, everything about Portugal's drug policies changed at the turn of the millennium. While needle exchanges had existed since 1993, with the slogan "Say NO! to a used syringe," they were expanded and actively promoted after 2001. Access to methadone and then buprenorphine was widely pushed, and the number of patients on opioid substitution increased fourfold between 2000 and 2008. Harm reduction and drug treatment were pushed concurrently with decriminalization. Addictions and drugs continue to affect the lives of Portuguese people; they have not slayed the dragon, but they have found a way to tame its rampages for now.

One beautiful spring day, I was on my way to the clinic. As I locked my bike and hurried down the street, I saw a familiar-looking man pulling a small suitcase and smiling in my direction.

"Haven't I seen you in a TED Talk?" I asked as Mark Tyndall walked toward me. Mark and I had worked together on some addiction and HIV projects when he came to run the infectious diseases department at my hospital in Ottawa in 2012. He had since been recruited back to Vancouver, where his track record included starting the Insite safe injection site. He was now the head of the BC Centre for Disease Control. I had just watched his recent TED Talk on addiction and harm reduction a few weeks earlier, and I was delighted to see him in person.

"What brings you back to town?" I asked.

"I'm here for a bunch of meetings with Health Canada. I had an idea to put up vending machines that dispense opioids."

I smiled and thought how typically Mark Tyndall such an idea was. Since I had first met him, I had been impressed by his bold vision to mitigate risks to people who use drugs: promoting needle exchanges, starting up safe injection sites, and now trying to convince governments that it was a good idea to give away opioids in order to prevent users from purchasing heroin and fentanyl.

Over the next year, I followed the progress of his vending machines. The idea was to have highly secure steel units dispense doses of hydromorphone to users registered to the system. The machines would use biometrics to verify the identity of registered users and then dispense their dose.

Mark told an interviewer in 2018, "We're at a point now where the drug supply is so toxic that we're really talking seriously about how to get people access to a safer supply of drugs."[17] When asked in another interview about diversion and people selling their hydromorphone, he responded, "Could I say that would never happen? No. Could I say that it would be the worst thing in the world that people were selling safe drugs on the street?"[18]

A few months later I learned that, as usual, Mark Tyndall was ahead of the game. In 2019 a new term entered the harm-reduction landscape: *safe supply*. His idea of using vending machines to dispense safe opioids fits exactly with the movement's argument that because fentanyl and carfentanil have poisoned North America's drug supply, it is crucial, in order to prevent overdose deaths, to provide a safe supply of opioids such as morphine and hydromorphone to those who use drugs. The model of safe supply used most often is to provide opioids to people at safe consumption sites for use on site, instead of them having to bring in contaminated forms of fentanyl.

In January 2019, Vancouver's Portland Hotel Society began to distribute hydromorphone at one of its overdose prevention sites; patients ingest it on site. Over the rest of 2019, calls for safe supply blended with calls to decriminalize drug possession. In July 2019, Vancouver's overdose emergency task force endorsed both safe supply and the decriminalization of drug possession, while also calling for more funding from the provincial and federal governments. Canada's federal government voiced support for safe supply, particularly in the form of injectable hydromorphone and heroin, but stopped short of moving toward drug decriminalization.

However, Dr. Bonnie Henry, British Columbia's provincial health officer, the top physician in the provincial bureaucracy, did not shy away from decriminalization. Instead, she released a fifty-page report in April 2019 calling for exactly that, even laying out some strategies for the province to decriminalize drugs without help from the federal government. She argued that decriminalizing personal possession along the same lines as Portugal did was an important step needed to reduce the deaths in British Columbia. Despite the report, the province's minister of public safety shot the idea down, stating that while law enforcement in the province would continue to help link people who use drugs with treatment, only the federal government could decriminalize drugs.

The idea of safe supply sounds to some like a return to the freewheeling opioid prescribing of the last two decades. Isn't opening the spigot on the opioid supply exactly what got us into this problem in the first place? The parallel does not hold up, however, as safe supply advocates are looking to prevent death in those already using high-risk opioids, rather than introducing new people to opioid use. The details of any programs will need to be carefully planned, and the programs will need to be monitored and then regularly re-evaluated. The goal this time around will be to save lives, not to maximize Purdue's profits.

I think the most valuable forms of safe supply are the ones that have been the most studied: prescribed and monitored methadone, buprenorphine, slow-release oral morphine, and injectable opioids such as hydromorphone and diacetylmorphine. If there is a lack of access to safe opioid substitution therapies, then the focus should be first on increasing access to care. When HIV treatment was introduced in the mid-1990s, it was unimaginable that we could get treatment to developing countries with crumbling health infrastructure. And although we aren't close to getting HIV drugs to everyone who needs them, we have made huge progress. The same can be done with opioid substitution treatment in North America. We need more types of treatment that work for everyone, and we need much more access to treatment.

Ultimately, there are many ways to get drug policy wrong. The tough-on-drug-user policies such as those espoused by the U.S. Department of Justice purport to promote public health and safety, but the evidence shows repeatedly that they do the opposite. Restrictive policies contribute to the spread of infectious diseases, create barriers to accessing health care, increase lethal violence, increase incarceration, and lead to more criminal charges and more overdose deaths.

Europe again shows us the way toward creating better drug policies. Decriminalization of drug possession is supported by the knowledge that the sickest people who use drugs commit a large fraction of non-violent, drug-related crime, and connecting those users to effective treatment is a humane and cost-effective intervention. Europe has also minimized the transmission of HIV by connecting those same people to HIV medications and a broad suite of free primary health care. North Americans need a bigger tool kit and better tools.

CHAPTER 9

Expanding the Treatment Tool Kit

One day on vacation last summer, I did something stupid. As the sun was just beginning to rise and while everyone else was sleeping, I sat outside in the cool morning, looked up briefly at Lake Ontario stretching toward the horizon, and began to read *Mayhem* by Sigrid Rausing. I had pre-ordered the book months earlier, so when it arrived a few days before we left for the cottage, I decided to bring it along. As I read the first sentence, I had a premonition that it might not be vacation reading. The book began like this: "Now that it's all over I find myself thinking about family history and family memories; the stories that hold a family together, and the acts that can split it apart."[1] But it was what followed that should have set off an alarm and led me to put the book away until I was back at work, surrounded by the daily grind of emergency room reports and letters from the coroner. Rausing wrote, "I used to think that no act was irreversible; that decisions taken and mistakes made could, on the whole, be put right. Now I know that certain acts in life are irreversible and lead you to landscapes you never dreamt of."[2]

I barely slept that night. After finishing the book just before midnight, I spent the next few hours in a terrorized sleep, haunted by the images and emotions the book had unleashed. More than anything else I'd ever read, the book showed me there was a dimension to my work in addictions that I had seen only in glimpses and at moments of crisis: the dimension of the family. Sigrid Rausing did not have an addiction; she was fantastically wealthy and successful in her work. It was her brother, Hans, and his wife, Eva, who were addicted to heroin and cocaine. Eva was found dead in 2012. The basic narrative is not uncommon — husband and wife struggle with addiction, have periods of remission, attend many rehabs until finally one dies and the other enters a fragile recovery. But life is not experienced as a narrative; life is about details. It was the details that made this book so disturbing even after I had borne witness to so many deaths. It was the details that made me want to lock it away and forget every word.

Perhaps not every word. The week after my vacation, the lesson I learned from Sigrid was brought back to me as Lucy told me about why she wanted to stop using heroin.

"This girl owed me money so I called her house, but instead I got her mom," Lucy said. "Her mom was really nice and gave me the money. She told me she was shaking when I called her because every time she gets a call from a number she doesn't recognize, she thinks it's someone calling to tell her that her daughter died. After she left I thought about that, about what it's like for my mom and dad. I used to think it didn't hurt other people. I was the one doing drugs — I wasn't making anyone else do them. But it's not like that, so I called my dad and told him I was okay."

I nodded, remembering that day at the cottage with *Mayhem*. Addiction, more than other diseases, leads to mayhem for a family. It is worse than other diseases because parents blame themselves or each other for their children's actions. Parents, brothers, sisters, friends feel they have the power to stage an intervention, to use love or tough love, to break the addiction. We are bound together in relationships, and our actions have an impact on each other; the closer the relationship, the greater the impact, both good and bad. It is not just death that affects families. It is every stage of the addiction.

I felt further stung as I read Chapter 63 in my addiction medicine textbook a few days later. It began with the admonishment, "Many physicians neither assess nor attend to the impact of chronic illness on a patient's family, nor do they consider, conversely, the family's impact on a patient's illness; this oversight is a grave error, and nowhere has its significance been better elucidated than in the treatment of the chronic illness of addiction."[3] Was I guilty of this oversight, of this grave error? I did think about my patients' families; I often asked patients to bring in family members to discuss their treatment plans. I asked about drug use in their family. *But*, I asked myself, *should I be doing more?*

One-quarter of families are affected by addiction in a first-degree relative. Family members can help or harm the course of addiction. Beyond the obvious genetic connection between patients and their parents and apart from the lingering effects on patients of early childhood experiences, I had seen family members start or perpetuate drug use in their relatives. Often older brothers would introduce their siblings to cannabis, or the cocaine habit of one sibling would trigger relapses in another sibling struggling with their own cocaine problem. Family members can become codependent and enable a substance use disorder. I thought that I had seen it all, but was I really seeing everything?

The attitudes of parents toward drugs can change a child's trajectory. One of my patients with the heaviest cannabis habit and the most anxiety and gastrointestinal consequences from cannabis told me, "My parents were very pro-weed. We used to sit around and all smoke at Christmas when I was a kid." Parents who are stricter about drug use typically have kids who use fewer drugs; it is a pattern repeated in homes across the world every day. I have seen opioid use passed down through three generations — from grandmother, to mother, to daughter. All three turned to street heroin, ended up on methadone, and also struggled with cocaine use.

The nightmare of watching a family member journey into the night of addiction is one that has been shared by many. Imagine a young man, with a young family, who begins to experiment with opioids. First, the drug coexists with his normal life like a secret girlfriend, barely making her presence known. Then the young man begins to miss family dinners, or forgets his daughter's birthday party, or doesn't come home for a few nights. Then the opioids displace and stress all other major relationships in the young man's life. The addiction continues to grow, affecting his parents, his siblings, his partner, and his children. They, all of them, especially his children, become increasingly neglected. Until it ends. Perhaps he recovers, perhaps he continues to use and becomes more and more distant from his family, or perhaps he dies.

I kept reading Chapter 63. In the cold, detached summary found only in medical textbooks and obituary notices, a lifetime of experience and suffering and a community of pain was parsed into two simple sentences: "Active addiction carries with it a sevenfold increase in risks of mortality, and families frequently experience the unexpected death of an addicted family member.... Some members may blame themselves or others in the family for the untimely death of the addicted parent, sibling, child or spouse."[4]

After reading this, I closed my textbook. The images of the mothers who had called me and showed up in my office after their sons and daughters had died from opioid addiction kept fighting their way into my consciousness — the spirits, the ghosts, and the survivors.

And then there was Rausing looking for meaning, trying to write down the truth, her truth, her reckoning of that moment when Eva died. Why could I not stop myself from thinking about her, about *Mayhem*, the mayhem of her life? Why had I been talking about the book to a young resident only the day before? Why was it still on the shelf, staring back at me, accusing me? What had I done to Rausing? To the mothers, to their sons and daughters? What was my responsibility?

I took a breath, looked out at the late-summer sky, and thought about why I was picking at these scabs and stirring the unwholesome pot of emotions and regrets. I remembered a line I had read: "The jackal rips out the hare's bowels, but the world rolls on." It was from J.M. Coetzee's book *Waiting for the Barbarians*, an allegorical novel about the fall of empire. Terrible things happen, terrible tragedies, but the survivors must keep living. Living and fighting. Fighting the war against opioids on many fronts — fighting against a new government hostile to harm reduction, against the suppliers and dealers, against ignorance and lies, and against despair. We can't let the ghosts hold us down, rob us of our will, push us into darkness. I decided to turn this new understanding of the role of the family and the impact of addiction on families into a weapon.

So for the next few weeks, I viewed each encounter with my patients through the lens of family. I asked Rachel about her relationship with her mother, and then I asked Ian about whether his older brother was still using cocaine at home and how that affected his own cocaine use. While part of me felt afraid as I used this new lens, as if I had suddenly realized the ocean was much deeper than I had previously imagined, I also felt empowered. As I came to learn more about each patient's family, I realized I could see my patients with new clarity, understand them and their context with a level of nuance I had missed in the past.

Sometimes what a family wants most is for their loved one to go to a traditional residential treatment program. The treatment journey usually starts with a phone call. The standard of care for addictions has been for a doctor to give the patient a list of numbers to call. Many detox or treatment centres won't even accept a referral from a doctor or family member because they want the patient to be motivated, to prove to themselves, and others, that they want to stop using. This attitude has always made me uncomfortable — we don't make patients call cardiologists on their own to deal with their heart disease. When someone has a stroke, we don't wait for them to call 911; we make the call because we know their illness makes it impossible for them to act promptly or rationally.

Slowly, this attitude is starting to change. Instead of letting the person hit rock bottom and decide to make a phone call, we are trying to redirect the trajectory of their addiction as much as possible. So if a person tells me about their drug use but does not feel it is causing them any harm and has no interest in stopping, I focus on harm reduction and education. Some simple education can go a long way, especially in areas where public opinion and media attitudes conflict with scientific reality.

If a patient recognizes they have a problem but doesn't want to do anything about it, I focus on what treatment options are out there: what meetings, what groups, what medications can help them. I start to work with them on achieving small reductions in use, and on harm reduction. I don't try to use fear as a motivator, but I do talk about how things could go from bad to worse based on what I've seen over the years. It takes only one drunken crash to ruin your life; it takes only one drug-impaired misjudgment to scuttle your career. I use the old Alcoholics Anonymous adage that you need to run the movie through to the end each time you begin to use.

When a patient is ready to stop using drugs, we quickly implement a plan. If they want to start opioid substitution therapy, we start right away. If they want to detox and go to treatment for alcohol or cocaine use, we make the referral immediately and get the process started. Addiction is a medical emergency and should be treated as such.

The type of psychosocial and residential treatment mixed into each treatment recipe varies by patient. In Ottawa, patients usually go to a central intake centre and meet with an addiction "navigator," who helps them decide on the type and intensity of treatment they require. They get plugged into the free Ontario system and either go to treatment in Ottawa or travel to treatment centres in other cities. Whether someone has private insurance or stable housing makes a difference, but most people can get the care they need.

We are lucky in Ottawa to have well-organized and well-funded homeless health and addiction programs, run by visionary leaders. Every morning on my way to work, I bike past the Ottawa Mission and see a handful of my patients chatting and smoking out front, regardless of the weather. The Mission is a homeless shelter for men. It has a stabilization unit for short-term stays as people prepare to enter into a five-month residential addiction program called LifeHouse. Each day, the men have sessions on mental health and addiction subjects, meet with their counsellors, and get connected to the health care they need. I worked as a resident in the clinic, and I have been so impressed by the care provided by its nurses, nurse practitioners, and doctors. I often speak to patients who long ago found housing but still go back to the addiction groups or the clinic at the Mission because they find them such valuable resources.

Sometimes my patients go away to publicly funded or private rehabs, which are located across Canada, as well as in more exotic places, such as Costa Rica, Thailand, and Bali. While the physical settings may be better than that of the Mission, I haven't seen much evidence that they lead to better outcomes for patients than the publicly funded system.

In 2013, I read the book *Inside Rehab* by Anne Fletcher, a *New York Times* journalist with her own history of substance use. I spoke to her about her experience writing the book, and we compared programs in Canada and the United States. Her book showed that the quality of rehabs varies considerably. There is also no good evidence that inpatient treatment is more effective than ongoing outpatient treatment. In fact, I think residential rehabs do more harm than good when they encourage patients to come off long-term opioid substitution therapy. This has become much less common in recent years in Canada, but is still common in the United States. Some see the U.S. private addiction treatment centres as being built on a multibillion-dollar lie that residential treatment works best. Like giving to charity, family members feel better the more money they spend on rehab for their loved one, a fact that some programs exploit.

Sarah Wakeman and Michael Barnett, both Harvard physicians, have asserted that one of the "tragic ironies" of the epidemic is that despite the fact that "with well-established medical treatment, opioid use disorder can have an excellent prognosis," there persists a "myth" that short-term, abstinence-based treatment is more effective than medication. The idea that more "treatment 'beds'" is a key to solving the epidemic is nonsense, in their view.[5]

Addiction is a chronic disease, and long-term treatment and follow-up are important variables in managing it. For example, doctors and nurses who develop addictions are usually treated with mandated programs for at least five years. These long-term programs allow them to get back to work safely and experience low rates of relapse. Longer treatment is better.

The first time I met Jim, he had just returned from a private rehab in Barbados. "It was great," he told me. "The people were amazing. I got to walk on the beach every day. But I relapsed the week after I got back."

He had come to see me to restart his methadone after it was tapered off to attend rehab. When Jim came back from Barbados, I asked him what he had learned. He told me he had attended group lectures on coping with cravings, identifying triggers for relapse, and coping with anxiety and boredom, and he had met with a counsellor and discussed his childhood issues of feeling neglected after his parents' divorce. These are the sort of topics that most rehabs teach, and I think they are very valuable.

As Jim experienced, an important piece of every patient's treatment plan is one-on-one counselling. This can be with an addiction counsellor, a social worker, or a psychologist. It can focus mostly on addiction; it can involve long journeys into one's childhood and psychological makeup; or it can be very present focused, helping a patient establish a routine, find a job, and develop healthy relationships. While the evidence supports opioid substitution as the most important part of recovery from opioid addiction, I always work to ensure my patients have someone to speak to regularly about their mental health and their inner life.

More complex patients need more support. These are the people about whom we say, "They fell through the cracks." Case management is one way to prevent people falling through these cracks. Case management takes many forms, but in essence it is about caring people going out of their way to support vulnerable patients who are trying to better their lives. Imagine you were living in shelter but had to attend appointments at court and at the hospital on the same day. Imagine you had to fill out reams of paperwork to apply for subsidized housing. Imagine you were a woman trying to leave an abusive partner, but you didn't know where to go. I have seen the case managers at my clinic help patients in each of these situations.

The opioid case managers at my clinic have a mandate to help patients struggling with opioid use. They hand out their cellphone numbers at detox and in community health centres. People call them and text them at all hours of the day, looking for support regarding access to treatment, housing problems, legal issues, and whatever else they want to talk about. The case managers in my clinic are some of the most caring and hardest-working people I know.

But even they cannot reverse major issues arising from poverty. To deal with those, poverty-reduction programs are necessary. For example, there is a growing interest in the idea of providing a basic income to all. One reason for this is the increasing dissatisfaction of many with the traditional welfare model. But providing a basic income does not solve the problem of meaning. As well as needing the basics for survival, patients trying to put their lives back together need to find ways to reconnect with the world beyond their addictions. Many of the community health centres in Canada have found ways for people who use drugs to positively engage with their community and peers. Social programs have an impact, rehabilitating and giving new meaning to lives that were previously dominated by drugs. I have seen tough guys serve pancakes to their fellow users after they were hired as peer workers at our clinic. My patients proudly tell me about the work they do as peer and support workers with such groups as Needle Hunters, which pays people to collect needles from parks and sidewalks, another blight that can be improved with access to safe injection sites.

Another fundamental part of a life, and of recovery from addictions, is having a home.

"Where are you living?" I asked Lincoln during a visit to restart his methadone after he had dropped out of treatment for a few weeks.

"That's the problem — I don't have anywhere to go. Sometimes I sleep at the shelter, sometimes I couch-surf," he told me.

I nodded, encouraging him to keep talking.

"Usually the people I'm staying with want to get high, shoot up, or smoke crack. Even if I was really ready to get clean, it makes it so much harder. I don't want to do this heroin anymore."

I had heard similar stories from other men and women in Lincoln's situation. To many, the discomfort and rampant drug use in shelters did nothing to help them stop using drugs. Even worse were the crack houses. Sometimes people would get housing only to lose it within a month or two because of violence or drug use or drug dealing. Often, to avoid the terrible environments of those places, they slept on the street, or in the ATM spaces in banks, or in parks. Housing wasn't always enough, but I came to see homelessness as another disease. I had seen the stats showing that around 60 percent of homeless people have a substance use disorder.[6] I had learned from my patients that when someone suffers from the triple burden of homelessness, mental illness, and addiction, recovery of any kind is that much harder. Eliminating homelessness completely is an obvious societal goal for many reasons, a mantle taken up by the Housing First movement, which advocates that "all people deserve housing, and that adequate housing is a precondition for recovery."[7]

When I next saw Lincoln, he had restarted his methadone and stopped using opioids, and he had a plan. "I talked to my worker and she told me I could go to treatment for a few months, and from there I can go to second-stage housing."

"Is that what you want?" I asked.

"I have to stop this bullshit. I'll never get clean where I'm staying. Actually, I don't even know where I'm staying tonight. It's so much easier to think when I'm on methadone. When I'm not on methadone, I get desperate. I shoplift. I don't care about anything other than getting heroin. But when I talked to my worker about housing yesterday, I felt different."

A month later, he had travelled to a government-funded treatment centre a six-hour drive north of the city. Three months later, he was back in town, living in a sober-living house and working on quitting smoking. He had been abstinent from opioids for more than one hundred days.

Sean has a long ponytail of unruly blond hair with tinges of red. In late 2018, his story appeared in the Opioid Chapters, a public-awareness campaign about the epidemic in Ontario. Each chapter tells the story of someone whose life has been touched by opioids. In his video, which I showed to a class of medical students at the University of Ottawa a few weeks after it was published, he told his story:

> I grew up on a Canadian Armed Forces base. I left home at the age of 13 to escape an abusive situation. I was put into emergency care and I was sexually abused there. It really took away a lot of my trust in the system. I put myself through high school. After that, I hitchhiked from Nova Scotia to San Francisco,

and got into university. It was going really well. I had a security job at a bar in town, I was a disc jockey and I fell in love. I finished two years of school and my girlfriend got pregnant. Unfortunately, she drowned seven months into the pregnancy. Out of that sprung my addiction. I turned first to alcohol, then opiates. Long story short, it turned into a pretty bad addiction. I pretty well lost everything that I worked for all those years, and ended up homeless and addicted to opiates.

I was in and out of shelters for about nine years. A huge step in improving my health was being housed. Initially, when I got out of one of the shelters, they put me into housing where there was still a lot of drug use going on. Every day and on every floor, there was a dealer. I eventually got back into drugs and lost my housing.

The next time, I decided to do it myself. To pay my rent, I delivered flyers for six cents a flyer. I lived in a really modest place. Where I am now is pretty modest, but that was pretty well a closet. I lived there for three years and it gave me privacy and safety and security. That was really huge. …

Another really important step for me was going on methadone. My methadone practitioner was a fantastic doctor. He never judged me. He always believed in me. I didn't even necessarily deserve the faith he put in me. Your priorities are really messed up when you're using. I had this infection on my elbow. It was very deep, and it was basically six weeks of antibiotics. But I was more worried about getting the drugs I needed to get through the day than my health care. I can't believe I was like that, but I was.

There are some hospitals and clinics in this city that are really good, and some that aren't very good

> toward people that use drugs. Some of the things they said to me in regards to the infections I had when I was using IV drugs — they were just horrible. The first time I went to get a blood test to start on methadone, the nurse or the technician was having problems finding a vein. She asked me how I could do this to myself. I was embarrassed enough as it was — I really didn't need her saying that![8]

Housing was the key to Sean's recovery. He now lives close to his job, where he advocates for the health and well-being of people who use drugs in Ottawa.

Losing housing is a sign of instability — someone can't pay their rent or can't stop the dealers coming to their place at all hours of night and day — but it's also a multiplier of instability. Every time one of my patients loses their housing, everything in their life gets worse.

When I saw Jessica's urine drug test light up positive for fentanyl and morphine for the first time in months, I immediately knew something was wrong. I asked her what was going on.

She hesitated. "Can I be honest? I've got so much stress. I was evicted and I've got to find a new place."

It turned out that rent wasn't the problem; she had the rent deducted straight from her disability cheque. The problem was the dealing.

"They said I was dealing, but that's bullshit. I'm going to lose my mind because of all the bullshit. There's just too much bullshit."

After she was evicted, she continued to use heroin and fentanyl. Then, two months later, she found a new place. She didn't stop using right away, but she came to see me almost every week. She asked me to increase her doses of buprenorphine, and after another month, I picked up Jessica's urine drug screen, looked at it closely, turned it around, and looked up at her.

She was smiling. "It's clean, right?"

It was.

CHAPTER 10
Treating the Whole Person

When a person who uses drugs starts opioid substitution therapy and it works, their life is radically changed. This change permeates every aspect of their life.

Christopher described his own experience of recovery to a group of pharmacists and doctors learning to prescribe methadone in 2012. "I went from waking up every day, knowing exactly what I needed to do all day long — find drugs — to waking up and not knowing what to do with myself. I needed the structure of treatment to give me some kind of routine. I went to the pharmacy to get my methadone; I went to the clinic. I very quickly woke up and realized how fucked up my life had become. My apartment was a disaster. I was totally broke. And I had HIV, which I'd tried to ignore for eight years."

Christopher's experience reminds me of a soldier returning from the simplicity of war to the complexity of civilian life. Opioid users bring a variety of other medical and psychiatric illnesses, as well as the other addictions, to treatment. It is a cliché, but it's true: it's fundamentally important to understand that to help people who use drugs recover, we must treat the whole person, not just the addiction.

Christopher had HIV, an infection found much more often in people who use drugs than in the general population. My journey to addiction medicine began with my interest in HIV. I realized that while people who used injection drugs made up around one in five HIV-positive individuals in most populations, they were the sickest. They had worse addiction issues and worse HIV-related problems. I learned early on that needle exchange programs helped prevent the transmission of HIV. It was during my first project working with Mark Tyndall that I started seeing the effect of combining antiretrovirals used to treat HIV with opioid substitution therapy.

The ward at St. Michael's Hospital in Toronto was buzzing with the sounds of nurses and doctors going about their morning rounds. I was taking an elective in HIV medicine with a mentor of mine, Dr. Kevin Gough. We were just reviewing my list of patients for the day — John, who had an abscess from injecting morphine; Catherine, who had a fungal infection in her brain caused by untreated and advanced HIV; and about ten others — when my phone rang.

"Hello, Brodie. This is Vera Etches."

I sat down in an overstuffed armchair in the hall and motioned to the rest of the team that I would catch up with them later. Vera Etches was a top physician in Ottawa public health. She would go on to become the chief medical officer for the city a few years later. We had been in touch a few weeks earlier about working on a project together.

"I have an idea for a project tying together HIV and injection drug use that we could use your help on," she said.

I was intrigued. She told me she wanted me to look at the evidence of how best to provide HIV and addiction care, and she wanted me to see what was available in Ottawa and where there were unmet needs. I agreed immediately, and when I got back home a few weeks later, I sat in my study and began to pore over the impressively rich vein of research linking HIV and injection drug use.

From my training up to that point in HIV medicine, I already knew that a central goal in treating HIV is to get the patient's viral load as low as possible. While curing HIV is still beyond reach, using antiretrovirals — in most cases just one tablet per day — can bring the level of HIV in a patient's blood down from one million copies per millilitre to a handful of copies, perhaps five or ten. This is called an undetectable viral load and is as close to being HIV negative as is feasible with current medication.

When someone has an undetectable viral load, they will feel better and will have few, if any, health effects from HIV. Another important consequence is that it is extremely unlikely that a patient with an undetectable viral load can spread HIV to another person; less virus means less chance of exposing others, even from unprotected sex.

The challenge is to get people to that point of being undetectable. I used to believe that if an illness can be vaccinated against, cured, or treated with a simple intervention, then it will be wiped off the face of the earth, like smallpox was in 1980. But I've learned the hard way that medical interventions are so much more complicated than that.

You would think preventing obesity would be simple, but it's not. You would think tuberculosis, which can be cured with inexpensive antibiotics, would be gone, but it's not. Similarly, of the more than one million people with HIV in the United States in 2014, only 49 percent had undetectable viral loads.[1] This was in part because some of them were unaware of their diagnosis, because they didn't attend or couldn't afford health care, or because of problems taking or tolerating their medicine. So, even a treatment as simple as taking one pill a day is treating just under half the people with HIV in the United States. Globally, the situation is even worse.

My early research for Vera Etches showed me that the rates of HIV are higher in patients with unstable substance use disorders than among the general population. One of the recommendations that kept coming up in my research was the necessity of linking HIV care and substance use care — ideally, both would be available in the same building. We could also link them by providing both medicines together, so a patient could go to the pharmacy and get their methadone and HIV medicine dispensed to them every day.

My HIV textbooks argued that patients with substance use disorders were not able to start antiretroviral therapy because their lives were too chaotic for them to adhere to treatment. I have found this to be true for only one or two of my patients. One of them is Saul, who always has a reason not to restart his HIV therapy or do his blood work.

Recently, he came in looking depressed. His face was covered in beads of sweats and his nose was running. "I used some fentanyl last night around eleven. Now I'm dope sick," he said flatly.

We discussed restarting his buprenorphine, reconnecting with his case manager, and following up the next day. Then I asked if he was taking his HIV meds.

"I don't want to talk about my HIV now. I just want to get my meds," he told me. And he said the same thing at our follow-up.

"Why don't you take your HIV medicine at the same time as your buprenorphine? The pharmacy can give you both together," I said. This strategy was working well for a number of other patients.

"I don't want them," was all he would say.

Years of research looking into this kind of reluctance has found that with the right supports, people who inject drugs can, in fact, do very well on HIV treatment and achieve undetectable viral loads at very high rates.

The WHO and UNAIDS (the Joint United Nations Programme on HIV/AIDS) recommend a full suite of services for patients who use drugs, including needle exchange programs, opioid substitution therapy, HIV testing and counselling, HIV antiretroviral therapy, prevention and treatment of sexually transmitted infections, condom programs, and treatment for hepatitis and tuberculosis.[2] An innovative way that we have tried to stop the transmission of HIV to people who use drugs is to give the HIV-negative patients antiretrovirals. This is known as pre-exposure prophylaxis (PrEP) and has been studied for sexual risk and injection drug risk. In both cases, taking one tablet a day of Truvada significantly reduces a person's risk of contracting HIV. The challenges with PrEP include the cost and the difficulty of convincing people to take medicine when they are not sick. It really works best when someone is at sustained risk of contracting HIV. For example, someone who is not always using clean needles and lives in a community with high HIV rates would be a good candidate for PrEP.

A much more established way to care for patients with both HIV and opioid addiction is to get them on methadone or buprenorphine. In 2005, the WHO added both of those treatments to its essential medicine list, meaning the organization believes every country should make them available within their health care system. There is a lot of evidence that people with HIV who inject drugs are more likely to start antiretrovirals, stay on antiretrovirals, and get to that ultimate goal of an undetectable viral load if they are on opioid substitution therapy. A large study from France showed that being on methadone or buprenorphine for the long term was associated with increased rates of achieving undetectable HIV viral loads.[3] There are fewer new cases of HIV among people who use injection drugs when they receive addiction and HIV care, and these treatments result in twelve dollars in crime reduction and health care savings for every dollar spent.

The experience in Russia and Eastern Europe shows what happens when people don't get the care they need. While rates of new cases of HIV have declined globally since the turn of the millennium, they have actually been going up in Eastern Europe and Central Asia. Unsafe injection accounts for two-thirds of these new cases.

Russia faces the unenviable situation of widespread opioid use and only sporadic needle exchanges. Opioid addiction blossomed in Russia after the collapse of the Soviet Union. Even worse, opioid substitution is illegal. As a consequence, people don't receive the addiction or HIV care they require and HIV has spread rapidly, from 500,000 cases in 2010 to as many as 1.5 million by 2016.[4]

After a couple of weeks of exploring this research, I wrote my report and went to meet with Vera at the Ottawa public health office. I also showed her my survey of the types of clinics and treatment centres available for both HIV and addictions in Ottawa. We talked about the evidence and about the gaps in care. I have been fortunate since then to work in teams of doctors and nurse practitioners who are experts at treating HIV in our high-risk patients.

Given the media and academic interest in HIV, a statistic from the 2017 World Drug Report struck me. More people who use drugs die from hepatitis C than from HIV, and more years of healthy life are lost owing to hepatitis C than to HIV. In 2016, for example, the global death toll among people who inject drugs was 220,000 for people with hepatitis C and sixty thousand for people with HIV.[5] This statistic reminded me of how easy it is to become biased and to get sidetracked by headlines and political priorities. HIV has a cultural presence that hepatitis C lacks, but the global rise of the hepatitis C infection and its treatment is an incredible story of disease and science that deserves to be shared.

When most of my medical school professors were young, hepatitis C did not even exist. As the letters suggest, the viral illness causing hepatitis A was identified first, and then hepatitis B was isolated. In the mid-1970s, blood tests could detect hepatitis A virus and hepatitis B virus, but to the surprise of researchers in the field, most hepatitis infections spread through blood were actually neither A nor B. This led to the delightfully awkward term *non-A, non-B hepatitis* (NANBH).

This term was used to describe the growing epidemic until 1989, when a group from the Chiron Corporation in California finally named the virus in a paper in the journal *Science*.[6] In the paper, they described the terrible hepatitis situation in the United States: more than 90 percent of transfusion-associated cases of hepatitis at the time were due to NANBH, and up to 20 percent of infected patients would end up with cirrhosis. They announced that they had cloned the genome of a NANBH virus, which they called the hepatitis C virus. But identifying the virus was only the first step. Next, treatments were developed, and for many years, only toxic treatments were available.

A week after I spoke on the phone to Vera Etches, I was sitting in a small conference room in St. Michael's Hospital as a hepatitis specialist flashed a picture of a man and a woman riding their bikes on a quiet country lane. "This is what hepatitis C treatment has been like until now. A couple of agents, not very effective, lots of side effects," he said. Next he showed a picture of the starting line of the Tour de France. Row after row of elite cyclists were lined up, about to break through the starting line. He said, "This is what hepatitis C treatment is going to look like in the coming years — an array of new treatments that are better and better tolerated."

I realized I was living through yet another revolution in science and medicine.

A few years later, just a decade and a half after the identification of the hepatitis C virus, it was routine for my patients with hepatitis C to get approved for government-funded treatments, which resulted in cure rates above 90 percent. And there was a lot of need. Around seven in ten of my patients who had used needles to inject drugs had contracted the virus. But despite the need, the treatment still seemed too good to be true. People were hesitant to start it because they had heard horror stories about the bad old days on interferon.

"That interferon made my buddy break out in a rash," Leo recounted when I encouraged him to register with our hepatitis C treatment program. "All the skin came off his body. He didn't look normal for weeks."

I tried to reassure him. "Yes, but the new meds are so much better. You don't have to take interferon anymore. Most people don't have many side effects."

He agreed to go to an appointment and hear about the medicines for himself. When his FibroScan, a scan of his liver using a special ultrasound machine, showed significant scarring, he said he was ready to give treatment a shot. The team assessed him and counselled him that even if he was cured, he could be reinfected in the future if he relapsed to needles or shared crack pipes.

Like Leo, many of my patients receive free treatment for the disease, and more than 90 percent are cured. This prevents many cases of advancing liver disease and cirrhosis over their lifetime. It also helps create a psychological break with their past selves. They are now hepatitis C negative and drug free, and the cost and risk of relapse becomes less tolerable.

Beyond HIV and hepatitis C, people who use drugs suffer from infectious conditions like cellulitis, infected joints, and endocarditis. Using clean needles in clean conditions such as a safe injection site can significantly reduce the risks of contracting all these infections.

It is the mental health burden that is even harder to remedy, in particular PTSD, bipolar disorder, and schizophrenia.

Jessica's nightmares often followed the same pattern, but that didn't make them any less terrifying. She always saw him, his eyes bright and angry; she felt afraid but couldn't escape; she woke up with her heart racing and her pillow covered in sweat. Her nightmares had been getting more frequent recently because she was due to go to court in a month, where she would have to relive the whole experience, and he would be in the same room. Jessica's life before her sexual assault had been marked by depression and anxiety. Now she also suffered with PTSD, which magnified her anxiety symptoms and invaded her sleep. She experienced flashbacks while riding the bus to her job at a downtown coffee shop; she lost brief stretches of time; she jumped anytime a door slammed.

It was about three months after her assault that she started to snort oxycodone. Her friend told her it would calm her down, help her forget, help her go to sleep, and it worked. For a time she felt calmer. Her boss noticed that she performed better at work, smiled more, and didn't seem so jumpy. But within a couple of weeks, she stopped getting the benefits from the opioids and started to feel worse than ever. If she didn't have any oxycodone, she suffered terrible withdrawal. And even when she had some, she needed more and more to get any benefit. She didn't have a doctor, she didn't have a psychiatrist, and because she had never considered herself an addict, she had never been to an addiction clinic.

Six months after her first use of oxycodone, I found myself sitting with Jessica, a mountain lake scene behind me, hearing the whole story. She had heard there was a pill that she could take to make the oxycodone withdrawal stop. She thought maybe something could make the flashbacks stop, let her sleep. I learned that Jessica's life had been hard from the beginning. Her mother had been an alcoholic and her father was violent. She had started smoking weed when she was thirteen. She got drunk with her friends almost every weekend starting a few years later.

Jessica's life had been hard, but now it was unbearable. Over the next year, she got better. She wasn't cured, but she was managing. I treated her opioid use with buprenorphine, and along with her psychiatrist, I gave her medicine to improve her anxiety, control her PTSD symptoms, and block out her nightmares and flashbacks. She went to a residential program that allowed her to continue all her medications for eight weeks, and then she kept seeing her trauma and addiction counsellor every week. She got back to her job and started to spend time watching movies with her friends, going to recovery meetings, and thinking about her future.

In the past, the mental health community might have turned Jessica away, telling her to get "sober" before they would treat her mental health. And often just a few weeks of abstinence from alcohol or drugs does help people sleep better, have more energy, and feel much happier. But treating both substance use and mental health problems is the best way to heal a damaged mind. It's the most humane thing to do, and it works. I've met many men and women like Jessica, and most of them have dramatically improved their lives by combining addiction and mental health treatments.

PTSD manifests in many ways. John was angry, impulsive, and frightening, but he was also racked by trauma. If someone used the wrong tone of voice or looked at him the wrong way, he would snap. He had grown up around violent crime. He didn't take pleasure in seeing others suffer, but he felt more alive in the middle of a bare-knuckle fight for survival than he did during the long nights when he was visited by nightmares. In his dreams, he would see his mother's dead body; he would see men chasing him and would feel powerless to fight back. When he was awake, he knew how to fight.

Things began to change for John when he started to see a psychologist. At first, it was hard. "It made me cry, talking about childhood and shit like that," he told me. "But now I don't feel like using, which is good. I'm glad I'm going to see him."

Some days, he still couldn't cope with his feelings. "I put my fist through my own kitchen cupboard the other day. Of course, I regretted it afterwards."

But after a while, he noticed that he was starting to react differently to situations. He said, "I don't get angry like I used to. I think it was the Percocet that was making me angry. I haven't hurt anyone in over a year."

The overlap between mental health conditions and substance use disorders is immense. It's unusual to find someone with a severe mental illness who has never had problems with drugs or alcohol, and it's also rare to find someone who uses drugs who doesn't have bad depression, anxiety, or bipolar disorder. One in ten people will suffer from major depression during their lifetime. Among people suffering with depression, the chance of having a problem with substances is doubled. Bipolar disorder is much less common, found in around 2 percent of the population. But someone with bipolar is four times more likely to have a substance problem than the general population.[7]

For many years, bipolar disorder mystified me. Those suffering from the disease flip between the two poles of mood: the high and the low, mania and depression. Bipolar is hard to diagnose because patients tend to be depressed most of the time and are often misdiagnosed with depression and treated with typical antidepressants. Every once in a while, these medications will actually trigger someone to enter the manic phase, and it is in mania that bipolar disorder becomes a remarkable condition. Mania manifests as a good mood unlike any other. A manic person is full of energy, ideas, plans, and schemes, and talks constantly to share all these profound ideas. A manic person doesn't sleep for up to a week at a time; they do impulsive things like gamble, buy things they can't afford, and go through a rapid succession of sexual partners. They have delusions of grandeur.

One day in October, just as the leaves were turning crimson, I was crossing the street to go into my clinic when Jake ran up to me.

His words came streaming out. "Doc, you've got to see me, like right now. I've got so much to tell you. Doc, I've realized that I was king in my last life and that it's my destiny to take over everything. I can change things just with the power of my mind."

I realized something wasn't right. My first thought was that he had taken speed or cocaine. Both those stimulants would cause that sort of hyperactivity and can also lead to psychotic symptoms such as delusions and hallucinations.

"I'll see you in a minute, Jake," I reassured him as I went inside to have a very quick lunch and change into my work shoes.

Before I went to get him from the waiting room, I reviewed his chart. There was no mention of bipolar; nor was there any history of depression.

When I brought Jake into the office a few minutes later, the rapid speech and grand ideas continued. "Doc, when I go into any room, people know I'm royalty. Doc, everything you're doing here, the lights, the computers, you won't need it — energy comes straight out of my body. I know what happened on nine-eleven."

After a few more minutes, I had to interrupt him. "Jake, have you taken any drugs? Any cocaine or speed or crystal meth?"

He said he hadn't.

"Jake, what have you used in the past few weeks?"

He said he hadn't touched any drugs in months. He said he hadn't needed drugs because with his mind now on a higher level than other people's, he didn't need to sleep or eat.

"Have you ever felt like this before?" I asked, with bipolar disorder rising higher in my mind as a possible diagnosis. It was hard to get a clear history from him that day, but as I saw him in the following weeks and his symptoms resolved, it became clear that he had had similar cycles in the past. I had him seen by the psychiatrist in our clinic, and she confirmed he had bipolar disorder and started him on mood stabilizers.

Patients with mental health problems have much higher rates of substance use disorders. For example, someone with ADHD is eight times more likely to have a drug addiction than someone without ADHD. And someone with antisocial personality disorder is about seventeen times more likely to have a drug addiction.[8] While smoking rates have fallen in North America, they remain stubbornly high in patients with mental health conditions, with rates of smoking higher than 80 percent among people with some conditions, like schizophrenia.

Tom was forty years old and overweight and had the yellow-stained teeth and fingers of a heavy smoker.

"They're following me again, Doc," he said at our first meeting.

"Who's following you?" I asked, instantly aware that Tom was either in trouble with some bad people or suffering from a paranoid delusion.

"The FBI," he said slowly.

Given that we were sitting in downtown Ottawa, well outside the jurisdiction of the FBI, I suspected that paranoid delusion was the more likely problem. Now I needed to figure out if Tom suffered from schizophrenia or had stimulant-induced psychosis or some other problem. I looked at his urine drug screen, which was positive for morphine and fentanyl but negative for cocaine and amphetamines. So stimulant use was less likely.

"They're waiting for me outside. They're going to put me in a helicopter and fly me to Guantanamo. I've done some bad things and they're after me."

It was my first time meeting with Tom. He had missed his last two appointments with his usual doctor, and I had agreed to see him when he asked to be seen urgently. I looked through his chart and found the psychiatrist's note from a year earlier describing his schizophrenia, which was managed with an injection of an antipsychotic medication every two weeks. I scrolled down and saw that he had missed the last five appointments for his injection and that his case manager had been unable to reach him. He had also been off methadone for two months. After connecting him back with his psychiatrist and getting his medication restarted, I was also able to restart his methadone and help him control his opioid use.

The opioid epidemic did not happen in isolation. Waves of drugs have been crashing against our shores, and opioids have mixed with cocaine, benzodiazepines, and stimulants such as speed and crystal meth. Just as someone who is drinking alcohol is more likely to smoke, people who seek a "down" in the form of opioids will often seek other types of down or will mix uppers in the form of cocaine to counteract the effects of sedating medications.

The most toxic brew is made by mixing two or three types of down together, as Derrick had on the Tuesday night in July when he was found dead by his wife, Petra. Toxicology reports showed fentanyl and Valium in his bloodstream. I hadn't seen Derrick in more than a year and a half, so I had to piece the story together from second-hand accounts and old medical reports. It wasn't until later that fall that I had all the details and could tell the full story of Derrick's life and death.

I first met Derrick when he was in his late thirties. He had started smoking fentanyl patches and sniffing OxyContin three years before. He came to my clinic looking for treatment options. We started methadone and he immediately responded. A few months later, his urine drug tests showed only methadone and he was working full time as a mechanic. He told me that a few other guys from the shop would get together after work to snort cocaine or Percocets, but he was able to avoid that scene and go home to his wife. Soon afterward, he told me his wife was pregnant.

If anyone had asked me, I would have said Derrick was a star patient. In a short time, he was the proud and responsible dad of twin girls. He told me he had the occasional cravings to go back to his old way of life, particularly when he felt stressed at work or had a fight with his wife, but overall he was able to keep these feelings in check. At every visit for three years, he had normal urine drug screens and told me things were going well. While my clinic was stuffed full of chaos and suffering, Derrick was dependable. He was solid.

After he bought a bigger house for his growing family, he told me he was ready to start tapering off methadone because he felt he didn't need it anymore.

"There is a risk that coming down or off methadone will set you up to relapse to opioids, so you have to be careful," I warned him that first day.

I told him about the stats showing that a lot of people relapse, but I agreed that for someone like him, someone with years of stability, with a job, with a partner who didn't use drugs, it was reasonable to try a taper. We went down slowly: a few milligrams a week. Each time he sat in my office, he smiled. I looked closely at his face; I looked at his pupils. I searched for signs of withdrawal, but he told me he was fine.

"Let's keep going," he said when I asked if he was ready to come off the final few milligrams. "I'm ready to be done with this." He was looking forward to a life without drugs and without drug treatment, without reminders of his past, without pharmacy visits and urine tests. On our last visit, a freezing afternoon in early January, I felt like a parent sending a child into the indifferent world, praying that his skills and his smarts and his wisdom would see him through.

Then there was silence. For a year and a half, I heard nothing. I didn't see his smile or hear his voice reassuring me that he was okay. There was so much need; there were so many other patients — I'm ashamed to say I forgot to think about him, to wonder where he was, what he was doing. It was the afternoon before a long weekend and I was thinking about another patient, Bradley. I had just started him on methadone and he had missed his first follow-up. I was worried, so I checked my inbox to see if he had contacted the clinic. But instead of Bradley's name, there was Derrick's. In the subject line, I read the dreaded phrase: "Patient overdosed."

After leaving my clinic eighteen months earlier, Derrick had ended up moving on with his life and staying away from drugs, for a time. Drugs were not a part of his life. He was earning more money and spending time with his young family. He was coping with everyday stressors of bills and parenting and rebuilding the relationships with his family, which had been fragmented during his years using drugs.

Some days the old demons would return to haunt him. He would be tormented by cravings. One night, he found himself walking toward the house of his old dealer, but then he turned toward the river and just walked off his frustrations instead. Another day, he passed by a pizzeria that sold heroin and cocaine to those who knew the right words and didn't look like cops. He even came by the clinic and thought about coming in to talk about going back on methadone. But he hadn't used, so he decided he didn't need to go back down that road.

He became more irritable with his wife. He would stay late at work, hanging out with the other guys. Petra's growing resentment pushed him away even more. They had a big fight late one night, and he stormed out. He would show her; he would show everyone. First, he just had a few drinks. Then he had a few more. Then someone offered him some Valium to take the edge off his frustrations. That feeling of Valium mixing with alcohol reminded him of another feeling, like a memory of a dream. Heroin.

This time he didn't turn away from the dealer's house. He dialed all the numbers he knew. His wife saw the calls on his phone, and the toxicology report told the rest of the story. In the end, one lapse was all it took to end Derrick's life.

Adding alcohol to another sedative has a deadly effect. Benzodiazepines are the class of sedatives that include sleep and anxiety medications such as Valium (diazepam) and Rivotril (clonazepam), and, perhaps most fatal of all, Xanax (alprazolam). The opioid and addiction guidelines are full of warnings not to combine any opioid with any benzodiazepine. But patients who like sedatives often do not discriminate. When you are shot through with psychic pain and anxiety, any substance that makes you feel calm and worry free, even for an hour or two, is a powerful salve.

A few days after Derrick died, Nadia told me that she had stopped using any benzos at all. "They were killing me. They were blacking me out."

"What do you mean? What happened?" I asked.

"I had a really bad experience with Xanax. I lost two weeks. I don't know what happened or what I did. I lost my wallet, and then for the last week, lots of people have been calling me and showing up at my door, but I don't know who they are. I'm afraid of what I did. I'm afraid of benzos."

I thought of Derrick and reflected how Nadia could easily have ended up another victim. We came up with a plan to control her use. She agreed to increase her dose of buprenorphine and to apply to go into a women's-only treatment centre as soon as a bed became available.

Mixing benzos and opioids is not new. Valium was the first billion-dollar drug; it was brought to North America and marketed by Arthur Sackler in the 1960s. Benzos have an important role to play in alcohol withdrawal and, if used judiciously, are very effective anti-anxiety agents. But the same phenomenon that brought us the opioid epidemic — the use of pharmaceuticals to try to eradicate all suffering — has also brought us a mini-epidemic of benzos. The death rate from benzos has been rising for years.

Ben fixed his eyes on me and said loudly, "I can't come down on my diazepam. I can't. Please, Doc, please."

I had been working with Ben for several months to get him off his dose of diazepam, but he was fighting me at every turn. "I need it. I'm going to have a heart attack if I go any lower," he said.

Ben was on methadone for a severe opioid addiction and had been started on diazepam more than ten years before by another doctor. He never felt it was enough and would buy extra tablets of Xanax and Ativan on the street. I told him we had to get him off diazepam, slowly and safely, but completely off.

The intoxication of benzos leads people to make bad decisions, get into fights, and crash their cars. One patient told me they called benzos "war pills" in jail, because guys would get into bad fights when they were high. Early in medical school, we studied a legal case of a patient in Germany who left the operating room with benzos in his body, crashed his car, and died. Michael Jackson allegedly died from a combination of the anesthetic agent propofol and two benzodiazepines (midazolam and lorazepam). Benzos sedate people — that's why they are used in the operating room. Combining sedatives usually leads to worse sedation, to a dangerous degree. Another case study in medical school described a young man who took his own life by combining Valium with large amounts of alcohol.

As opioid prescriptions have been rising, so have prescriptions for benzodiazepines. In 1996, 8.1 million Americans filled a benzo prescription. By 2013, that number was 13.5 million, and their doses went up as well; the total quantity of benzodiazepines prescribed in the United States tripled during that time. The higher the dose of opioid and the higher the dose of benzo, the more likely a patient is to suffer from falls, cognitive impairment, sedation, or death.[9]

When I first met Ben, he would stagger into the clinic unsteadily, he would miss appointments, he was confused, and his speech was sometimes slurred. It was alarming. I wasn't sure what was making him like this, but I had an idea. I knew he was at high risk of death.

A study in North Carolina showed that patients receiving benzos and opioids were ten times more likely to overdose than those receiving opioids alone.[10] A Canadian study showed that in six out of ten overdose deaths among patients prescribed opioids for pain, the patients were also on benzodiazepines.[11] The 2016 CDC opioid guidelines explicitly discussed the risks of combining the two classes of medicine, telling doctors to avoid the lethal combination. In August 2016, the FDA added this black-box warning to both classes: "FDA is warning patients and their caregivers about the serious risks of taking opioids along with benzodiazepines or other central nervous system (CNS) depressant medicines, including alcohol. Serious risks include unusual dizziness or light-headedness, extreme sleepiness, slowed or difficult breathing, coma, and death. These risks result because both opioids and benzodiazepines impact the CNS, which controls most of the functions of the brain and body."[12]

Even with the statistics and the warnings, the lure of benzos is so strong for patients like Ben. But despite his cravings, he agreed to try to reduce his consumption of benzos. Over a few months, we slowly decreased his dosages and he slowly started to wake up. One day, a few weeks after he had come off the diazepam, he sat upright in the chair facing me, the lake and mountain photo behind me, and said simply, "I feel like I've woken up. I had no idea how fucking out of it I was."

Stimulants like cocaine, speed, and crystal meth have the opposite effects of benzodiazepines. They wake you up, give you energy and focus, make you anxious, and cause insomnia. Too often they lead to panic attacks, paranoia, psychosis, heart attacks, or strokes. Before the opioid epidemic, cocaine was the drug that resulted in the most emergency room visits, usually for chest pain, heart attacks, panic attacks, or psychosis.

Something has been happening to cocaine use in America. It declined between 2006 and 2010 as supply decreased and the price went up. But this trend has reversed since 2010. Cocaine is found in more and more overdose cases. There was a huge jump in overdose deaths involving cocaine in the United States between 2015 and 2017. In 2016 there were more than ten thousand overdose deaths involving cocaine; in 2017, there were over fourteen thousand.[13] One reason this is happening is that people are using cocaine at the same time as heroin and fentanyl. This may or may not be intentional, as sometimes fentanyl is a contaminant in cocaine — something we've found with our drug-testing machine.

When I noted that Steve's urine test showed amphetamines, he said, "I took some bad speed, and I was just pacing around my room, shouting and screaming. My face was all messed up. I was real mad."

Cocaine and speed are the most common street drugs I find in my patients' urine drug tests once they are on a stable dose of opioid substitution. The opioid substitution takes care of the opioids, but the stimulants are still out there.

Steve struggled more than most with injecting cocaine. "It really messes with your mind. All you care about is your next hit. I've let everything else slide — my apartment is a mess."

I knew from my addiction textbooks that cocaine overwhelms the brain with massively high levels of dopamine, then leaves the brain devastated like a post-tsunami landscape. Hence the term *crash* for the feeling after cocaine intoxication.

A few months later, Steve stopped using cocaine and things got a lot better. "I didn't realize how bad things were until I stopped," he told me. "Now I don't get as depressed, I can think, I actually enjoy doing stuff."

A big problem in addiction medicine is that we don't have very good treatments for cocaine and speed use. There are counselling and group therapy, but it's hard for people to attend this treatment when they are actively using. People will often stop using after a bad experience, which was Steve's motivation, or if they run out of money or if they go to jail. Getting them into stable housing helps, as does a stay at rehab. Some patients stop using as a result of the deals made in the drug-court system.

One study showed that giving ADHD medication called lisdexamfetamine to patients who are using both opioids and cocaine can help them reduce their cocaine use, but for now there is no methadone for cocaine users.[14] At one point, it looked like a vaccine would block the ability of cocaine to get into the brain, but the studies never worked out. Ronald Crystal, the Cornell physician who led a cocaine vaccine study, narrowly escaped death while climbing Mount Everest in April 2018. The results from his study are still pending.

But even a vaccine or a new pill would not be a complete solution. To treat addiction, we have to treat the whole patient, the whole person, their mind and body. We have to meet them where they are and ask them about their needs, priorities, and values. Sometimes they want help to stop smoking crack; sometimes they don't. Sometimes they have a pretty good place to live, but they can't control their anxiety symptoms. The holy grail for decades has been to link addiction care with mental health care with medical care for complications of drug use such as infectious diseases. It sounds like a lofty goal, but it's not. Caring for the whole person should be the default. If we can provide good care to this generation, we may be able to prevent addiction from spreading down to the next. We may be able to break the cycle.

CHAPTER 11
Breaking the Cycle

Longfellow Elementary School in Oakland, California, was closed down in 2004. It lives on in addiction mythology because it is the setting of a famous exchange between Nancy Reagan and a fourth grader who, during a discussion about the dangers of drug use in 1984, asked the First Lady, "But Mrs. Reagan, what should I say if someone offers me drugs, if someone wants to give them to me?"

"Just say NO!" she responded. "That's all you have to do. Just say no and walk away."[1]

However history judges the Just Say No campaign, we can say with certainty that to end the opioid epidemic, we need to prevent it from infecting the next generation, the fourth graders of today. Childhood and adolescence are the periods of greatest risk. The brain does not fully mature until a person reaches their early twenties. By age twenty-one, it's getting there, but young people often do not possess adult-level judgment. It is the prefrontal cortex, the region that governs judgment and self-regulation, that is last to fully develop.

Young people may have difficulty regulating their emotions, indulge in increased risk-taking and novelty-seeking, and be more sensitive to peer pressure. Their brains are also more malleable and will develop differently in the presence of a drug. Imagine a young man, filled with strong emotions and trying to learn to deal with challenging experiences, who uses cannabis every day from the age of fourteen. Ideally, that young man will learn to cope with those feelings and achieve his goals using healthy coping skills like exercising, spending time with his family and friends, and working through his feelings. If, instead, he gets high every time he feels a strong emotion and every time he faces a challenge, his brain and his tool kit of coping strategies will be radically changed and weakened by the time he reaches adulthood.

The more young people reduce their use of drugs and alcohol, the better for their brains, for their future well-being, and for society. A truism in addiction medicine is that the later a person starts drinking alcohol, smoking, or using drugs, the lower the risk they will become addicted. Nora Volkow and her colleagues have used the later development of the prefrontal cortex to justify leaving the drinking age in the United States at twenty-one. They pointed out that this change led to a significant reduction in highway deaths. They even made a case for increasing the legal smoking age to twenty-one.[2] When cannabis legalization was pushed through in Canada, public health experts advocated for a legal age of twenty-one to twenty-five, while the cannabis industry argued for eighteen. In the end, the age was set at eighteen.

While most teens like to take risks, they are not all thoughtlessly reckless. Teens all over the developed world are becoming more responsible. Overall, teen drug and alcohol use has been declining in recent years. The biggest drop has been in smoking. A generation ago in the United States, 10 percent of fourteen-year-olds were daily smokers. That means about two or three students in every ninth-grade class smoked every day. Now that number is down to less than 1 percent. And as smoking has declined, so has other drug use. Teens are trying alcohol later. They are drinking less, getting drunk much less often, and abstaining more often. In Sweden, the rate of complete abstention from drugs and alcohol rose from one in ten in 2003 to three in ten by 2015.[3] Critically, teen use of opioids in the United States is declining after hitting a peak in 2007.

In 2017, the National Institute on Drug Abuse's massive Monitoring the Future survey asked more than forty-three thousand high-school students about their drug and alcohol use, and the news was mostly good.[4] In a video on the NIDA website, Nora Volkow commented, "This year we have very good news, because overall we are observing that the pattern of drug use among teenagers in the United States has continued to go down, and it is most notable, for example, in the case of opioid drugs."[5]

I had seen some media coverage of the survey when the results were released, so I looked in detail to see if the data were really that good. The use of heroin and other opioids by twelfth graders had fallen from the worst years, the period from 2003 to 2009. Use of the opioid Vicodin fell from 10.5 percent in 2003 to 1.7 percent by 2018 among twelfth graders. Nicotine levels were also at the lowest level ever seen. Overall, alcohol use continued to decline and the rate of binge drinking among twelfth graders was down to half its peak level, which occurred in 1997. Marijuana use and vaping, by contrast, continued to remain high; indeed, they were seen to increase.[6]

And as most drug and alcohol use has declined, so has antisocial behaviour like getting into fights and bullying. Other risky behaviour, such as drunk driving, has declined, and teens have become less sexually promiscuous. Between 1991 and 2015, America's teenage birth rate crashed by two-thirds.[7]

These are positive trends. We need to understand them to nurture this progress. There are a number of theories about why this is happening; there are likely several factors working together. One factor is the overall decline in smoking. As smoking rates have declined, many fewer teens are exposed to smoking and become regular users. Nicotine exposure may prime the brain to be more susceptible to other drugs, and learning to break the rules to smoke may lead many teens to break other rules and experiment with other drugs.

Another major change is parenting. American parents on average spent forty-one minutes a day looking after their children in 1965, a number that more than doubled to eighty-eight minutes by 2012. Families are also smaller, so children are getting more focused attention from their parents.[8] Fathers are playing a larger role in the family, and their own tobacco use is down. Teens are hanging out less in groups late at night, partly because of changing parental expectations and partly because their internet use has increased. Attitudes against smoking and teen drinking have shifted and become stricter.

But an improvement is not good enough for the parents of addicted children. Every day in North America, far too many young people pick up their first joint or pop their first opioid, setting themselves up for addiction and death. Communities that have been hit hard are looking for solutions. One night in November 2018, I drove to a small town outside of Ottawa that is struggling with a spike in overdose deaths and is looking to a program called Planet Youth for solutions. The meeting was held in an old stone church. A late-autumn rain fell outside as cold air seeped into the ancient building. The pews were stuffed with community activists and parents. Down the aisle from me sat a police officer in full uniform, leaning forward intently and writing notes in his small notebook. Everyone was hungry for solutions.

Planet Youth is an organization that was founded in Iceland to prevent teens from initiating substance use. In the 1990s, Iceland had a serious problem with substance abuse among teens. It had the highest rate of teen drinking in Europe, and it also had a high rate of teen marijuana use and smoking initiation. Health and addiction researchers promoted the idea of letting teens get high on the euphoria of exercise and self-expression rather than on illicit drugs. They looked at surveys showing the difference between teens who had problematic substance use and those who didn't and found a few important protective factors. The kids without problems were more likely to be involved in organized sports three or four times per week, spent more time with their parents, felt cared about at school, and were not out late in the evenings.

Using this information, a lot was done to educate parents about the importance of physical activity for kids and the importance of spending quality time with their kids. The government made physical activity for youth easier and cheaper. It created subsidies and encouraged youth to join teams. You don't find Icelandic teens loitering around after school anymore; they are all doing something active or creative. Interestingly, a curfew was also put into place for teens. So instead of hanging out and looking for trouble, teens were either participating in sports or at home with their families. The results were incredible. Alcohol use, cannabis use, and smoking all declined dramatically.

That night, the Icelandic researcher Alfgeir Kristjansson stood in front of the immense church organ and told the story of Iceland's victory against an epidemic of drug and alcohol use. He spelled out the best way to end an epidemic of addiction: preventing or delaying the recruitment of new users. This is the heart of primary prevention, the cheapest and most long-lasting type of intervention in medicine and public health. Prevention is cheap; treatment is expensive. The challenge is to find prevention strategies that work. Professor Kristjansson said that the key to the Icelandic model was working on the whole peer group rather than trying to change the behaviour of individual teens. Teens have a very hard time resisting peer pressure, but if you change the behaviour of the whole group, you take peer pressure out of the equation.

Think of a child or teen as a character in a drama, in the middle of two other characters: their family and their peer group. Their decisions take place in two key settings: at school and at after-school leisure activities. Trying to change the child without changing their context is very hard.

In the afterword to *Dreamland*, Sam Quinones reflected on the links between parenting, community, and preventing another opioid epidemic. He wondered if keeping boys inside, bouncing off the walls, and then treating them with ADHD medications is part of the problem. He wrote, "Keeping kids cooped up seems to me connected to the idea that we can avoid pain, avoid danger." He recalled playing outdoors in the park constantly during his own childhood, whereas now that park is empty. He bemoaned that "we have built isolation into our suburbs and called it prosperity," before concluding, "I believe more strongly than ever that the antidote to heroin is community."[9]

While the road to addiction is different for every young person, there are many commonalities. The risk factors for youth substance use are divided into four domains: the community, the peer group, the family, and individual. In the community, violence, poverty, easy access to alcohol and drugs, and norms that favour substance use are most significant. That's why laws that limit the opening hours and density of stores selling alcohol or other legal drugs can be very effective. Reducing norms that favour access to opioid prescriptions also reduces the chance that young people will access opioids.

Within peer groups, substance use among peers and the attitudes of peers toward drugs are important. Parent who know their kids' friends and know those friends' parents can create a community where the well-being of children and teens is paramount. Communities are made up of families; thus the alcohol and drug use of each family influences what is seen as normal in a community. Parents who have strict norms against alcohol and drug use can influence their kids and the friends of their kids in healthy ways.[10]

Both the quality and quantity of parenting matters. Good attachment to at least one parent is the foundation of a healthy emotional life. Good attachment grows from consistent care, warmth, affection, fair and consistent discipline, adequate supervision, and never threatening to abandon a child. Teens need parents just as much as young children do; even if they say they don't want their parents around, they need their parents around. In a sense, parents should be like "potted plants"[11] — present at home and in the teen's life, but unobtrusive until the teen needs help.

The psychologist Lisa Damour has written about the research supporting just the presence of a parent in the same space as their teen: "One friend of mine quietly folds laundry each evening in the den where her teenagers watch TV. They enjoy one another's company without any pressure to make conversation. Another routinely accepts his daughter's invitation to work or read nearby while she sits and does her homework."[12]

Teens feel more stressed and have worse health when they routinely come home to an empty home and do not eat meals with their parents. Our children need us as a dependable foundation, from which they can build their own life, explore the world, and assert their independence. Damour contended that teenagers "like toddlers, feel most at ease when their folks balance active engagement with detached availability."[13]

But parents also need to talk to their teens and their younger children. One lesson from the Iceland program that Professor Kristjansson highlighted was the recognition that alcohol is a gateway drug. Parents and policy-makers alike were concerned about the state of mind of young kids when they started to drink, particularly when they began to binge drink to the point of intoxication. Drunk teens make very bad decisions, including the decision to use other drugs. Stemming underage drinking is a key to reducing all drug use, including opioid use. Knowing how and when to have productive conversations with kids about substance use is a critical, and sometimes neglected, skill for any parent.

On May 13, 2013, the U.S. Substance Abuse and Mental Health Services Administration (SAMHSA) launched a prevention program for underage drinking called "Talk. They Hear You." A public-service ad began with a woman's voice laying out the background: "Underage drinking is a serious problem with severe consequences. We know that children who drink alcohol are more likely to use drugs, get bad grades, engage in risky sexual activity, and even suffer injury or death."

At the launch event, SAMHSA administrator Pamela Hyde cited research showing that more than 80 percent of children said their parents were the leading influence in their decision to use alcohol. She said that interviews with children showed that most six-year-olds knew alcohol is only for adults, but between ages nine and thirteen, more kids thought drinking was okay for them and some began to use alcohol. While most parents want to talk to their kids about substance use, few know how to do so. Thus, the program launched an app that parents can use to practise having a productive conversation with their children about drinking. Parents use a "parent avatar" and then practise having the conversation, with feedback designed to make them more effective at having productive conversations about alcohol use. Pamela Hyde emphasized to parents, "When you talk, your children do listen."

During the launch, a youth advocate named Michelle Nicholas told the story of how, on May 15, 2011, three of her friends died in a drunk-driving crash. "No one should have to go through what my community has gone through," she said. She urged parents not to avoid the issue until it's too late. "Parents, please talk to your kids about underage drinking. You won't ever regret telling your kids to be safe."

Parents and teachers need to be particularly alert to children who have a predisposition to developing substance use problems. A child with ADHD by definition has worse impulse control and is therefore at higher risk of using substances. Children who are naturally sad, irritable, passive, or withdrawn, or those who have low self-esteem, poor social skills, or poor social problem-solving skills are more likely to turn to substances to numb their feelings and increase their comfort in social settings.[14]

Parents need to be alert to the warning signs of early drug use. First, they can ask their children about substance use, but if their children are not ready to open up, they can look for the expected signs, such as new or worsening irritability, isolation, withdrawal from family activities, decline in school performance, or dropping of social activities or extracurriculars such as team sports. Always needing money, to the extent of stealing money or shoplifting, is also a clear warning sign. Blackouts can be caused by intoxication or withdrawal.

The child's primary-care provider or pediatrician can play an important role in identifying problematic substance use and can work with the child and parents to make healthy choices. The American Academy of Pediatrics recommends screening for the use of alcohol, tobacco, and other drugs annually, beginning as early as eleven years of age. The academy recognizes that "compared to people in other age groups, adolescents are at the highest risk for experiencing health problems related to substance use."[15]

In 2017 SAMHSA published a booklet for parents titled *Keeping Youth Drug Free*. The guide included a number of tips, including "establish and maintain good communication with your child," "get involved in your child's life," and "be a positive role model."[16] The advice echoes that from Planet Youth, the program developed in Iceland, such as the importance of giving young people opportunities to pursue "interesting activities to keep them busy, happy, and productive."[17] It focuses on the importance of the peer group and encourages parents to help shape their child's peer group and also to get to know the other kids and parents in the community, advising that as a parent you should "help your child develop healthy, wholesome relationships with other happy kids and you will make it less likely that she will turn to drugs or alcohol for comfort."[18]

The U.S. federal government's Office of Adolescent Health also listed the importance of treating pain cautiously, specifically to prevent opioid use among teens. The office warns, "Adolescents often are initially exposed to opioids through prescriptions; dentist prescriptions account for 31 percent of adolescents' first exposure to opioids."[19]

The risks of opioid exposure from dental procedures was confirmed by a study from Stanford published in December 2018, which showed that among almost fifteen thousand young people prescribed opioids by dentists, 5.8 percent were diagnosed with opioid abuse in the twelve months after the initial prescription, while only 0.4 percent of a control group that was not given opioids went on to be diagnosed with opioid abuse. This is a very significant difference, as all those additional cases of addiction could have been prevented by not prescribing opioids to youth in the first place.[20]

But even well-meaning parents feel overwhelmed when confronted by drug use in their children. "I think my daughter is using drugs," Carlos said to me one afternoon as the hot July sun shone outside.

Carlos had himself experimented with cocaine and cannabis as a teenager. He also drank heavily and went on to develop a serious drinking problem. However, when he came to see me, he had been sober for ten years and was vigilant about looking for signs that his teenage daughter, Kelsey, was heading down the same path.

"She doesn't talk to me anymore, she stays out late, and if I ground her, it doesn't make any difference," he said. "She tells me I'm stupid and I don't understand her, but I think I do understand her. I've been there. Last week she was confused, she looked horrible, she wasn't herself. She said she was just tired, that she hadn't eaten all day, but I don't know — something doesn't seem right."

I talked to Carlos about the other warning signs, about talking openly with Kelsey, about being a potted plant. He agreed to bring her in so she could talk to me on my own.

When Kelsey came in a few weeks later, I could tell she hadn't come willingly. Her mouth was pursed; she kept looking away; she looked sad; she looked tired. Her father's instincts had been right. Something was going on.

I made some small talk, trying to get through the wall I sensed. After a few minutes, I used a teen substance use questionnaire called CRAFFT that I had learned about at a conference in Boston a few years earlier. I asked Kelsey if she had ever ridden in a car driven by someone who was high, if she ever used substances to relax, if she had ever used alone, if she forgot things she had done while using, if family or friends had ever told her to cut down, and if she had ever gotten into trouble while using. She told me she had been in a car with a boy who'd had too much to drink and that she did like to use weed to relax sometimes. I asked her about opioids, listing them all: Tylenol 3, Percocet, OxyContin, dilaudid, fentanyl. She looked up when I said the word *fentanyl* — there was fear in her eyes.

"I would never take fentanyl. That stuff kills."

"What about the other opioids? What about pills?" I asked.

Yes, she had taken Percocet, she admitted, her voice hushed, her eyes fixed intently on the floor. "It was only a few times."

I waited a moment, but she didn't speak. Then I suppressed my brain's impulse to press her for more details, to confront her with all the dangers of opioid use, and to tell her about the risk of overdose, of addiction, and of death. I knew if I pushed too hard, she would shut down and never open up like this again.

"I'm not going to do it again," she said quietly, after a long pause. "I overdosed and went to the ER last week. I'm too scared to do that again."

I thought about her father. If he had not raised his concerns with me, Kelsey would still be carrying this secret alone.

The ventilation system hummed through the silence, and as the warm sunlight shone on her face, I could see little beads of sweat mixing with the tears forming around her eyes. As the tears flowed down her cheeks, I sighed. I was relieved to have gotten through to her, but I was also afraid. Kelsey had almost died; her life could have been another link in the chain of death dragging down families and communities across the continent.

And the risks to Kelsey weren't over yet. I knew that a teenager's desire to stop using, even more than an adult's, is not enough. She needed every tool, every weapon we could muster, to combat opioids. To save kids like Kelsey, we need to make changes fast. We need to be Iceland; we need to be brave; we need to think of every risk and every technology; we need to spend money; we need to take every step we can toward a better future.

Conclusion: Ten Steps Toward a Better Future

In March 1988, Gary Henderson, a professor of pharmacology at the University of California in Davis, saw the future. He saw that the "future drugs of abuse will be synthetics rather than plant products"; he saw that they would be extremely potent and would be designed by chemists in drug labs. In particular, he warned the readers of *The Journal of Forensic Sciences* about fentanyl. "It is important to remember that any chemist who is successful in achieving even a nominal yield of a few hundred milligrams of any of the potent fentanyls has at his disposal many millions of individual doses of a synthetic heroin substitute," he wrote in a paper titled "Designer Drugs: Past History and Future Prospects." While fentanyl had been detected predominantly in California in the mid-1980s, he warned that "fentanyls could reappear at any time and would probably not be restricted to California."[1] What is surprising about the thirty years since Professor Henderson made his warning is not that fentanyl has inundated North America, but that it took so long to arrive.

When the writer Patrick Lane went to rehab for his alcohol use disorder over Christmas one year, he looked around at his fellow travellers. Next to him was a young woman, singing softly with her eyes half closed. He wrote, "She's only a step away from a room of crack pipes and seizures, a broken bottle in the back seat of a car, a needle hanging from her arm. She's only a step away from being clean, too, but that's a big step, and I don't know if she'll take it."[2] Was the prescription-opioid epidemic and the subsequent wave of fentanyl deaths inevitable? Are we now trapped in an endless cycle of despair and relapse spreading down through subsequent generations? Or can we beat the epidemic?

There are many ways to get drug policy wrong; there are many steps we should not take. One wrong step would be to introduce harsher penalties for people who use drugs. That would push them further underground and further from treatment and recovery. Another wrong step would be to put more resources into short-term, abstinence-based rehabs when we know that long-term medications and harm reduction are more effective. And finally, we do not need more stigma regarding addiction or addiction treatments; we do not need fear, and we do not need moral panic.

Too many lives have been lost. When the epidemic ends, it won't be soon enough — but the end will come. Just look at what has happened with HIV. Before fentanyl there was heroin, and before heroin there was HIV/AIDS. HIV spread from chimpanzees and gorillas to humans in the Congo in the early twentieth century. Cases slowly spread out of Africa, concentrating in gay men and people who used injection drugs. After the CDC recognized the disease in 1981, it continued to spread. HIV became a moral panic and a true global pandemic. Globally, new HIV infections peaked at 3.5 million new cases per year in 1997 and deaths at two million a year in 2005.

There are now more than thirty-seven million people living with HIV, and people are still dying. Over thirty-two million have died from HIV.[3] The disease blossomed from a few cases in the jungle to a global pandemic. The fear, stigma, and hysteria of the 1980s and 1990s have largely been forgotten, but there was a real moral panic in North America and around the world. A famous photo from the early days shows a group of men holding a banner as they march. The banner reads "A.I.D.S.: WE NEED RESEARCH, NOT HYSTERIA."

HIV is still with us, but we are beating back the epidemic. As research replaced hysteria and advocacy supplanted ignorance, scientists and clinicians made previously unfathomable strides forward. Effective medications were introduced in the mid-1990s, and public health officials systematically looked for ways to stop the epidemic. First it was the ABC strategy: abstinence, be faithful, use condoms. Then clean needles and addiction supports were added to the mix. Then governments stepped up and funded global treatment. Then early treatment was shown to reduce transmission. Then pre-exposure prophylaxis was added. Public-awareness campaigns, the internet, phone support, and apps: everything was mobilized.

A goal for those trying to eradicate any disease is to find a vaccine to prevent it in the first place. After the HIV virus was identified in 1983, officials announced that a vaccine would be only two years away. But developing effective vaccines is difficult. Every few years, a new HIV vaccine has been announced amid great fanfare. When tested, however, these vaccines have been found to work not much better than placebos.

As we saw with the cocaine vaccine, developing effective vaccines for addictive drugs is also very difficult. Pharmaceutical companies could make a fortune selling vaccines for nicotine to the hundreds of millions of smokers around the world. Kim Janda is a chemist at the Scripps Research Institute in La Jolla, California, who has worked on vaccines for nearly every addictive substance, beginning in the 1980s. "I'd love to be able to tell you I could create a vaccine against alcohol but I'm not that clever," he said to an interviewer in 2014.[4]

In the past decade, Dr. Janda has worked on a heroin vaccine. Such a vaccine could change the course of the opioid epidemic. It could work by stimulating the immune system to recognize heroin and other opioids as foreign and therefore block them from entering the brain. This could take away the high, reduce relapse rates, and reduce the risk of overdose. In 2013 Janda and his team reported that the vaccine reduced drug-seeking behaviour and relapse in rats.[5] "We had to train the immune system to recognize heroin as being foreign; furthermore we had to train the immune system such that we got a very high response to a particular drug of abuse," Janda explained in a video for Scripps.

In February 2018, Scripps announced that the vaccine had passed another milestone. A team led by Candy Hwang found that using the tetanus toxoid carrier protein resulted in the optimal vaccine and that that formulation protected against otherwise lethal doses of heroin. "The heroin vaccine is one step closer to clinical evaluation," Dr. Hwang said in a press release.[6]

In December 2018, the Virginia Commonwealth University announced that its researchers were testing the Scripps opioid vaccine. "If a person injects heroin or fentanyl after they have been vaccinated, those antibodies are there to capture the drugs in the bloodstream, which should prevent people from getting high," said Matthew Banks, professor in the Department of Pharmacology and Toxicology in the Virginia Commonwealth University School of Medicine.[7]

As work on the Scripps vaccine continues, researchers at the Walter Reed Army Institute of Research are testing other anti-heroin and anti-oxycodone vaccines. The maker of naloxone overdose kits (sold under the brand name Narcan) is Opiant Pharmaceuticals. In 2016, Opiant licensed OPNT005, the heroin vaccine developed by Walter Reed, acquiring exclusive development and commercialization rights. Walter Reed scientists, with collaborators from the State University of New York Upstate Medical University, were then given funding by the National Institutes of Health in late 2018 to conduct clinical trials of OPNT005.[8]

Opiant is also working on new antidotes for fentanyl overdoses. The U.S. Biomedical Advanced Research and Development Authority is concerned about weaponized fentanyl. Imagining scenarios such as the hostage rescue operation in Moscow, where aerosolized carfentanil deployed by security services killed more than a hundred innocent people, they have entered into a contract potentially worth $4.6 million with Opiant to develop a single-dose antidote to fentanyl. Opiant also received a $7.4 million grant from NIDA to develop the fentanyl antidote. The company is investigating a nasal form of nalmefene, a drug which "is five times more potent than naloxone."[9]

Nalmefene was approved by the FDA for use in an injectable form in 1995, but was discontinued in 2008. It has a longer duration of action compared with naloxone, and it causes less fluctuation in a subject's level of consciousness. Whether the intranasal formulation will be safer or more effective than existing naloxone kits remains to be seen, but it may offer another overdose prevention tool in the near future.[10]

Epidemics can be beaten, but it takes a rich mixture of scientific breakthroughs, advocacy, education, and brave policy to do so. We have to figure out what works and then scale it up rapidly. We have to shed tradition and superstition. We have to involve young people to try to break transmission to the next generation. There is still so far to go in eradicating HIV, as science has done with smallpox, but we have already come so far.

The news about the tobacco epidemic is rather different. For North America, tobacco is a very good news story. Driven by science and employing the same creative mixture of policies employed against HIV, we have reduced smoking rates from a peak of 42 percent of U.S. adults in the 1960s to 14 percent in 2017. Half of smokers die from a tobacco-related cause, so this is an important accomplishment. But there is still work to be done, as there remain more than thirty million smokers in the United States.

While there has been success in reducing smoking rates in North America, global smoking rates have barely changed in the past twenty years. As their profits have been squeezed in Europe and North America, tobacco companies have shifted their focus to Asia and Africa. More than a billion people smoke worldwide, and the death rate has continued to climb. Today, more than seven million deaths a year can be attributed to tobacco use. There are signs that, like the tobacco epidemic, the opioid epidemic is spreading abroad as Big Pharma aggressively markets opioids in countries with historically low rates of opioid use.

As well as encouraging smoking in countries outside of North America and Europe, the tobacco industry has tried to circumvent anti-smoking laws by introducing vaping devices marketed as healthier alternatives to tobacco combustion. Young teenagers ask their parents for vaping devices now because all their friends have one, showing, once again, the power of the peer group. Vaping devices, also known as e-cigarettes, are sold with very little regulation and contain carcinogens and additives with unknown long-term health impacts. The e-cigarette industry is booming and is even working with the cannabis industry to create synergies that may very well fuel the addictions of the next generation.

On December 17, 2018, the Monitoring the Future Program released an alarming press release that began, "Increases in adolescent vaping from 2017 to 2018 were the largest ever recorded in the past 43 years for any adolescent substance use outcome in the U.S."[11] Vaping is on the rise. I have seen it among my patients, heard it from concerned parents, and driven by dozens of vape stores as every strip mall and city block has added another outlet. And all these stores have meant more access for young people. Monitoring the Future reported that the number of twelfth graders in the survey who said they had vaped nicotine in the previous thirty days almost doubled in a year, from 11 percent in 2017 to 21 percent in 2018. No substance had ever become so popular so quickly among American teens. Vaping cannabis also increased from 4.9 percent to 7.5 percent among twelfth graders, and was at an unbelievably high 7 percent among tenth graders — children as young as fifteen.[12]

The lead author of this Monitoring the Future study is Richard Miech from the University of Michigan in Ann Arbor. "Vaping is making substantial inroads among adolescents, no matter the substance vaped," he said in a press release. He lamented that vaping has been eroding the gains made in reducing nicotine use among adolescents, concluding that "the policies and procedures in place to prevent youth vaping clearly haven't worked."[13] The epidemic of vaping-related hospitalizations in 2019 across North America confirmed that public health experts were right to be concerned about the unknown risks of vaping.

So will the future of the opioid epidemic look like that of HIV or tobacco, or of smallpox, which was completely eradicated in 1980? If we have an idea what kind of future we want for ourselves and our children, we have a much better chance of getting there. We know the policies that work; we see them work in Europe and in small pockets of North America. Some policies can be changed with the stroke of a pen, some will take years and a cultural shift, and others will require major redistributions of wealth and changes to the social safety net.

The situation reminds me of the Monty Python skit "Great Actors," in which John Cleese plays an actor who is learning lines for the theatre. He says, "I don't want you to get the impression it's just a question of the number of words. I mean, getting them in the right order is just as important. Old Peter Hall used to say to me, 'They're all there, Eddie. Now we've got to get them in the right order.'"[14] We have all the policies at our fingertips; we just need to implement them. Of course, this is harder than learning lines, but listing the steps we need to take will get us on the right path. Here's where I think we should be heading.

First, we need to make sure everyone has access to effective treatment. When someone has a heart attack in North America, they will get essentially the same treatment no matter which emergency room they land in. They will get supportive care and medications, and they will be seen by a cardiologist. But when someone lands in an emergency room or in a clinic with opioid addiction, there is no telling what will happen next. That must change. There must be implementation of standard opioid treatment guidelines everywhere. In Ontario, this is being driven by a visionary program called META:PHI (Mentoring, Education, and Clinical Tools for Addiction: Primary Care–Hospital Integration), which is making it easier for hospitals to immediately start patients on opioid substitution and connect them to rapid-access addiction medicine clinics in the community. In the United States, this means free and universal access to these treatments.

Second, we need more and better treatments. Methadone and buprenorphine work, but we can do better. Injectable naltrexone should be used more, and it should be available in Canada. Injectable and implantable buprenorphine needs to be affordable and widely available. The use of injectable opioids should be scaled up. Where conventional treatment is hard to access, we should build an evidence base so we can understand the effect of providing a safe supply of opioids, such as Mark Tyndall's opioid vending machines. Vaccine research must be supported and expedited. Insurance plans, regulators, and governments must improve access to treatment free of ideological and stigma-driven bias. Addictions are medical conditions, and governments and insurance companies should never justify the denial of coverage or treatment.

Third, needle exchanges and naloxone kits are evidence based and cost effective. They should be free and universally available. They are among the most cost-effective interventions in public health. Paraphernalia laws should be changed across the board to remove any charges associated with carrying drug-use paraphernalia. These laws drive users to reuse dirty equipment, which results in more HIV and hepatitis C transmission. Naloxone kits have been shown to reduce overdose death rates and have already saved thousands of lives.

Fourth, supervised consumption sites are also evidence based and cost effective. Everyone who needs it should be able to access a supervised consumption site twenty-four hours a day, and the culture among people who use drugs needs to change so that they both know and choose not to use outside of a supervised consumption site and never use alone. Myths about injection sites need to be dispelled. They do not encourage drug use or ruin neighbourhoods; instead, they prevent overdose, create a culture of safety among people who use drugs, and connect active users to addiction treatment and primary health care services such as HIV and hepatitis C testing, contraception, and other preventive care services.

Fifth, more must be done to prevent overdoses. A device that could detect overdoses and auto-inject naloxone is technologically feasible and has been floated by researchers at the University of New Mexico. Such a device would detect if a wearer stops breathing and inject doses of naloxone until the wearer begins to breathe normally. At the same time, an alarm could sound or a signal could be sent to emergency medical services. In January 2019, researchers from the University of Washington in Seattle published a proof of concept of software that converts an ordinary smartphone into a short-range sonar system that can detect potential opioid overdoses by measuring respiration and gross motor movement. They proposed that smartphones used with such an application could provide another form of harm reduction by alerting friends, family, shelter personnel, or emergency medical services of a potential overdose requiring naloxone.[15]

Furthermore, simple and accessible tools that enable someone to test a drug to detect high levels of fentanyl or other dangerous contaminants may also save lives. Fentanyl test strips are available, but they tell us only if fentanyl is present, not how much or what types. Something that can be plugged into a smartphone and can list contaminants and quantify different drug levels would be a more useful tool.

Sixth, we should employ the Portuguese model to decriminalize non-violent drug crimes such as use, possession, and petty sale, and connect people to treatment and drug courts instead of prison. The aggressive criminalization of drug use is not a deterrent, and it hurts the most vulnerable members of society, who are more likely to suffer from drug-related disease and end up in prison and without appropriate addiction or other medical care. Connecting people to care could actually reduce a root cause of crime.

Seventh, treatment for HIV and hepatitis C should be universal and free for people who use drugs — and for the entire population, for that matter. Treatment for HIV has advanced to the point where a single pill a day controls the disease indefinitely. Yet despite this simple treatment, too many people in Canada and the United States do not have their HIV under control. There are a number of reasons for this: a lack of testing; a lack of care; and barriers, including financial barriers, to starting and continuing on HIV medications. Hepatitis C can now be cured with a relatively simple twelve-week course of medications. Treating hepatitis C among people who use drugs can prevent both the onward transmission of the disease and its expensive and painful consequences, such as cirrhosis and liver failure.

Eighth, treatment and harm-reduction services should be available in all correctional systems. Prisoners are at great risk for drug-related harms, including contraction of HIV and hepatitis C, if they do not have clean needles. Furthermore, providing prisoners with drug treatment options and naloxone kits can prevent overdose deaths upon their release from prison.

Ninth, we in the medical profession need to avoid over-prescribing addictive medications, including opioids, benzodiazepines, and stimulants. The tide is turning against opioids, but too many doctors continue to believe opioids should be used over the long term at high doses. Furthermore, exposure to even a short course of opioids can set someone on the path to addiction. We must not abandon patients with pain, but we must learn from the European and Japanese health care systems that treat pain in more holistic ways while using fewer opioids.

At the same time, we must insulate ourselves against future epidemics of over-prescribing, by building a firewall between clinicians and any business or individual that puts profits before health. This means ensuring regulators hold Big Pharma accountable for its marketing strategies. It also means that the clinical guidelines recommending medications should be developed by people without financial ties to industry. It means that the medical professions, hospitals, and universities should enforce codes of conduct that make the ethical choice the default choice, without stifling research or innovation.

And tenth, we need to prevent the transmission of the epidemic to the next generation by raising young people with healthy coping skills, good self-esteem, meaningful life choices, and hope for the future. We need to build a healthy generation of children who have strong attachment to their family members, especially their parents; a love of positive activities; peer groups that celebrate healthy choices; and a community that steers them away from early initiation into drugs and alcohol. We must ensure that the legalization of cannabis and the rising use of vaping devices do not undermine the work we have done to denormalize smoking and drug use in general.

There are many challenges, and these are ten hard steps to take, but there is hope. In August 2019, a report from the British Columbia Coroners Service showed a one-third reduction in overdose deaths in that province, compared with 2018.[16] The overdose rate in the United States is also beginning to fall. This may be the end of the beginning. Has a corner been turned? Are investments in treatment and harm reduction across North America beginning to pay off? Every epidemic, like every fire, has to end at some point. The number of new HIV infections in the world began to fall in the late 1990s, and the number of deaths from HIV began to fall a few years after that. We have contained epidemics of sudden acute respiratory syndrome (SARS) and, more recently, Ebola. The North American opioid epidemic has to end; we need to take only ten steps to help make that happen.

The first chapter of Beth Macy's book on the opioid epidemic, borrowing from Gore Vidal, is titled the "United States of Amnesia." It's a packed phrase, full of meaning and double entendre. It suggests that America forgets the past, that it paves over the past and builds a new suburban development. It also suggests that America is a place where people use pills to change how they feel, to quiet their pain, to forget. The medical profession has also forgotten; so have the regulators and the corporations out for profit. Doctors forgot about the risks of addiction, and we swung from zero opioids to too many opioids, pushed by Big Pharma, pulled by patient expectations, and free from our usual restraint. Ariana DeBoo sings that her drug dealer was her doctor, in the Macklemore song "Drug Dealer."

It was prescription opioids that started this epidemic. We must prevent the infection of the next generation. There will always be illicit drugs on the street and on the dark web, but most people won't buy and snort or inject a sketchy white or pink or purple powder if they've never tasted the fake bliss of prescription opioids.

This epidemic will leave us with a stronger and more robust addiction treatment system. Just a few years ago, there were no guidelines for treating opioid addiction in Canada or the United States; there were only guidelines telling us how to get people on to high doses of opioids. Just a few years ago, there was no widespread access to naloxone kits, there was no general knowledge about methadone or buprenorphine, and there were no safe injection sites. There was stigma, there was ignorance, there was pressure to prescribe, and there were threats from patients and incentives from Big Pharma. Everything is pushing in the opposite direction now.

I sometimes wonder what happened to Amber, after all these years. I think about that day in Toronto in 2009 when I first came face to face with overdose. I remember the frantic voice of the nurse, the smell of urine in the hallway, Amber's sterile hospital room, her long black hair on the pillow. I remember the blue sapphires under her nails, her unhurried breathing, how quickly she woke up from the naloxone. When she wasn't angry anymore, once the heroin had left her body, we talked about her going to treatment. After a few more days of IV antibiotics, she was discharged from the hospital.

Before she left, we made an appointment for her to follow up in the clinic to review the antibiotics for her heart. I didn't know how to say it, but I said something about starting methadone. "It might help you; it might help you stop using drugs. That's very important for your heart, to prevent you from getting the infection again," I said slowly, trying to find the right words.

As we looked toward her future on that last day, we didn't know that fentanyl was about to arrive, that things were going to get worse before they got better. Her boyfriend was still using. Without medication, without support, she could have relapsed so easily. On darker days I think that it could all have ended for her in a single instant. But when I see signs of change, people working together to make our world a little bit safer for Amber and for every person who struggles with addiction, I feel hope.

Amber could be in recovery now; she could be putting a buprenorphine tablet under her tongue every morning, waiting for that bitter lemon flavour to dissolve into nothing. She could have an apartment where she lives with her family. She could have kids by now. I wonder what they're like. They can't be older than eight or nine. I hope we meet one day.

Acknowledgements

My own patients have inspired me to write this book, through their stories and through their examples. I have changed all names and identifying details to protect their privacy. My teachers and colleagues have also been an inspiration, in both Toronto and Ottawa. Lisa Bromley, above all others, has been patient, kind, wise and brilliant. I am privileged to work with an amazing team of nurses, nurse practitioners, case managers, and pharmacists. Rob Boyd read an earlier draft of the manuscript and gave me much valued feedback. Special thanks to my agent, Lloyd Kelly, for believing in this project and providing me with valuable advice and guidance. I want to thank the whole team at Dundurn. The editing and guidance my editors at Dundurn provided me has been nothing short of outstanding. Finally, my family has supported me at every step, and I can't thank you enough for everything you have given me.

Notes

Introduction

1. Seth et al., "Overdose Deaths."
2. Bagnall, "Counterfeit Pills Carry Overdose Risk, Police, Health Officials Warn."
3. Quinones, *Dreamland*, 7.
4. Quinones, 8–9.
5. Wood, "Lessons from Canada," 1567.
6. This image is borrowed from the writings of David Courtwright. See *The Age of Addiction*, 2019.

Chapter 1: Knocking at the Door

1. Zuger, "General in the Drug War."
2. Crozier, "Introduction," xi.
3. Volkow, Koob, and McLellan, "Neurobiologic Advances," 368.
4. Compton, Jones, and Baldwin, "Nonmedical Prescription-Opioid Use."
5. Borg et al., "The Pharmacology of Opioids."
6. Strain, "Opioid Use Disorder."
7. Volkow and Warren, "Drug Addiction."
8. Marlowe, *How to Stop Time.*
9. Volkow, Koob, and McLellan, "Neurobiologic Advances."
10. Schuckit, "Treatment of Opioid Use Disorders."
11. Snyder, "Nora Volkow."
12. Kendler et al., "Genetic and Environmental Influences."
13. Chang, 2018.

14. Volkow and Warren, "Drug Addiction."
15. Strain, "Opioid Use Disorder."
16. Becker and Starrels, 2018.
17. Quoted in Scarborough, "The Opium Poppy," 11.
18. Barash et al., "Acute Amnestic Syndrome."

Chapter 2: The Story of Opium

1. Inglis, *Milk of Paradise.*
2. Inglis.
3. Aristotle, *On Sleep and Sleeplessness.*
4. Carter, "Dwale," 1623.
5. Power, "Early Anaesthesia," 6.
6. Booth, xi.
7. Dover, *Ancient Physician's Legacy*, 10–11.
8. Quoted in Inglis, *Milk of Paradise*, 206.
9. Museum of Health Care, "Mrs. Winslow's Soothing Syrup."
10. Quoted in Tinniswood, *His Invention So Fertile*, 36.
11. Tinniswood, *His Invention So Fertile.*
12. Inglis, *Milk of Paradise.*
13. Inglis, 186.
14. Inglis.
15. White and Callahan, "Addiction Medicine in America," 366.
16. Booth, 36.
17. Doyle, *The Adventures of Sherlock Holmes.*
18. Inglis, *Milk of Paradise.*
19. Gibbons, "Letheomania," 481.
20. Borg et al., "The Pharmacology of Opioids."
21. Inglis, *Milk of Paradise.*
22. Courtwright, *Dark Paradise*, 1.
23. Courtwright.
24. Inglis, *Milk of Paradise.*

Chapter 3: The Engine of the Epidemic

1. Quinones, *Dreamland.*
2. Quinones.

3. Porter and Jick, "Addiction Rare."
4. Leung et al., "A 1980 Letter."
5. Quinones, *Dreamland*, 108.
6. Quinones, *Dreamland*, 95.
7. Van Zee, "Promotion and Marketing of OxyContin."
8. Van Zee.
9. Quinones, *Dreamland.*
10. Van Zee, "Promotion and Marketing of OxyContin."
11. Macy, *Dopesick.*
12. Macy.
13. Frieden and Houry, "Reducing the Risks of Relief."
14. Zuger, "A Doctor's Guide."
15. Frieden and Houry, "Reducing the Risks of Relief."
16. Compton, Jones, and Baldwin, "Nonmedical Prescription-Opioid Use."
17. Quinones, *Dreamland.*
18. Strain, 2017.
19. Berthiaume, "U.S. Raises Alarm."

Chapter 4: Fentanyl Arrives

1. Berman, "Addiction Ground Zero."
2. British Columbia Coroners Service, *Illicit Drug Overdose Deaths.*
3. British Columbia Coroners Service, *Illicit Drug Overdose Deaths.*
4. "High Levels of Fentanyl."
5. Lupick, "Vancouver's Rate."
6. Howlett et al., "How Canada Got Addicted to Fentanyl."
7. Inglis, *Milk of Paradise*, 373.
8. Cooper, "How Chinese Gangs."
9. Romanish, "Fentanyl Info and Response," 10.
10. Wood, "Lessons from Canada."
11. NDEWS Coordinating Center, *Increase in Fentanyl Overdoses.*
12. Leins, "New Hampshire."
13. Stanley, Egan, and Van Aken, "Tribute to Dr. Paul A.J. Janssen."
14. Stanley, Egan, and Van Aken.
15. Henderson, "Designer Drugs."

16. United States Drug Enforcement Administration, *Fentanyl.*
17. Guan, Schneider, and Patterson, "'I Am in Pain!"
18. Mansfield and Jatoi, "Asphyxiation with a Fentanyl Patch."
19. Mansfield and Jatoi, Discussion section.
20. Arens et al., "Adverse Effects," Discussion section.
21. United States Drug Enforcement Administration, *Fentanyl*, 11.
22. United States Drug Enforcement Administration, 15.
23. United States Drug Enforcement Administration.
24. Port et al., "Intravenous Carfentanil."
25. Riches et al., "Analysis of Clothing and Urine."
26. "Demand Unexpectedly High."

Chapter 5: Explaining the Epidemic

1. Defoe, 27.
2. Defoe, 5.
3. Defoe, 17.
4. Hidaka, "Depression as a Disease of Modernity."
5. Richtie and Roser, "Drug Use."
6. Murphy et al., "40-Year Perspective."
7. Statistics Canada.
8. Xu et al., "Attention-Deficit/Hyperactivity Disorder."
9. Kirkey, "Canadian Children Now Take."
10. Van Amsterdam and van den Brink, "Misuse of Prescription Opioids," 10.
11. Green, "Cat Marnell."
12. Inglis, *Milk of Paradise.*
13. Macy, *Dopesick, 137.*
14. Courtwright, *Dark Paradise*, 6.
15. Cicero, 2014.
16. Unick et al., "Heroin Market Dynamics."
17. Jones et al., "Vital Signs."
18. Gutierrez, Reiss, and Siemaszko, "Welcome to Williamson, W.Va."
19. Lembke, "Why Doctors Prescribe Opioids," para. 1.
20. Lembke, para. 2.

21. European Monitoring Centre for Drugs and Drug Addiction, *European Drug Report.*
22. Dasgupta, Beletsky, and Ciccarone, "No Easy Fix."
23. Bershidsky, "Supply, Not Despair."
24. Onishi et al., "Comparison of Opioid Prescribing Patterns."
25. Matsuyama, "Japan Is Discovering."
26. Compton, Jones, and Baldwin, "Nonmedical Prescription-Opioid Use."
27. Csete et al., "International Drug Policy."
28. Wakeman and Barnett, "Primary Care."
29. Courtwright, *Forces of Habit*, 80–81.

Chapter 6: Treating Addiction

1. Streatfeild, *Cocaine*, 84.
2. Kleber, "Methadone Maintenance."
3. Kleber, Commentary section.
4. Dole and Nyswander, "Medical Treatment."
5. Kleber, "Methadone Maintenance," Methadone Maintenance section.
6. Metzger et al., 1993.
7. R.A. Rettig and A. Yarmolinsky, *Federal Regulation of Methadone Treatment, Washington, DC: Institute of Medicine National Academy Press*, 1995, quoted in Kleber, "Methadone Maintenance," Federal Regulations section.
8. Kleber, "Methadone Maintenance," Methadone: Terminable or Interminable section.
9. "Kicking the Habit."
10. "Kicking the Habit."
11. Csete et al., "International Drug Policy."
12. Kakko et al., "1-Year Retention and Social Function."
13. Hämmig et al., "Use of Microdoses."
14. Wakeman and Barnett, "Primary Care," para. 2.
15. Saloner, Stoller, and Alexander, "Moving Addiction Care," para. 1.
16. Saloner, Stoller, and Alexander.
17. "Detox Is Not the Answer."
18. Peles, Schreiber, and Adelson, "Opiate-Dependent Patients on Waiting List."

19. Van Amsterdam and van den Brink, "The Misuse of Prescription Opioids."
20. Wakeman and Barnett, "Primary Care."
21. Provenzano, "Caring for Ms. L."
22. Provenzano.

Chapter 7: Rethinking Our Relationship with Opioids and Big Pharma

1. Angell, 199.
2. Angell, "No Choice."
3. Angell, *The Truth*, xxv–xxvi.
4. Angell, *The Truth*, 20.
5. PBS, 2003.
6. PBS, 2003.
7. Kamal, Cox, and McDermott, "Recent and Forecasted Trends."
8. Angell, "NEJM200 Marcia Angell Full Interview."
9. Angell, "NEJM200 Marcia Angell Full Interview."
10. Frieden and Houry, "Reducing the Risks of Relief," para. 6.
11. Chang et al., "Effect of a Single Dose."
12. Centers for Disease Control, "Opioid Prescribing Rate Maps."
13. Frieden and Houry, "Reducing the Risks of Relief."
14. Frieden and Houry, para. 4.
15. Volkow and McLellan, 2016.
16. Gallagher and Hatcher, "Will the New Opioid Guidelines."
17. Persaud, "Will the New Opioid Guidelines," para. 9.
18. Persaud, "Rebuttal," para. 6.
19. Silverman, "Doctor's Wallet."
20. Grant, "The Pressure of Big Pharma."
21. Manglik et al., "Structure-Based Discovery."
22. Hill et al., "The Novel μ-Opioid Receptor."
23. Rosenquist, "Management of Chronic Non-Cancer Pain."
24. Rapoport and Rowley, 2017.

Chapter 8: Searching for Solutions

1. Khoury, 2017.

2. Csete et al., "International Drug Policy," 1441.
3. Csete et al.
4. Wood, "Lessons from Canada."
5. *New York Times* Editorial Board, "Safe Injection Sites."
6. Rosenstein, "Fight Drug Abuse."
7. Ng, Sutherland, and Kolber, "Does Evidence Support?"
8. Rosenstein, "Fight Drug Abuse."
9. Kleiman, Caulkins, and Hawken, *Drugs and Drug Policy*.
10. Gossop, Marsden, and Stewart, "Drug Selling."
11. Gossop et al., "Reductions in Criminal Convictions."
12. Kleiman, Caulkins, and Hawken, *Drugs and Drug Policy*.
13. Volkow and Warren, "Drug Addiction."
14. Csete et al., "International Drug Policy."
15. Csete et al.
16. Volkow and Warren, "Drug Addiction."
17. Little, "Opioid Vending Machines."
18. Woodward, "Safe Opioid Vending Machine."

Chapter 9: Expanding the Treatment Tool Kit

1. Rausing, *Mayhem*, 3.
2. Rausing, 3.
3. Leipman et al., "Family Involvement," 958.
4. Leipman et al., 959.
5. Wakeman and Barnett, "Primary Care," para. 7, 9.
6. Baggett and O'Connell, "Health Care of Homeless Persons."
7. Housing First.
8. "Scan," *The Opioid Chapters*.

Chapter 10: Treating the Whole Person

1. Altice et al., 2010.
2. Csete et al., "International Drug Policy."
3. Moatti et al, 2000.
4. Csete et al.
5. 2017 World Drug Report.
6. Choo et al., "Isolation of a cDNA Clone."

7. Nunes and Weiss, "Co-Occurring Addictive and Mood Disorders."
8. Nunes and Weiss.
9. National Institute on Drug Abuse.
10. Dasgupta et al.
11. Gomes et al.
12. Food and Drug Administration, "New Safety Measures Announced."
13. Seth et al., "Overdose Deaths."
14. Nuijten et al., "Sustained-Release Dexamfetamine."

Chapter 11: Breaking the Cycle

1. Frances Spatz Leighton, *The Search for the Real Nancy Reagan* (New York: Macmillan, 1987), 365, quoted in Loizeau, *Nancy Reagan in Perspective*, 105.
2. Volkow, Koob, and McLellan, "Neurobiologic Advances."
3. "Teenagers Are Better Behaved."
4. Johnston et al., *Monitoring the Future.*
5. Volkow, *Dr. Nora Volkow Discusses.*
6. Johnston et al., *Monitoring the Future.*
7. "Teenagers Are Better Behaved."
8. "Teenagers Are Better Behaved."
9. Quinones, 352–53.
10. Bukstein, "Substance Use Disorder."
11. Damour, "What Do Teenagers Want?"
12. Damour.
13. Damour.
14. Bukstein, "Substance Use Disorder."
15. American Academy of Pediatrics.
16. Center for Substance Abuse Prevention, *Keeping Youth Drug Free*, 4, 6, 7.
17. Center for Substance Abuse Prevention, 6.
18. Center for Substance Abuse Prevention, 11.
19. Office of Adolescent Health, "Opioids and Adolescents."
20. Schroeder et al., "Opioid Prescriptions from Dental Clinicians."

Conclusion: Ten Steps Toward a Better Future

1. Henderson, "Designer Drugs."
2. Lane, "Afterword," 226.
3. UNAIDS 2019 Fact Sheet.
4. "Vaccine for Heroin Addiction."
5. Willyard, "Pharmacotherapy."
6. Scripps Research Institute, "Heroin Vaccine Blocks Lethal Overdose."
7. Virginia Commonwealth University, "VCU Researchers Test Effectiveness."
8. Mayani, "Opiant Pharmaceuticals' OPNT005."
9. Edney, "This Killer Opioid."
10. Edney.
11. Monitoring the Future, "National Adolescent Drug Trends," 1.
12. Monitoring the Future, 1–2.
13. Monitoring the Future, 2.
14. Monty Python, *Matching Tie and Handkerchief*, side 1, track 12.
15. Nandakumar, Gollakota, and Sunshine, "Overdose Detection Using Smartphones."
16. British Columbia Coroners Service, *Illicit Drug Toxicity Deaths*.

Bibliography

Altice, Frederick, A. Kamarulzaman, V.V. Soriano, et al. "Treatment of Medical, Psychiatric, and Substance-Use Comorbidities in People Infected with HIV Who Use Drugs." *Lancet* 376 (2010): 59–79.

American Academy of Pediatrics. "Substance Use Screening and Brief Intervention for Youth." 2019. aap.org/en-us/advocacy-and-policy /aap-health-initiatives/Pages/Substance-Use-Screening.aspx.

Angell, Marcia. "NEJM200 Marcia Angell Full Interview." YouTube. youtube.com/watch?v=0F080FNyB-Y.

Angell, Marcia. "No Choice but to Die Alone." *Washington Post*, February 24, 2002. Accessed December 30, 2018. washingtonpost. com/archive/opinions/2002/02/24/no-choice-but-to-die-alone/ e685dd88-45ba-4418-8414-0d8dd59f664c/?noredirect=on&utm_ term=.dca62c975e6b.

Angell, Marcia. "The Supreme Court and Physician-Assisted Suicide—The Ultimate Right." *New England Journal of Medicine* 336 (1997): 50–53.

———. *The Truth about the Drug Companies: How They Deceive Us and What to Do About It*. New York: Random House, 2004.

Arens, Ann M., Xander M.R. van Wijk, Kathy T. Vo, Kara L. Lynch, Alan H.B. Wu, and Craig G. Smollin. "Adverse Effects from Counterfeit Alprazolam Tablets." *JAMA Internal Medicine* 176, no. 10 (2016): 1554–55.

Aristotle. *On Sleep and Sleeplessness*. Accessed November 14, 2018. classics.mit.edu/Aristotle/sleep.html.

Baggett, Travis P., and James J. O'Connell. "Health Care of Homeless Persons in the United States." *UpToDate*. Updated 2017. Accessed April 4, 2018.

Bagnall, James. "Counterfeit Pills Carry Overdose Risk, Police, Health Officials Warn." *Ottawa Citizen*. Updated February 13, 2017. ottawacitizen.com/news/local-news/counterfeit-pills-carry-overdose-risk-police-health-officials-warn.

Barash, Jed A., Michael Ganetsky, Katherine L. Boyle, Vinod Raman, Michael S. Toce, Scott Kaplan, Michael H. Lev, Jonathan L. Worth, and Alfred DeMaria Jr. "Acute Amnestic Syndrome Associated with Fentanyl Overdose: Letter to the Editor." *New England Journal of Medicine* 378 (March 22, 2018): 1157–58.

Becker, William and Joanna Starrels. "Prescription Drug Misuse: Epidemiology, Prevention, Identification, and Management." *UpToDate*. Updated 2018. Accessed April 4, 2018.

Berman, Sarah. "Why Vancouver Has Always Been an Addiction Ground Zero." *Vice*, July 13, 2017. Accessed October 27, 2018. vice.com/en_ca/article/nev4p8/why-vancouver-has-always-been-an-addiction-ground-zero.

Bershidsky, Leonid. "Supply, Not Despair, Caused the Opioid Epidemic." *Bloomberg*, January 10, 2018. Accessed July 4, 2018. bloomberg.com/view/articles/2018-01-10/supply-not-despair-caused-the-opioid-epidemic.

Berthiaume, Lee. "U.S. Raises Alarm over Afghan Heroin Flowing through Canada." *Ottawa Citizen*, November 20, 2014. Accessed January 10, 2018. ottawacitizen.com/news/politics/u-s-raises-alarm-over-afghan-heroin-flowing-through-canada.

Booth, Martin. *Opium: A History*. New York: St. Martin's Press, 1998.

Borg, L., M. Buonora, E.R. Butelman, E. Ducat, B.M. Ray, and M.J. Kreek. "The Pharmacology of Opioids." In *The ASAM Principles of Addiction Medicine*, 5th ed., edited by Richard K. Ries, David Fiellin, Shannon C. Miller, and Richard Saitz, 135–50. Philadelphia: Wolters Kluwer Health, 2014.

British Columbia Coroners Service. *Illicit Drug Overdose Deaths in B.C.: Findings of Coroners' Investigations*. Victoria: Ministry of Public Safety and Solicitor General, September 27, 2018.

———. *Illicit Drug Toxicity Deaths in BC: January 1, 2009–June 30, 2019*. Victoria: Ministry of Public Safety and Solicitor General, August 16, 2019. gov.bc.ca/assets/gov/birth-adoption-death-marriage-and-divorce/deaths/coroners-service/statistical/illicit-drug.pdf.

Bukstein, Oscar. "Substance Use Disorder in Adolescents: Epidemiology, Pathogenesis, Clinical Manifestations, Course, Assessment, and Diagnosis." *UpToDate*. Last modified 2019. Accessed January 19, 2019.

Carter, Anthony. "Dwale: An Anaesthetic from Old England." *BMJ* 319, no. 7225 (December 18, 1999): 1623–26.

Center for Substance Abuse Prevention. *Keeping Youth Drug Free*. HHS Publication No. (SMA) 17-3772. (Rockville, MD: Center for Substance Abuse Prevention, Substance Abuse and Mental Health Services Administration, 2017).

Centers for Disease Control. "U.S. Opioid Prescribing Rate Maps." Updated October 3, 2018. cdc.gov/drugoverdose/maps/rxrate-maps.html.

Chang, Andrew K., Polly E. Bijur, David Esses, Douglas P. Barnaby, Jesse Baer. "Effect of a Single Dose of Oral Opioid and Nonopioid Analgesics on Acute Extremity Pain in the Emergency Department: A Randomized Clinical Trial." *JAMA* 318, no. 17 (2017): 1661–67. DOI:10.1001/jama.2017.16190.

Chang, Grace. "Substance Use by Pregnant Women." *UpToDate*. Updated 2018. Accessed December 4, 2018.

Choo, Qui-Lim, George Kuo, Amy J. Weiner, Lacy R. Overby, Daniel W. Bradley, and Michael Houghton. "Isolation of a cDNA Clone Derived from a Blood-Borne Non-A, Non-B Viral Hepatitis Genome." *Science* 244, no. 4902 (April 21, 1989): 359–62.

Cicero, T.J., Ellis, M.S., Surratt, H.L., Kurtz, S.P. "The Changing Face of Heroin Use in the United States: A Retrospective Analysis of the Past 50 Years." *JAMA Psychiatry* 71, no. 7 (2014): 821–26.

Coetzee, J.M. *Waiting for the Barbarians*. London: Vintage, 2004.

Compton, Wilson M., Christopher M. Jones, and Grant T. Baldwin. "Relationship between Nonmedical Prescription-Opioid Use and Heroin Use." *New England Journal of Medicine* 374 (January 14, 2016): 154–63.

Cooper, Sam. "How Chinese Gangs Are Laundering Drug Money through Vancouver Real Estate." *Globe and Mail*, April 19, 2018. Updated June 5, 2018. globalnews.ca/news/4149818/vancouver-cautionary-tale-money-laundering-drugs/.

Courtwright, David. *Dark Paradise: A History of Opiate Addiction in America*. Cambridge: Harvard University Press, 2001.

———. *Forces of Habit: Drugs and the Making of the Modern World*. Cambridge: Harvard University Press, 2001.

Crozier, Lorna. "Introduction." In *Addicted: Notes from the Belly of the Beast*, edited by Lorna Crozier and Patrick Lane, ix–xii. Vancouver: Greystone Books, 2016.

Csete, J., A. Kamarulzaman, M. Kazatchkine, F. Altice, M. Balicki, J. Buxton, J. Cepeda, et al. "Public Health and International Drug Policy." *Lancet* 387, no. 10026 (April 2, 2016): 1427–80.

Damour, Lisa. "What Do Teenagers Want? Potted Plant Parents." *New York Times*, December 14, 2016. Accessed December 19, 2018. nytimes.com/2016/12/14/well/family/what-do-teenagers-want-potted-plant-parents.html.

Dasgupta, N., L. Beletsky, and D. Ciccarone. "Opioid Crisis: No Easy Fix to Its Social and Economic Determinants." *American Journal of Public Health* 108, no. 2 (2018): 182–86.

Dasgupta N., M.J. Funk, S. Proescholdbell, A. Hirsch, K.M. Ribisl, S. Marshall. "Cohort Study of the Impact of High-Dose Opioid Analgesics on Overdose Mortality." *Pain Medicine Malden Mass* 17, no. 1 (2016): 85–98. DOI:10.1111/pme.12907.

Defoe, Daniel. *A Journal of the Plague Year*. Mineola, NY: Dover Thrift Editions, 2001.

"Demand Unexpectedly High at Year-Old Supervised Injection Trailer." *CBC News*. Posted November 7, 2018. cbc.ca/news/canada/ottawa/shepherds-good-hope-supervised-injection-anniversary-1.4894516.

"Detox Is Not the Answer for Opiate Addiction." *CBC News*. Posted February 26, 2016. cbc.ca/radio/the180/rewrite-the-criminal-code-stop-detoxing-opiate-addicts-and-build-an-oil-railroad-to-alaska-1.3464524/detox-is-not-the-answer-for-opiate-addiction-1.3464693.

Dole, Vincent P., and Marie Nyswander. "A Medical Treatment for Diacetylmorphine (Heroin) Addiction: A Clinical Trial with Methadone Hydrochloride." *JAMA* 193, no. 8 (1965): 646–50.

Dover, Thomas. *The Ancient Physician's Legacy to His Country: Being What He Has Collected in Forty-Nine Years Practice*, 6th ed. Dublin: George Faulkner, 1734. Accessed November 14, 2018. books.google.ca/books?id=MSYZKW snKbcC&printsec=frontcover&dq=inauthor:%22Thomas +Dover+(M.+B.)%22&hl=en&sa=X&ved =0ahUKEwiL4-TdzNTeAhXrdN8KHVItCY0 Q6AEIKjAA#v=onepage&q&f=false.

Doyle, Arthur Conan. *The Adventures of Sherlock Holmes*. Accessed October 7, 2019. gutenberg.org/files/1661/1661-h/1661-h.htm#chap06.

Edney, Anna. "This Killer Opioid Could Become a Weapon of Mass Destruction." Bloomberg, December 12, 2018. Accessed January 19, 2019. bloomberg.com/news/features/2018-12-12/killer-opioid-fentanyl-could-be-a-weapon-of-mass-destruction.

European Monitoring Centre for Drugs and Drug Addiction. European Drug Report 2017: Trends and Developments. Luxembourg: Publications Office of the European Union, 2017.

Fletcher, Anne M. Inside Rehab: *The Surprising Truth About Addiction Treatment — And How to Get Help That Works*. New York: Viking, 2013.

Food and Drug Administration. "New Safety Measures Announced for Opioid Analgesics, Prescription Opioid Cough Products, and Benzodiazepines." August 31, 2016. fda.gov/drugs/information-drug-class/new-safety-measures-announced-opioid-analgesics-prescription-opioid-cough-products-and.

Frieden, T.R., and D. Houry. "Reducing the Risks of Relief — The CDC Opioid-Prescribing Guideline." *New England Journal of Medicine* 374 (April 21, 2016): 1501–4.

Gallagher, Romayne, and Lydia Hatcher. "Will the New Opioid Guidelines Harm More People Than They Help? Yes." *Canadian Family Physician* 64, no. 2 (February 2018): 101–2.

Gibbons, H. "Letheomania: The Results of the Hypodermin Injection of Morphia." *Pacific Medical and Surgical Journal* 12 (1870): 481–95. nlm.nih.gov/exhibition/pickyourpoison/digitalgallery/gibbons/html5/index.html

Gomes, T., M.M. Mamdani, I.A. Dhalla, J.M. Paterson, D.N. Juurlink. "Opioid Dose and Drug-Related Mortality in Patients with Nonmalignant Pain." *Archives of Internal Medicine* 171, no. 7 (2011): 686–91. DOI:10.1001/archinternmed.2011.117.

Gossop, M., J. Marsden, and D. Stewart. "Drug Selling Among Drug Misusers Before Intake to Treatment and at 1-Year Follow-Up: Results from the National Treatment Outcome Research Study (NTORS)." *Drug and Alcohol Review* 19, no. 2 (June 2000): 143–51.

Gossop, M., K. Trakada, D. Stewart, and J. Witton. "Reductions in Criminal Convictions after Addiction Treatment: 5-Year Follow-Up." *Drug and Alcohol Dependence* 79, no. 3 (September 1, 2005): 295–302.

Grant, Kelly. "The Pressure of Big Pharma." *Globe and Mail*, June 19, 2017. Accessed December 30, 2018. theglobeandmail.com/news/national/the-pressure-of-big-pharma-financial-conflicts-of-interest-common-on-medical-guidelinepanels/article35389639/.

Green, Penelope. "Cat Marnell, a Former Beauty Editor, on Her New Addiction Memoir." *New York Times*, January 27, 2017. nytimes.com/2017/01/27/style/cat-marnell-addiction-memoir-how-to-murder-your-life.html.

Guan, Wei, Ronald Schneider, and James Patterson. "'I Am in Pain!' — A Case Report of Illicit Use of Transdermal Fentanyl Patches." *Primary Care Companion for CNS Disorders* 13, no. 5 (2011). DOI:10.4088/PCC.11l01196.

Gutierrez, Gabe, Adam Reiss, and Corky Siemaszko. "Welcome to Williamson, W.Va., Where There Are 6,500 Opioid Pills Per Person." *NBC News*, February 1, 2018. Accessed November 13, 2018. nbcnews.com/news/us-news/welcome-williamson-w-va-where-there-are-6-500-opioid-n843821.

Hämmig, Robert, Antje Kemter, Johannes Strasser, Ulrich von Bardeleben, Barbara Gugger, Marc Walter, Kenneth M. Dürsteler, and Marc Vogel. "Use of Microdoses for Induction of Buprenorphine Treatment with Overlapping Full Opioid Agonist Use: The Bernese Method." *Substance Abuse and Rehabilitation* 7 (2016): 99–105.

Henderson, G.L. "Designer Drugs: Past History and Future Prospects." *Journal of Forensic Sciences* 33, no. 2 (1988): 569–75.

Hidaka, B.H. "Depression as a Disease of Modernity: Explanations for Increasing Prevalence." *Journal of Affective Disorders* 140, no. 3 (2012): 205–14.

"High Levels of Fentanyl — and Deceit — Detected in Vancouver Street-Drug Supply." *CBC News*. Posted May 18, 2018. Accessed October 26, 2018. cbc.ca/news/canada/british-columbia/high-levels-of-fentanyl-and-deceit-detected-in-vancouver-street-drug-supply-1.4668895.

Hill, R., A. Disney, A. Conibear, K. Sutcliffe, W. Dewey, S. Husbands, C. Bailey, E. Kelly, and G. Henderson. "The Novel μ-Opioid Receptor Agonist PZM21 Depresses Respiration and Induces Tolerance to Antinociception." *British Journal of Pharmacology* 175, no. 13 (2018): 2653–61.

"Housing First." Homeless Hub. Accessed June 1, 2018. homelesshub.ca/solutions/housing-accommodation-and-supports/housing-first.

Howlett, Karen, Justin Giovannetti, Nathan Vanderklippe, and Les Perreaux. "How Canada Got Addicted to Fentanyl." *Globe and Mail*, April 8, 2016. Updated November 12, 2017. theglobeandmail.com/news/investigations/a-killer-high-how-canada-got-addicted-tofentanyl/article29570025/.

Inglis, Lucy. *Milk of Paradise: A History of Opium*. London: Macmillan, 2018.

"Interview: Marcia Angell." *Frontline*, PBS, June 19, 2003. Accessed December 30, 2018. pbs.org/wgbh/pages/frontline/shows/other/interviews/angell.html.

Johnston, Lloyd D., Richard A. Miech, Patrick M. O'Malley, Jerald G. Bachman, John E. Schulenberg, and Megan E. Patrick. "Monitoring the Future: National Survey Results on Drug Use — 2017 Overview, Key Finding on Adolescent Drug Use." *University of Michigan Institute for Social Research*, January 2018. Accessed July 18, 2018. deepblue.lib.umich.edu/bitstream/handle/2027.42/142406/Overview%202017%20FINAL.pdf?sequence=1&isAllowed=y.

Jones, Christopher M., Joseph Logan, R. Matthew Gladden, and Michele K. Bohm. "Vital Signs: Demographic and Substance Use Trends among Heroin Users — United States, 2002–2013." *Morbidity and Mortality Weekly Report* 64, no. 26 (July 10, 2015): 719–25.

Kakko J., K.D. Svanborg, M.J. Kreek, and M. Heilig. "1-Year Retention and Social Function after Buprenorphine-Assisted Relapse Prevention Treatment for Heroin Dependence in Sweden: A Randomised, Placebo-Controlled Trial." *Lancet* 361, no. 9358 (February 22, 2003): 662–68.

Kamal, Rabah, Cynthia Cox, and Daniel McDermott. "What Are the Recent and Forecasted Trends in Prescription Drug Spending?" *Health System Tracker*. Accessed December 22, 2018. healthsystemtracker.org/chart-collection/recent-forecasted-trends-prescription-drug-spending/#item-nominal-and-inflation-adjusted-increase-in-rx-spending_2017.

Kendler, K.S., E. Schmitt, S.H. Aggen, and C.A. Prescott. "Genetic and Environmental Influences on Alcohol, Caffeine, Cannabis, and Nicotine Use from Early Adolescence to Middle Adulthood." *Archives of General Psychiatry* 65, no. 6 (2008): 674–82.

Khoury, George. "Is Possession of Drug Paraphernalia a Felony?" *Findlaw Blogger*. Posted January 26, 2017. blogs.findlaw.com/

blotter/2017/01/is-possession-of-drug-paraphernalia-a-felony.html.

"Kicking the Habit." *Economist*, September 15, 2012. Accessed October 28, 2018. economist.com/china/2012/09/15/kicking-the-habit.

Kirkey, Sharon. "Canadian Children Now Take Far More Mood-Altering Drugs, Prescription Count Shows." *National Post*, November 13, 2016. Accessed October 27, 2018. nationalpost.com/health/canadian-children-now-take-far-more-mood-altering-drugs.

Kleber, Herbert D. "Methadone Maintenance 4 Decades Later." *JAMA* 300, no. 19 (2008): 2303–5. jamanetwork.com/journals/jama/fullarticle/182898.

Kleiman, Mark, Jonathan Caulkins, and Angel Hawken. *Drugs and Drug Policy: What Everyone Needs to Know.* New York: Oxford University Press, 2011.

Lane, Patrick. "Afterword." In *Addicted: Notes from the Belly of the Beast*, edited by Lorna Crozier and Patrick Lane, 223–25. Vancouver: Greystone Books, 2016.

Leins, Casey. "New Hampshire: Ground Zero for Opioids." *US News and World Report*, June 28, 2017. usnews.com/news/best-states/articles/2017-06-28/why-new-hampshire-has-one-of-the-highest-rates-of-opioid-related-deaths.

Leipman, Michael R., Kathleen A. Gross, Maritza M. Lagos, Theodore V. Parran Jr., and Kathleen J. Farkas. "Family Involvement in Addiction, Treatment, and Recovery." In *The ASAM Principles of Addiction Medicine*, 5th ed., edited by Richard K. Ries, David Fiellin, Shannon C. Miller, and Richard Saitz, 958–74. Philadelphia: Wolters Kluwer Health, 2014.

Lembke, Anna. "Why Doctors Prescribe Opioids to Known Opioid Abusers." *New England Journal of Medicine* 367 (October 25, 2012): 1580–81.

Leung, P.T.M., E.M. MacDonald, M.B. Stanbrook, I.A. Dhalla, and D.N. Juurlink. "A 1980 Letter on the Risk of Opioid Addiction." *New England Journal of Medicine* 376, no. 22 (June 1, 2017): 2194–95.

Little, Simon. "Opioid Vending Machines among 'Out of the Box' Overdose Solutions at Vancouver Forum." *Global News*, June 7, 2018. globalnews.ca/news/4261182/opioid-vending-machines-vancouver/.

Loizeau, Pierre-Marie. *Nancy Reagan in Perspective*. New York: Nova History Publishers, 2005.

Lupick, Travis. "Vancouver's Rate of Drug-Overdose Deaths Now Ranks among Highest in North America." *Georgia Straight*, May 10, 2018. Accessed October 26, 2018. straight.com/news/1074336/vancouvers-rate-drug-overdose-deaths-now-ranks-among-highest-north-america.

Macklemore. "Drug Dealer." Featuring Ariana DeBoo. 2016, single.

Macy, Beth. *Dopesick: Dealers, Doctors, and the Drug Company That Addicted America*. New York: Little, Brown and Company, 2018.

Manglik, A., H. Lin, D.K. Aryal, J.D. McCorvy, D. Dengler, G. Corder, A. Levit, et al. "Structure-Based Discovery of Opioid Analgesics with Reduced Side Effects." *Nature* 537, no. 7619 (2016): 185–90.

Mansfield, A.S., and A. Jatoi. "Asphyxiation with a Fentanyl Patch." *Case Reports in Oncology* 6 (2013): 242–44.

Marlowe, Ann. *How to Stop Time: Heroin from A to Z*. archive.nytimes.com/www.nytimes.com/books/first/m/marlowe-time.html.

Matsuyama, Kanoko. "Japan Is Discovering the Power of Painkillers." *Bloomberg*, September 21, 2017. Accessed October 17, 2018. bloomberg.com/news/articles/2017-09-21/painkiller-sales-take-off-as-japan-s-baby-boomers-demand-relief.

Mayani, Mamta. "Opiant Pharmaceuticals' OPNT005 Receives Grant for Development of a Heroin Vaccine." *Seeking Alpha*, October 18, 2018. Accessed Jan 19, 2019. seekingalpha.com/news/3398493-opiant-pharmaceuticals-opnt005-receives-grant-development-heroin-vaccine.

Metzger, D.S., G.E. Woody, A.T. McLellan, et al. "Human Immunodeficiency Virus Seroconversion Among Intravenous Drug Users In and Out of Treatment: An 18 Month Prospective Follow-Up." *Journal of Acquired Immune Deficiency Syndromes* 6, no. 9 (1993): 1049–56.

Moatti JP, MP Carrieri, B Spire B, et al. "Adherence to HAART in French HIV-infected injecting drug users: the contribution of buprenorphine drug maintenance treatment." The Manif 2000 study group. AIDS 14 (2000): 151–55.

Monitoring the Future, University of Michigan Institute for Social Research. "National Adolescent Drug Trends in 2018." Press release, December 17, 2018. monitoringthefuture.org/pressreleases/18drugpr.pdf.

Monty Python. *Matching Tie and Handkerchief.* Charisma Records, 1973, album.

Murphy, Francois. "U.N. Drugs Body Places Fentanyl Ingredients on Control List." *Reuters*, March 16, 2017. Accessed June 27, 2018. reuters.com/article/us-un-drugs-fentanyl/u-n-drugs-body-places-fentanyl-ingredients-on-control-list-idUSKBN16N2MB.

Murphy, J.M., N.M. Laird, R.R. Monson, A.M. Sobol, and A.H. Leighton. "A 40-Year Perspective on the Prevalence of Depression: The Stirling County Study." *Archives of General Psychiatry* 57 (2000): 209–15.

Museum of Health Care. "Mrs. Winslow's Soothing Syrup: The Baby Killer." *Museum of Health Care Blog*, July 28, 2017. Accessed October 10, 2018. museumofhealthcare.wordpress.com/2017/07/28/mrs-winslows-soothing-syrup-the-baby-killer.

Nandakumar, Rajalakshmi, Shyamnath Gollakota, and Jacob E. Sunshine. "Opioid Overdose Detection Using Smartphones." *Science Translational Medicine* 11, no. 474 (2019): eaau8914.

National Institute on Drug Abuse. "Benzodiazepines and Opioids." Revised March 2018. drugabuse.gov/drugs-abuse/opioids/benzodiazepines-opioids.

NDEWS Coordinating Center. *The Increase in Fentanyl Overdoses.* NDEWS New Hampshire HotSpot Report, October 14, 2016. ndews.umd.edu/sites/ndews.umd.edu/files/pubs/newhampshirehotspotreportphase1final.pdf.

New York Times Editorial Board. "Let Cities Open Safe Injection Sites." *New York Times*, February 24, 2018. Accessed March

7, 2018. nytimes.com/2018/02/24/opinion/sunday/drugs-safe-injection-sites.html.

Ng, Jennifer, Christy Sutherland, and Michael R. Kolber. "Does Evidence Support Supervised Injection Sites?" *Canadian Family Physician* 63, no. 11 (November 2017): 866.

Nuijten, M., P. Blanken, B. van de Wetering, B. Nuijen, W. van den Brink, and V.M. Hendriks. "Sustained-Release Dexamfetamine in the Treatment of Chronic Cocaine-Dependent Patients on Heroin-Assisted Treatment: A Randomised, Double-Blind, Placebo-Controlled Trial." *Lancet* 387, no. 10034: 2226–34.

Nunes, E.V., and R. Weiss. "Co-Occurring Addictive and Mood Disorders." In *The ASAM Principles of Addiction Medicine*, 5th ed., edited by Richard K. Ries, David Fiellin, Shannon C. Miller, and Richard Saitz, 1300–32. Philadelphia: Wolters Kluwer Health, 2014.

Office of Adolescent Health. "Opioids and Adolescents." Office of Population Affairs. 2017. Accessed January 9, 2019. hhs.gov/ash/oah/adolescent-development/substance-use/drugs/opioids/index.html.

Oliver, John. "Marketing to Doctors." *Last Week Tonight*, HBO, February 25, 2015. youtube.com/watch?time_continue=975&v=YQZ2UeOTO3I.

Onishi, E., T. Kobayashi, E. Dexter, M. Marino, T. Maeno, and R.A. Devo. "Comparison of Opioid Prescribing Patterns in the United States and Japan: Primary Care Physicians' Attitudes and Perceptions." *Journal of the American Board of Family Medicine* 30, no. 2 (2017): 248–54.

PBS. 2003. The Other Drug War. Interview: Marcia Angell. Accessed December 30, 2018. pbs.org/wgbh/pages/frontline/shows/other/interviews/angell.html.

Peles, E., S. Schreiber, and M. Adelson. "Opiate-Dependent Patients on a Waiting List for Methadone Maintenance Treatment Are at High Risk for Mortality until Treatment Entry." *Journal of Addiction Medicine* 7, no. 3 (2013): 177–82.

Persaud, Nav. "Rebuttal: Will the New Opioid Guidelines Harm More People Than They Help? No." *Canadian Family Physician* 64, no. 2 (February 2018): e59–e60.

———. "Will the New Opioid Guidelines Harm More People Than They Help? No." *Canadian Family Physician* 64, no. 2 (February 2018): 102–4.

Port, J.D., T.H. Stanley, E.P. Steffey, N.L. Pace, R. Henrickson, and S.W. McJames. "Intravenous Carfentanil in the Dog and Rhesus Monkey." *Anesthesiology* 61 (1984): A378.

Porter, Jane, and Hershel Jick. "Addiction Rare in Patients Treated with Narcotics." *New England Journal of Medicine* 302 (1980): 123.

Power, D'Arcy. "Early Anaesthesia." *British Journal of Anaesthesia* 1, no. 1 (1923): 4–7. bjanaesthesia.org/article/S0007-0912(17)51851-6/pdf.

Provenzano, Audrey M. "Caring for Ms. L. — Overcoming My Fear of Treating Opioid Use Disorder." *New England Journal of Medicine* 378 (2018): 600–601.

Quinones, Sam. *Dreamland: The True Tale of America's Opiate Epidemic*. New York: Bloomsbury, 2016.

Rapoport, Alison, and C. Rowley. "Stretching the Scope — Becoming Frontline Addiction-Medicine Providers." *New England Journal of Medicine* 377 (2017): 705–70.

Rausing, Sigrid. *Mayhem*. New York: Knopf, 2017.

Riches, James R., Robert W. Read, Robin M. Black, Nicholas J. Cooper, and Christopher M. Timperley. "Case Report Analysis of Clothing and Urine from Moscow Theatre Siege Casualties Reveals Carfentanil and Remifentanil Use." *Journal of Analytical Toxicology* 36 (2012): 647–56.

Richtie, Hannah, and Max Roser. "Illicit Drug Use." *Our World in Data*, April 2018. ourworldindata.org/drug-use.

Romanish, Daria. "Fentanyl Info and Response: With Case Studies" PowerPoint CRRA presentation, October 19, 2017. Accessed October 26, 2018. albertahealthservices.ca/assets/wf/eph/wf-eph-fentanyl-info-response.pdf.

Rosenquist, Richard. "Use of Opioids in the Management of Chronic Non-Cancer Pain." *UpToDate*. Accessed November 15, 2018. uptodate.com/contents/use-of-opioids-in-the-management-of-chronic-non-cancer-pain.

Rosenstein, Rod J. "Fight Drug Abuse, Don't Subsidize It." *New York Times*, August 28, 2018. nytimes.com/2018/08/27/opinion/opioids-heroin-injection-sites.html.

Saloner, Brendan, Kenneth B. Stoller, and G. Caleb Alexander. "Moving Addiction Care to the Mainstream — Improving the Quality of Buprenorphine Treatment." *New England Journal of Medicine* 379 (July 5, 2018): 4–6.

Scarborough, John. "The Opium Poppy in Hellenistic and Roman Medicine." In *Drugs and Narcotics in History*, edited by Roy Porter and Mikuláš Teich, 4–23. Cambridge: Cambridge University Press, 1995.

Schroeder, A.R., M. Dehghan, T.B. Newman, J.P. Bentley, and K.T. Park. "Association of Opioid Prescriptions from Dental Clinicians for U.S. Adolescents and Young Adults with Subsequent Opioid Use and Abuse." *JAMA Internal Medicine* 179, no. 2 (2019): 145–52. Published online December 3, 2018. DOI:10.1001/jamainternmed.2018.5419.

Schuckit, Mark A. "Treatment of Opioid Use Disorders." *New England Journal of Medicine* 375, no. 4 (July 28, 2016): 357–68.

Scripps Research Institute. "Heroin Vaccine Blocks Lethal Overdose." Press release, February 13, 2018. Accessed January 10, 2019. scripps.edu/news-and-events/press-room/2018/20180213janda.html.

Sean. *The Opioid Chapters*. Ontario Drug Policy Research Network and Healthy Debate: Faces of Health Care. N.d. theopioidchapters.com/sean.

Seth, Puja M., Lawrence Scholl, Rose A. Rudd, and Sarah Bacon. "Overdose Deaths Involving Opioids, Cocaine, and Psychostimulants — United States, 2015–2016." *Morbidity and Mortality Weekly Report* 67, no. 12 (March 30, 2018): 349–58. cdc.gov/mmwr/volumes/67/wr/mm6712a1.htm.

Silverman, Ed. "Does Pharma Money Mix with Cash Receptors in Your Doctor's Wallet?" *Wall Street Journal*, February 9, 2015. Accessed January 6, 2019. blogs.wsj.com/pharmalot/2015/02/09/does-pharma-money-mix-with-cash-receptors-in-your-doctors-wallet/.

Snyder, Bill. "Nora Volkow: Two Paths to the Future." *Lens*, February 2006. Accessed January 3, 2018. mc.vanderbilt.edu/lens/article/?id=129&pg=999.

Stanley, Theodore H., Talmage D. Egan, and Hugo Van Aken. "A Tribute to Dr. Paul A.J. Janssen: Entrepreneur Extraordinaire, Innovative Scientist, and Significant Contributor to Anesthesiology." *Anesthesia and Analgesia* 106, no. 2 (2008): 451–62.

Statistics Canada. Table 13-10-0465-01 Mental Health Indicators. DOI: https://doi.org/10.25318/1310046501-eng.

Strain, Eric. "Opioid Use Disorder: Epidemiology, Pharmacology, Clinical Manifestations, Course, Screening, Assessment, and Diagnosis." *UpToDate*. Last modified 2017. Accessed February 14, 2018.

Streatfeild, Dominic. *Cocaine: An Unauthorized Biography*. New York: St. Martin's Press, 2001.

"Teenagers Are Better Behaved and Less Hedonistic Nowadays." *Economist*, January 10, 2018. economist.com/international/2018/01/10/teenagers-are-better-behaved-and-less-hedonistic-nowadays.

Tinniswood, Adrian. *His Invention So Fertile: A Life of Christopher Wren*. London: Jonathan Cape, 2001.

UNAIDS. Global HIV & AIDS Statistics — 2019 Fact Sheet. unaids.org/en/resources/fact-sheet.

Unick, G., D. Rosenblum, S. Mars, and D. Ciccarone. "The Relationship between U.S. Heroin Market Dynamics and Heroin-Related Overdose, 1992–2008." *Addiction* 109 (2014): 1889–98.

United Nations Office on Drugs and Crime. *World Drug Report 2017*. unodc.org/wdr2017/index.html.

United States Drug Enforcement Administration. *Fentanyl: A Briefing Guide for First Responders*. June 2017.

"Vaccine for Heroin Addiction." *Media Mayhem*. The Lip TV. YouTube video. Posted February 16, 2014. youtube.com/watch?v=V0pUpVQf42Y.

Van Amsterdam, J., and W. van den Brink. "The Misuse of Prescription Opioids: A Threat for Europe?" *Current Drug Abuse Reviews* 8 (2015): 3–14.

Van Zee, Art. "The Promotion and Marketing of OxyContin: Commercial Triumph, Public Health Tragedy." *American Journal of Public Health* 99, no. 2 (2009): 221–27.

Virginia Commonwealth University. "VCU Researchers Test Effectiveness of Anti-Opioid Vaccine." *EurekAlert!* December 6, 2018. Accessed January 10, 2019. eurekalert.org/pub_releases/2018-12/vcu-vrt120618.php.

Volkow, Nora. *Dr. Nora Volkow Discusses the 2017 MTF Survey Results*. National Institute on Drug Abuse. Video, May 16, 2018. drugabuse.gov/nida-tv/director-remarks-interviews.

Volkow, Nora, George F. Koob, and A. Thomas McLellan. "Neurobiologic Advances from the Brain Disease Model of Addiction." *New England Journal of Medicine* 374 (January 28, 2016): 363–71.

Volkow, Nora, and A. Thomas McLellan. "Opioid Abuse in Chronic Pain — Misconceptions and Mitigation Strategies." *New England Journal of Medicine 374* (2016):1253–63

Volkow, Nora, and K. Warren. "Drug Addiction: The Neurobiology of Behavior Gone Awry." In *The ASAM Principles of Addiction Medicine*, 5th ed., edited by Richard K. Ries, David Fiellin, Shannon C. Miller, and Richard Saitz, 3–18. Philadelphia: Wolters Kluwer Health, 2014.

Walley, A.Y., Z. Xuan, H.H. Hackman, E. Quinn, M. Doe-Simkins, A. Sorensen-Alawad, S. Ruiz, et al. "Opioid Overdose Rates and Implementation of Overdose Education and Nasal Naloxone Distribution in Massachusetts: Interrupted Time Series Analysis." *BMJ* 346 (2013): f174.

White, William L., and James F. Callahan. "Addiction Medicine in America: Its Birth and Early History (1750–1935) with a Modern Postscript." In *The ASAM Principles of Addiction Medicine*, 5th ed., edited by Richard K. Ries, David Fiellin, Shannon C. Miller, and Richard Saitz, 365–74. Philadelphia: Wolters Kluwer Health, 2014.

Willyard, Cassandra. "Pharmacotherapy: Quest for the Quitting Pill." *Nature* 522, no. 7557 (June 25, 2015): S53–S55.

Wood, Evan. "Strategies for Reducing Opioid-Overdose Deaths — Lessons from Canada." *New England Journal of Medicine* 378 (April 26, 2018): 1565–67.

Woodward, Jon. "Safe Opioid Vending Machine Closer to Reality: BCCDC." *CTV News*, January 17, 2018. Accessed October 28, 2018. bc.ctvnews.ca/safe-opioid-vending-machine-closer-to-reality-bccdc-1.3763945.

Xu, Guifeng, Lane Strathearn, Buyun Liu, Binrang Yang, and Wei Bao. "Twenty-Year Trends in Diagnosed Attention-Deficit/Hyperactivity Disorder among U.S. Children and Adolescents, 1997–2016." *JAMA Network Open* 1, no. 4 (2018): e181471. DOI:10.1001/jamanetworkopen.2018.1471.

Zuger, Abigail. "A Doctor's Guide to What to Read on the Opioid Crisis." *New York Times*, December 17, 2018. Accessed December 30, 2018. nytimes.com/2018/12/17/books/review/opioid-abuse-drug-dealer-anna-lembke.html.

———. "A General in the Drug War." *New York Times*, June 13, 2011. nytimes.com/2011/06/14/science/14volkow.html.

Index